Who Needs a New Covenant?

Princeton Theological Monograph Series

K. C. Hanson, Charles M. Collier, and
D. Christopher Spinks, Series Editors

Recent volumes in the series

Kevin Twain Lowery
Salvaging Wesley's Agenda: A New Paradigm for Wesleyan Virtue Ethics

Matthew J. Marohl
Faithfulness and the Purpose of Hebrews: A Social Identity Approach

D. Seiple and Frederick W. Weidmann, editors
Enigmas and Powers: Engaging the Work of Walter Wink for Classroom, Church, and World

Stanley D. Walters
Go Figure!: Figuration in Biblical Interpretation

Paul S. Chung
Martin Luther and Buddhism: Aesthetics of Suffering, Second Edition

Ralph M. Wiltgen
The Founding of the Roman Catholic Church in Melanesia and Micronesia, 1850–1875

Steven B. Sherman
Revitalizing Theological Epistemology: Holistic Evangelical Approaches to the Knowledge of God

David Hein
Geoffrey Fisher: Archbishop of Canterbury, 1945–1961

Mary Clark Moschella
Living Devotions: Reflections on Immigration, Identity, and Religious Imagination

Who Needs a New Covenant?

*Rhetorical Function of the Covenant Motif
in the Argument of Hebrews*

MICHAEL D. MORRISON

⌐PICKWICK *Publications* • Eugene, Oregon

WHO NEEDS A NEW COVENANT?
Rhetorical Function of the Covenant Motif in the Argument of Hebrews

Princeton Theological Monograph Series 85

Copyright © 2008 Michael D. Morrison. All rights reserved. Except for brief quotations in critical articles or reviews, no part of this book may be reproduced in any manner without prior written permission from the publisher. Write: Permissions, Wipf and Stock Publishers, 199 W. 8th Ave., Suite 3, Eugene, OR 97401.

www.wipfandstock.com

Pickwick Publications
A Division of Wipf and Stock Publishers
199 W. 8th Ave., Suite 3
Eugene, OR 97401

ISBN 13: 978-1-55635-804-3

Unless noted otherwise, translations from the Bible are from the *New Revised Standard Version Bible*, copyright © 1989, Division of Christian Education of the National Council of the Churches of Christ in the United States of America. Used by permission. All rights reserved.

Cataloging-in-Publication data:

Morrison, Michael D.
    Who needs a new covenant? : rhetorical function of the covenant motif in the argument of Hebrews / Michael D. Morrison.

    Princeton Theological Monograph Series 85

    xiv + 212 p. ; 23 cm.

    Eugene, Ore.: Pickwick Publications

    Includes bibliography

    ISBN 13: 978-1-55635-804-3

    1. Bible. N.T. Hebrews—Socio-rhetorical criticism. 2. Covenants—Biblical teaching. 3. Covenants—Religious aspects—Christianity. I. Title. II. Series.

BS2775.2 M80 2008

Manufactured in the U.S.A.

Contents

Acknowledgments / vii

Abbreviations / viii

Introduction / xi

1. Jews and/or Gentiles: The Ethnic Identity of the Recipients of Hebrews / 1
2. The Occasion of Hebrews / 23
3. Religious Beliefs of the Readers / 44
4. "Covenant" in Jewish Literature / 84
5. "Covenant" in the New Testament / 126
6. Conclusion: Role of the Covenant Motif in the Exhortations in Hebrews / 153

APPENDIX A: *The Text of Hebrews with All References to Covenant Removed / 161*

APPENDIX B: *The Rhetorical Genre of Hebrews / 171*

APPENDIX C: *Date of the Epistle / 177*

APPENDIX D: *Translation Irregularities of* ברית *and* Διαθήκη */ 181*

APPENDIX E: *"Covenant" in the Epistle of Barnabas / 194*

Bibliography / 199

Acknowledgements

THIS BOOK ORIGINATED AS A DOCTORAL DISSERTATION AT FULLER Theological Seminary, and I am happy to thank my employer, the Worldwide Church of God, for substantial tuition assistance, and my supervisors, J. Michael Feazell and Joseph Tkach, for their encouragement and the flexibility they gave me on the job.

I thank Lynn A. Losie, Chair of the Department of Biblical Studies at Haggard Graduate School of Theology, Azusa Pacific University, for encouraging me to begin and continue my doctoral studies. David M. Scholer and Donald A. Hagner at Fuller helped me develop and improve the dissertation. I thank K. C. Hanson and Chris Spinks at Wipf and Stock for their role in making this book part of the Princeton Theological Monograph Series.

The research was done primarily in 2002–2005; I have edited it again in 2007 to improve the wording and readability, remove some errors, and to interact with some of the more recent literature, including several commentaries and monographs relevant to the focus of this research. Hebrews was ignored for much of the 20th century, but has been the subject of numerous commentaries and books in the last 20 years. I hope that my monograph will be of some use among this flood of companions, and will help guide some of the future discussion.

I am especially grateful to my family, and I dedicate this book to my son, Steven, as he considers the options set before him in coming years. May his academic, social, and occupational choices serve him and others well; may he continue to be faithful to the confession, covenant, and community.

Abbreviations

AB	Anchor Bible
ABD	*Anchor Bible Dictionary*. Edited by David Noel Freedman. 6 vols. New York: Doubleday, 1992
ACNT	Augsburg Commentaries on the New Testament
AGJU	Arbeiten zur Geschichte des antiken Judentums und des Urchristentums
ANRW	*Aufstieg und Niedergang der römischen Welt: Geschichte und Kultur Roms im Spiegel der neueren Forschung*. Edited by H. Temporini and W. Haase. New York: de Gruyter, 1972–
AnSBF	Analecta (Studium Biblicum Franciscanum)
AsTJ	*Asbury Theological Journal*
BBR	*Bulletin for Biblical Research*
BDAG	Danker, F. W., W. Bauer, W. F. Arndt, and F. W. Gingrich. *Greek-English Lexicon of the New Testament and Other Early Christian Literature*. 3rd ed. Chicago: University of Chicago Press, 2000
BETL	Bibliotheca ephemeridum theologicarum lovaniensium
BR	*Biblical Research*
BZNW	Beihefte zur Zeitschrift für neutestamentliche Wissenschaft
CBC	Cambridge Bible Commentary
CBET	Contributions to Biblical Exegesis and Theology
CBQ	*Catholic Biblical Quarterly*
ConBNT	Coniectanea biblica: New Testament Series
CurBS	*Currents in Research: Biblical Studies*
EDNT	*Exegetical Dictionary of the New Testament*. Edited by Horst Balz and Gerhard Schneider. Translated by Virgil P. Howard, James W. Thompson, John W. Medendorp, and Douglas W. Stott. 3 vols. Grand Rapids: Eerdmans, 1990–93
EKKNT	Evangelisch-katholischer Kommentar zum Neuen Testament
ETL	*Ephemerides theologicae lovanienses*
GOTR	*Greek Orthodox Theological Review*
HNT	Handbuch zum Neuen Testament
HTR	*Harvard Theological Review*
HUT	Hermeneutische Untersuchungen zur Theologie
IBS	*Irish Biblical Studies*
Int	*Interpretation*
JAOS	*Journal of the American Oriental Society*

JBL	*Journal of Biblical Literature*
JETS	*Journal of the Evangelical Theological Society*
JJS	*Journal of Jewish Studies*
JSNTSup	Journal for the Study of the New Testament: Supplement Series
JSOTSup	Journal for the Study of the Old Testament: Supplement Series
JSP	*Journal for the Study of the Pseudepigrapha*
JTS	*Journal of Theological Studies*
KEK	Kritisch-exegetischer Kommentar über das Neue Testament (Meyer-Kommentar)
LEC	Library of Early Christianity
NIBCNT	New International Biblical Commentary on the New Testament
NICNT	New International Commentary on the New Testament
NIDNTT	*New International Dictionary of New Testament Theology*. Edited by Colin Brown. 4 vols. Grand Rapids: Zondervan, 1975–1985
NIDOTTE	*New International Dictionary of Old Testament Theology and Exegesis*. Edited by W. A. VanGemeren. 5 vols. Grand Rapids: Zondervan, 1997
NIGTC	New International Greek Testament Commentary
NovT	*Novum Testamentum*
NTC	New Testament Commentary
NTL	New Testament Library
NTM	New Testament Message
NTS	*New Testament Studies*
OTP	*The Old Testament Pseudepigrapha*. Edited by J. H. Charlesworth. 2 vols. New York: Doubleday, 1983, 1985
PTMS	Princeton Theological Monograph Series
QD	Quaestiones Disputatae
RCT	*Revista catalana de teología*
ResQ	*Restoration Quarterly*
SBLDS	Society of Biblical Literature Dissertation Series
SJSJ	Supplements to the Journal for the Study of Judaism
SNTSMS	Society for New Testament Studies Monograph Series
SP	Sacra pagina
SR	*Studies in Religion*
TDNT	*Theological Dictionary of the New Testament*. Edited by Gerhard Kittel and Gerhard Friedrich. Translated by Geoffrey W. Bromiley. 10 vols. Grand Rapids: Eerdmans, 1964–1976
TDOT	*Theological Dictionary of the Old Testament*. Edited by G. Johannes Botterweck, Helmer Ringgren, and Heinz-Josef Fabry. Translated by John T. Willis, David E. Green, and Douglas W. Stott. 15 vols. Grand Rapids: Eerdmans, 1974–2006
TLOT	*Theological Lexicon of the Old Testament*. Edited by Ernst Jenni and Claus Westermann. Translated by Mark E. Biddle. 3 vols. Peabody: Hendrickson, 1997

TNTC	Tyndale New Testament Commentaries
TRE	*Theologische Realenzyklopädie*. Edited by Gerhard Krause and Gerhard Müller. 36 vols. Berlin: de Gruyter, 1976–2006
TUGAL	Texte und Untersuchungen zur Geschichte der altchristlichen Literatur
TynBul	*Tyndale Bulletin*
VT	*Vetus Testamentum*
VTSup	Supplements to Vetus Testamentum
WBC	Word Biblical Commentary
WTJ	*Westminster Theological Journal*
WUNT	Wissenschaftliche Untersuchungen zum Neuen Testament
ZBKNT	Zürcher Bibelkommentare zum Neuen Testament

Introduction

Covenant is a prominent motif in Hebrews. Although this document comprises only 4.5 percent of the New Testament, it has 52 percent of all NT occurrences of διαθήκη.[1] It is also well known that Hebrews alternates between doctrine and exhortation, but the link between the epistle's use of διαθήκη and its exhortations needs to be explored. Covenant is important doctrinally, and exhortation is a major purpose of the epistle,[2] but how do the two relate to one another?

The need for this investigation becomes more apparent when we observe that the covenant motif could be eliminated from Hebrews, as shown in Appendix A, without damaging the coherence of the epistle or its major christological conclusions. The author does not need the covenant motif to extol the superiority of Jesus or the superiority of his sacrifice.[3] Indeed, he argues that Jesus is superior long before he even mentions the covenant.

Hebrews 7:22 is the first use of διαθήκη: "accordingly Jesus has also become the guarantee of a better covenant." In this verse, the author does not argue that Jesus is better because his covenant is better. Rather, the logic is the reverse: Jesus is better; therefore his covenant is also better. In this passage, the covenant motif is not a step toward

---

1. Although Hebrews has characteristics of a written sermon, or a series of sermons, the document is traditionally called an epistle due to its epistolary ending. I call it an epistle for the sake of convenience, not to categorize its genre. Hebrews calls itself a "word of exhortation" (13:22), a phrase used in Acts 13:15 for a synagogue message. For an attempt to define this genre, see Wills, "The Form of the Sermon," 177–99, and Black, "The Rhetorical Form," 1–18.

2. My initial interest in covenant was due to a doctrinal controversy within my denomination, but as I became convinced that exhortation is the primary purpose of Hebrews, I began to ponder the link between these two.

3. Throughout this work, "author" refers to the author of Hebrews. I refer to myself in the first person, and to other scholars by surname. Hebrews 13 implies that the author was known to the recipients, and had no need to hide his identity, so the masculine self-reference in 11:32 can be taken as accurate. I therefore use masculine pronouns for the author.

a christological conclusion. Instead, the Christology here functions as a step toward a point that the author wishes to make about the covenants.⁴ The covenant motif does not directly support other themes; it is a point in itself. This can also be seen in the fact that the author goes out of his way to include the covenant motif. There is no explicit need for it—the word is not found in Ps 110 (the key scripture of the epistle and the context of Heb 7:22). Also, the author introduces the covenant motif in the context of priesthood and sacrifice even though Jer 31 (the key "covenant" scripture) says nothing about priesthood and sacrifice.⁵

Hebrews has a parenetic purpose. The author repeatedly goes from exposition to exhortation, generally linked by some form of "therefore." The author urges the readers to respond to the explanations of Scripture that he has given—but how does the covenant motif support the author's exhortations? Why has the author included this theme when it is seemingly not necessary for his other themes?

To investigate this question, this study begins with a preliminary examination of the situation in which Hebrews was written. Of particular interest is the ethnicity of the intended recipients, the situation that prompted the author to write, and the questions that the readers faced. Scholars are divided on these questions and have used a variety of methodological approaches to answer them. In chapters 1 and 2, I survey their conclusions and evaluate their reasons. I find that answers become more evident when we use a tool of literary criticism—the concept of implied reader. In chapter 3, I examine various arguments in Hebrews to discern some of the beliefs that the author assumed the readers had. From this examination we may retrieve more evidence about ethnicity and situation. I conclude that the readers are most likely Jewish, they believe in Jesus as the Messiah, and they are attracted to the old covenant.

---

4. The Christology of the epistle does not *always* serve to support a point about covenants. The author clearly wants to make certain christological points in addition to what he says about covenants.

5. "Lorsque ce livre décrit les sacrifices, il ne les présente pas comme ayant un rapport avec l'alliance. Notre auteur, au contraire, a tenu à exprimer et à souligner le rapport qui existe entre le culte et l'alliance . . . . Après avoir cite l'oracle de la 'nouvelle alliance', qui, répétons-le, ne contient pas la moindre allusion au culte sacrificiel, l'auteur réaffirme immédiatement le rapport qui lie alliance et culte" (Vanhoye, "La 'teliôsis," 337).

I next examine the concept of covenant in first-century Jewish thought, which would have been based on the Scriptures and reflected in writings of the Second-Temple period. Since the author quotes from the Septuagint rather than the Masoretic text, I have based my analysis of Scripture on the LXX,[6] and rather than using a historical-critical analysis, I have analyzed the Jewish Scriptures from the pre-critical perspective of a first-century person who accepted them as divinely initiated words. Although some of these observations are not directly relevant to Hebrews, I have tried to be comprehensive in this study because scholars have significant disagreements about the issues involved, and all the documents are potentially part of the conceptual background relevant to the readers of Hebrews, shaping their understanding of the word διαθήκη when it is used in the epistle. Of particular interest in this study are the predictions of an eschatological covenant, since the "new covenant" has an important role in Hebrews. It can then be seen how the conclusions of this historical inquiry converge with the conclusions coming from the study of the implied readers.

In chapter 5, I survey the New Testament to see what concept of "covenant" is implied in these writings.[7] Chapter 6 then considers how the covenant motif supports the argument of the epistle, including its exhortations. Assuming that the author did not put a major motif in this epistle without purpose, I conclude that the readers had a specific need for doctrinal instruction about the covenant, and that this theme had important behavioral implications for the readers. This conclusion gives further evidence in support of the ethnicity of the readers and the occasion of the epistle.

---

6. At this point, I switch investigative methods, from an analysis of the implied reader to a more historical word study. Although we can ascertain some of the readers' beliefs about covenant simply from the way Hebrews uses the term, Hebrews by itself does not give us a complete picture. Therefore I broaden the scope of the study and switch to a method more appropriate to the question of what would likely come to the mind of first-century Jews when they heard the term *covenant*. Although the concept of covenant among Greek-speaking Jews would have been influenced by the Hebrew Scriptures and the Hebrew word בְּרִית, the most immediate influence on their thinking would have been the LXX. Although I cannot verify that the author had read all the books included in the LXX today, I analyze the entire LXX.

7. "Covenant" is used once in the Apocalypse, in the phrase "ark of the covenant" (Rev 11:19), but it is impossible to use this as a window into what people thought about covenant itself.

1

Jews and/or Gentiles

The Ethnic Identity of the Recipients of Hebrews

THE TRADITIONAL VIEW HAS BEEN THAT HEBREWS WAS WRITTEN TO Jews. However, starting in the 19th century, a number of commentators have argued that the audience contained Gentiles also. Some argue for an exclusively Gentile audience.[1] If we can find clues in the text to help us ascertain the ethnicity of the recipients, we will improve our understanding of the situation the author addressed, and from that, the message he wanted to convey. I will begin with a survey of opinions and reasons offered, looking largely at secondary sources. (I will present my own analysis of Hebrews in chapter 3.) Asking about the readers *implied by the text* gives us several lines of evidence relevant to the ethnicity of the readers. Of the various methods that have been used to ascertain the ethnicity of the readers, this approach seems to offer the most substantial evidence and a more defensible conclusion, suggesting that it is a better tool for the inquiry.[2]

---

1. Scholars who support the various views are listed in Koester, *Hebrews*, 46–48; McCullough, "Hebrews," 78; and Schmithals, "Über Empfänger," 321–42. In most cases, scholars are discussing ethnic rather than religious categories. By Jews, they usually mean Jews who believe in Jesus as the Messiah, and Gentiles mean Gentiles who believe in Jesus. I will discuss the readers' religious beliefs in chapter 3.

2. In *Faithfulness and the Purpose of Hebrews*, Marohl surveys dozens of commentators and concludes that a consensus is impossible because the historical-critical method is simply unable to answer the question of ethnicity with the data provided in the text (p. xiv). He argues that the best we can do is to find out how the readers categorized themselves—and that is as "the faithful." I agree that the author wanted the readers to think of themselves in this way, but I believe that a rhetorical analysis will provide evidence for their ethnicity as well.

Arguments for Gentiles

To argue for a Gentile audience, commentators must counter the arguments traditionally assumed to indicate a Jewish audience and offer evidence that suggests Gentile readers. The following are traditionally cited as evidence for a Jewish audience: 1) extensive use of the Jewish Scriptures; 2) use of Jewish exegetical methods; 3) sustained concern with the Levitical worship system; and 4) the author's assumption that the readers would view the Jewish Scriptures as authoritative. However, these points are countered by the simple observation that Gentiles often attended synagogues and could be familiar with the Scriptures, Jewish exegesis, and the Levitical cult, and could view the Scriptures as authoritative. George Guthrie states it well:

> Although some scholars have taken these insights to indicate a thoroughly Jewish audience for Hebrews, one must remember that many Gentiles affiliated themselves with first-century synagogues, either as proselytes or God-fearers. Consequently, some Gentiles came to Christ with a rich background in Jewish worship and extensive knowledge of the Jewish Scriptures. Therefore, the exact mix of Jews and Gentiles in this church group must remain a mystery.[3]

DeSilva notes that a Gentile did not even have to first attend a synagogue to acquire a Jewish perspective. It could have been acquired through new groups, those who accepted Jesus as the Messiah and used the Jewish Scriptures:

> The Gentile entering the Christian community became an "heir of the promise," a "child of Abraham," the "Israel of God," the "circumcision" and the "royal priesthood, God's holy nation." That is to say, the Gentile Christian was socialized to view himself or herself as the heir to the titles and promises that belonged to God's chosen people (historically, the Jewish people). The Gentile Christian was also enculturated to regard the Jewish Scriptures as the "oracles of God."[4]

Through their worship meetings, Gentile believers could have been familiar with the Scriptures,[5] could respect them as authoritative,

---

3. Guthrie, *Hebrews*, 20.
4. deSilva, *Perseverance in Gratitude*, 3.
5. I use the word "believers" to refer to people who believed in Jesus as the Savior,

and could be familiar with Jewish exegetical methods. DeSilva cites examples from Galatians, 1 Peter, and 1 Corinthians to show that Gentile believers were assumed to have a good knowledge of the Scriptures. "The use of the OT in Hebrews, then, does not necessitate or even suggest an audience made up primarily of Jewish Christians."[6] Trotter likewise notes that many Gentiles were familiar with the Scriptures, priests, and sacrifices.[7]

However, it could be argued that a Gentile who was wavering in allegiance to Christ (or at least in allegiance to the community of believers, as Heb 10:25 indicates) might also be wavering in allegiance to the Scriptures, but since Hebrews *assumes* their continuing acceptance of the Scriptures, Gentiles are not likely to be in the audience. DeSilva responds to this argument:

> If their temptation to defect, however, is primarily social (yielding to society's shaming techniques at last) rather than ideological (rejecting the message about Christ and the texts in which it was grounded), then the OT would remain a valid body of texts from which to elevate ideological considerations over considerations of social well-being.[8]

The traditional evidence in favor of Jewish readers is weak. But, what is the evidence in favor of *Gentile* readers? Bruce reports the arguments of scholars who favor a Gentile audience: Jews going back to Judaism would not likely be described as "turning away from the living

---

Lord and/or Messiah. Hebrews most often calls them ἀδελφοί. Although Hebrews implies a strong group boundary marker—those who confess (Christ) vs. those who do not—it does not give us a distinctive term by which the group identified itself vis-à-vis others. Although people today often use the term "Christian" as a category for first-century believers, the term may import anachronistic concepts of a well-developed religious system into the readers of Hebrews, who may not have perceived the boundaries in the same way.

Anderson illustrates the difficulty of categorizing the readers: "Rather than 'Judaism' being considered a foreign religion in Hebrews, the epistle testifies to a type of 'Christianity' which is oriented primarily if not exclusively toward Jews. This form of Christianity, while opposing cultic or temple Judaism in the strongest possible terms, nevertheless considers itself Jewish" ("Who Are the Heirs?" 258). Similar definitional problems exist for "Jewish Christian." See Paget, "Jewish Christianity," 741.

6. deSilva, *Perseverance*, 4.

7. Trotter, *Interpreting the Epistle*, 29.

8. deSilva, *Perseverance*, 5. But the social pressures probably included pressure for ideological conformity.

God" (3:12), nor would they be accused of having performed "dead works" before they believed in Christ (6:1; 9:14).[9] Braun argues that Hebrews addresses Gentile Christians because 1) the six topics of Heb 6:1 are teachings given to Gentiles who were becoming proselytes to Judaism, and 2) the warnings in Hebrews about apostasy never mention a return to Judaism.[10] Weiss also argues for Gentile readers on the basis of Heb 6:1 as a proselyte catechism.[11] Davies gives two additional reasons:

> There are in fact two indications that the readers were Gentile:
>
> (a) The writer never says or implies that their turning away would be a turning *back*, as he surely would if they had been Jews before conversion. Judaism is presented as an obsolete religion, but not as their own previous religion.
>
> (b) The warning about holiness of life in 12:14, and about sexual immorality in 13:4, seems unlikely to be directed to Jews, who were conspicuous in the ancient world for their ethical religion and their standards of sexual morality.[12]

Davies also suggests that the readers "were not sufficiently aware of the connection between religion and morality" and needed instruction in basic morality—something that would not be necessary for Jewish readers.[13] Montefiore uses a similar argument: "The warning about pre-

---

9. Bruce, *Hebrews*, 5. Bruce rejects these arguments and concludes that the readers were Jewish.

10. "Der Text wendet sich an Heidenchristen, wie die an sie gerichtete Bekehrungspredigt zeigt, die unter den Primärbelehrungen die Abkehr von den toten Werken, also dem Götterdienst, und den Glauben an Gott nennt 6,1. Die häufigen Warnungen vor Abfall sprechen nie von Rückfall ins Judentum" (Braun, *An die Hebräer*, 2). Unfortunately, even though he notes that it is understandable that early commentators gave it the title πρὸς Ἑβραίους, his introduction does not give any further rationale for his conclusion. Bénétreau also observes that Braun does little to support his opinion: "Braun opte encore pour une origine païenne, sans faire un gros effort pour fonder son opinion" (*L'Épître aux Hébreux*, 1:18).

11. Weiss, *Der Brief an die Hebräer*, 71. März gives an equally brief explanation for why he claims that the readers were Gentiles: that Hebrews shows little interest in differentiating Jews and Gentiles, and does not accuse the readers of returning to Judaism (*Hebräerbrief*, 19). Grässer merely notes that the old covenant-new covenant comparison is meaningful to Gentile Christians, too (*An die Hebräer*, 1:23). None of these commentators gives an adequate discussion of the possibilities.

12. Davies, *Hebrews*, 6.

13. Ibid., 123.

marital and extra-marital sexual relationships . . . could hardly have been intended for Jewish Christians, but rather for former pagans."[14] Although he says that the readers are "predominantly Jewish in origin," he believes the audience must have contained some Gentiles as well.[15]

Delville, like Davies, argues that the readers were Gentiles attracted to Judaism.[16] Like Braun, he builds his case largely on 6:1–2, saying that these elementary doctrines were similar to the main teachings Jews taught to pagan proselytes. These Gentiles were immersed in a Jewish culture and had come to believe in Christ, but were now being troubled by people who wanted them to follow the Torah, be circumcised, and participate in sacrifices. Delville argues that Hebrews responds to this by showing that each of the basic teachings (6:1–2) finds fulfillment in Jesus Christ.[17]

Moffatt asserts that the readers were Gentile, but does not offer much evidence. "The writer never mentions Jews or Christians . . . . They are in danger of relapsing, but there is not a suggestion that the relapse is into Judaism."[18] "Had the danger been a relapse into Judaism of any kind, it would have implied a repudiation of Jesus Christ as messiah and divine—the very truth which the writer can assume!"[19] However,

14. Montefiore, *Hebrews*, 16.

15. Ibid.

16. Delville, "L'Épître aux Hébreux," 323–68. Schmithals similarly argues from Heb 5:11—6:3 that the readers were Gentiles who had accepted Christ after being God-fearers ("Über Empfänger," 335).

17. Delville shows that Jewish teaching for proselytes often included repentance, faith, circumcision, ablutions, resurrection and judgment. He then posits that early Christians taught a similar pattern, substituting baptisms and the laying on of hands as initiation rites instead of circumcision and ablutions. He assumes that Heb 6:2 shows the catechism the readers had already been taught. Delville posits the improbable situation of 1) a Gentile audience "qu'ils ont vécu en contact avec le judaïsme, qu'ils ont reçu un enseignement de base semblable à celui des prosélytes convertis au judaïsme" and 2) an author who wanted to fight "une propagande juive qui devait tenter son auditoire et voulait le convaincre que la conversion et le salut véritable ne se faisaient qu'à travers le rituel juif" ("L'épître," 356, 262), and yet 3) an author who does not address circumcision, the very ritual that distinguished the groups. Delville does not discuss how the epistle might dissuade Gentiles from going into Judaism.

18. Moffatt, *Commentary*, xvi. In response, I note that there is no suggestion of relapse into paganism, either. I do not know what sort of "relapse" Moffatt is proposing.

19. Ibid., xxvii. As I argue below, an attraction to old covenant rituals would not necessarily involve an overt repudiation of Jesus as the Messiah or as divine. First-century Judaism had a wide variety of beliefs, and there was more concern for orthopraxy than

he does not give any evidence *in favor of* Gentile readers. Similarly, Schierse supports his conclusion with only one sentence: "There is not a single passage which speaks of reverting to Judaism; nor is there any reference to Herod's temple."[20]

Scott argues the case in more detail, giving these reasons: 1) The extensive use of Jewish Scriptures could be appropriate for Gentiles as well as Jews; 2) Hebrews says nothing about an apostasy to Judaism; 3) First-century Judaism was a matter of law, not worship ritual; 4) Hebrews deals with the tabernacle, not the temple; and 5) Hebrews does not refer to Jews or Gentiles, implying an audience unconcerned about the distinction.[21] However, he does not offer any positive evidence in favor of Gentiles.

Without endorsing the view, Koester adds another argument in favor of Gentile readers:

> Those who think that the addressees were of Gentile background often hold that Hebrews was written rather late, probably in the final decades of the first century. Since Hebrews does not reflect the tensions between Jewish and Gentile Christianity that are evident in Paul's letters, one can argue that the distinction between Jewish and Gentile Christians had become a thing of the past . . . . Those who favor a Gentile Christian readership generally argue that the listeners were not in danger of reverting to Judaism, but of giving way to the fatigue and discouragement that was typical of second-generation Christians.[22]

---

for theological uniformity. See Barclay, *Jews in the Mediterranean Diaspora*, 413, and Paget, "Jewish Christianity," 734 n. 11.

20. Schierse, *Hebrews*, xii. Schierse rejects the "widely accepted" theory that the readers were Palestinian Jews and calls it "far-fetched" and "superficial." But that is a straw-man argument, since the Palestinian Jewish theory is not widely accepted. He has not addressed the evidence, nor given any evidence in favor of Gentiles.

21. Scott, *Hebrews*, 16–18. I grant most of these points, while denying that they lead to the conclusion that Scott draws. I will respond to them shortly.

22. Koester, *Hebrews*, 47. Scott is an example of a scholar who supports his view at several points by referring to a late date, based largely on the fact that the church has a history "apparently of some duration" (Scott, *Hebrews*, 5). This gives too much weight to the ambivalent evidence in 2:3 and 13:7.

Arguments Against Gentile Readers

There are weaknesses in the arguments for Gentile readership, and the case is often made with superficial discussion. Evidence against some of the arguments is offered even by scholars who agree that Gentiles were among the readers. Ellingworth, for example, rejects the argument that only Gentiles could "turn away from the living God," or that only Gentiles could be said to have "dead works."[23] In this he echoes Bruce, who points out that the author of Hebrews would regard *any* retrogression as a failure to hear the word of God, and therefore an apostasy against him.[24] "What was possible for Israelites then [in the wilderness] was equally possibly for Israelites now. And the 'dead works' are things which call for repentance and cleansing, on the part of Jews and Gentiles without discrimination."[25] Trotter writes, "A final argument for gentile readership comes from the reference to 'dead works' (Heb. 6:1; 9:14). Yet the author of Hebrews does not consider the works of Judaism to be alive either, as his calling those works a mere shadow makes abundantly clear."[26] Trotter eventually concludes that "the weight of evidence tends toward a congregation of mixed background."[27] Similarly, Ellingworth writes, "None of these references, therefore, absolutely requires an exclusively gentile readership; they do, perhaps, suggest that the addressees were not exclusively Jewish."[28]

Trotter mentions six arguments within Hebrews whose form might imply a Gentile background, but he also notes that Jews and Gentiles could understand the arguments equally well; none supports an exclusively Gentile readership.[29] Even if the teachings of 6:1–2 were a catechism that Jews gave to proselytes from paganism, it could still be possible to mention these teachings to Jewish believers as the foundation that does not need to be discussed. The teachings of 6:1–2 do not give us a clear indication of the ethnicity of the readers.

---

23. Ellingworth, *Hebrews*, 24.
24. Bruce, *Hebrews*, 5.
25. Ibid., 6.
26. Trotter, *Interpreting*, 30.
27. Ibid.
28. Ellingworth, *Hebrews*, 25.
29. Trotter, *Interpreting*, 30; see also Ellingworth, *Hebrews*, 24.

Ellingworth notes the "consistent avoidance both of distinctively 'Jewish' and also of distinctively 'gentile' language."[30] He writes,

> The argument for a mixed Jewish and gentile readership is strengthened by the systematic exclusion, from the author's OT quotations and verbal allusions, of negative references to Israel, and also references to gentiles, present in the OT contexts. The evidence for such exclusion, though by its nature negative [i.e., an argument from silence], is cumulatively very strong.... It is more likely that the author is avoiding references which might reawaken earlier tensions, now resolved, between Jews and gentiles within the Christian community.... The avoidance of potentially divisive references points to a mixed community.[31]

Let us review the arguments in favor of Gentile readership and note their weaknesses:

1) It is claimed that Jews going back to Judaism would not likely be described as "deserting the living God" (3:12). Bruce's response is valid: the author would regard any retrogression, any refusal to listen, as apostasy.[32] Even when people maintain the same behavior as before, they can be guilty of desertion if God is calling them to change. Indeed, the author's use of "living" may be a subtle reminder that God's instructions can change.

2) Several scholars claim that Jews would not be accused of having been involved in "dead works" (6:1; 9:14). Trotter gives a good response: The shadows of the Levitical cult could be called "dead," especially after the reality had arrived.[33] Hebrews argues that the Levitical rituals are *ineffective* and *obsolete*; it is only a small step further to call them dead. Also, as illustrated by John the Baptist, preachers could call Jewish audiences to repentance, implying that their previous activities were insufficient.[34] Just as

---

30. Ibid., 26.
31. Ibid., 25.
32. Bruce, *Hebrews*, 5.
33. Trotter, *Interpreting*, 30.
34. Koester gives further evidence that Jews could be involved in dead works: "The examples of unbelief in Hebrews are from Israel, not from the Gentile world" (*Hebrews*, 305).

faith could be called dead in Jas 2:17, ineffective works could be called dead in Jewish circles, even if those works were Jewish.

3) Many also claim that the elementary teachings of Heb 6:1–2 are appropriate for Jews to preach to Gentiles leaving paganism. However, Michel correctly observes that it is also appropriate for a Jew writing to Jews to call these teachings elementary and then, as our author does, not discuss them in any further detail.[35] The six teachings are remedial topics that the readers do not need to review.[36]

4) Several scholars note that the readers are not accused of turning back to a previous religion.[37] But nor are they accused of turning to a different religion or abandoning all religion. The author does not describe their situation in modern categories. We cannot expect the first-century author to mark the distinction between religious systems in the way we do today. As Attridge observes, the author is more concerned about the confession the readers are tempted to abandon than where they might go.[38] However, that does not mean that there are *no* clues about what they are tempted with. Does Hebrews completely lack a warning against reversion? Gordon argues that the reference to Abraham returning to a previous land (Heb 11:15) would not be relevant to the readers unless they were tempted with a religious return.[39]

35. "Der Brief will darum auch nicht die katechetischen Elementarstücke lehren, die für Heidenchristen wichtig, aber dem Judentum schon bekannt sind (6:1–2), sondern das apostolische Kerygma in einer neuen kultischen, diesen Lesern gemäßen Gestalt" (Michel, *Der Brief,* 45). Although the catechism could fit a Gentile readership, the reference to washings and the absence of a Christological statement calls that into question; it is not designed for Gentiles entering the church (ibid., 50).

36. Hebrews 1–5 includes several basic teachings about Christ. In 6:12, the author says that he will now leave that behind and go on to something more mature. He mentions but does not elaborate on the "foundation."

37. Davies, *Hebrews,* 6.

38. Attridge, *Hebrews,* 369.

39. Gordon, *Hebrews,* 14. Although deSilva does not advocate Jewish readers tempted with Judaism, he nevertheless (like Gordon) argues that 11:15 is crafted to be relevant to the readers, and that they looked back "wistfully to the homeland they left behind (socially if not spatially)" (*Hebrews,* 381, 400). Since religion is an essential part of the readers' social setting, this suggests a religious reversion, and Judaism is the only religious context discussed. Hagner says: "The implication can hardly be missed that our author does not want his readers to return to their previous Judaism" (*Encountering,* 149).

Bruce argues that the "camp" of 13:13 "stands for the established fellowship and ordinances of Judaism," which the readers were exhorted to leave.[40] They may not be accused of turning back, but in 13:13 they are told to turn *away* from something. Hagner writes about the contrast in chapter 12 between Sinai and Zion: "The purpose of the contrast is to indicate what the readers already enjoy, and what they necessarily return to if they abandon their Christian faith."[41] The author did not consider polytheism an option worth mentioning.

5) Davies claims that Jews would not be warned about holiness or sexual morality.[42] However, as Jewish literature shows, Jews were not immune from exhortations to morality. Matthew and James also have reminders against adultery for their Jewish readers. And if the readers did not know that faith was connected to morality, as Davies argues, the author would need to explain that connection, but he does not. He argues at length about cultic details, but mentions morality without supporting argumentation, as if it will be accepted without question.

6) Hebrews does not reflect tensions between Jewish and Gentile Christianity, and some claim this as evidence that the readers include both Jews and Gentiles.[43] However, the avoidance of Jew-Gentile tensions could be explained in several ways: a) the readers were mixed, and the author did not want to stir up any unnecessary controversy, b) the readers were of one ethnic group, yet living near believers of other ethnic groups, and again the author did not want to exacerbate tensions, or c) the

---

40. Bruce, *Hebrews*, 381. Thus the author might not be addressing a *return* to Judaism, but a failure to leave it in the first place. Stanley argues similarly: "The context makes it clear that the camp is Jerusalem, which they can abandon because the city they are seeking is not the earth-bound Jerusalem, but a heavenly city (v. 14, cf. also 11:14–16). In effect, the readers are being encouraged to break with the religious community of Israel" ("New Covenant Hermeneutic," 103). See also Hagner, *Encountering*, 173, and Salevao, *Legitimation*, 147.

41. Hagner, *Encountering*, 161. In his earlier commentary, Hagner refers to possibly "gnostic" views in 13:4, 9, but also notes that Judaism was influenced by similar ideas (*Hebrews*, 3). The presence or absence of (proto)gnostic views says little about the ethnicity of the readers. For a critique of gnostic theories, see Hurst, *Hebrews*, 67–75.

42. Davies, *Hebrews*, 6.

43. Koester, *Hebrews*, 47 and Ellingworth, *Hebrews*, 26.

readers were of one ethnic group and were not concerned about what other believers did (cf. Acts 21:20–25). In support of option b, I note that several commentators suggest that Hebrews was probably written to one house church in a city that had several[44]—and we could ask why Hebrews was written to the one rather than to them all. Could it be that this group was different in composition and needs from the others?[45]

7) Ellingworth notes that Hebrews avoids mentioning Gentiles in the quotes from Scripture, even when Gentiles are in the original context.[46] However, this could also suggest an exclusively Jewish audience, believers who needed to focus on Christology and worship without being reminded of their loss of special status. Moreover, if the audience were Gentile or mixed, it would be appropriate to remind them, even if subtly, that the Jewish Scriptures predicted the inclusion of Gentiles.[47] When mentioning Abraham's descendants (2:16), for example, it would seem appropriate to clarify, as other NT writers do, that this includes Gentiles. A systematic exclusion of Gentile references could be construed as an insult to Gentile readers; it suggests an entirely Jewish audience.

Scott argues that Judaism was not concerned about ritual, but about the law. "Paul, to whom the Jewish peril was a very real one, never deems it necessary even once to utter warnings against the attractions of the Temple worship."[48] But we should note that Gentiles were

---

44. Ellingworth, *Hebrews*, 24; Koester, *Hebrews*, 74; Trotter, *Interpreting*, 31; Weiss, *Der Brief*, 74–75, and Lane, *Hebrews 1–8*, liii.

45. The other congregations may have been Gentile, or perhaps Jewish believers who did not have the same doctrinal needs as the readers of Hebrews did.

46. Ellingworth, *Hebrews*, 25.

47. Anderson also views this as evidence of Jewish readers: "Nowhere in Hebrews is any interest shown in that part of Genesis 22 which refers to gentiles.... One would assume that any first century Christian concerned with a gentile mission would not leave out the one part of this passage connected with the blessing of Abraham with non-Jews" ("Heirs," 261–62). "The author of Hebrews gives not a hint that his gospel was directed to other than the children of Abraham in the traditional sense" (268).

48. Scott, *Hebrews*, 17. However, he later admits that Philo was a Jew who was "preoccupied with the idea of worship" (ibid., 52). There is a detailed critique of Scott's argument in Manson, *Hebrews*, 18–22.

generally not concerned with Jewish rituals, either. As Scott later admits, "the writer of Hebrews appears to acknowledge no valid religion outside of Judaism" and he "sees in worship the central fact of religion."[49] Whether the concern for worship was common among Jews or not, it is a possibility for the readers just as much as for the author, and Hebrews evidences an author with an interest in ritual. We should also note that the readers were confronted with strange teachings (13:9) that were not necessarily found in majority Judaism.

In short, the evidence for Gentiles in the audience is scanty and debatable. Each argument for Gentiles has a serious weakness, which means that even when they are put together, there is little evidence for the existence of *any* Gentiles among the readers. Nor is it legitimate to conclude that the audience is mixed merely because the evidence for neither group is conclusive. It would be more appropriate to remain undecided, as Koester is,[50] or to be silent, as some commentators are. Koester observes a few more objections:

> If the listeners were of Gentile background, one might expect a clearer indication of this, as in other NT letters (cf. 1 Thess 1:9; Gal 4:8; Rom 1:5–6; 1 Pet 4:3–4). If listeners were in danger of reverting to Greco-Roman religious beliefs, there would probably have been some clearer mention of threats posed by idolatry (cf. 1 Cor 8:1–13; 10:14–30).[51]

However, the possibility of idolatry is never addressed. The author never praises anyone for leaving idolatry, nor argues against idolatry. Manson observes, "There is not a word in Hebrews about unbelief in the sense of irreligion pure and simple, nor about pagan rites and mysteries."[52] Also lacking in Hebrews is any mention that old covenant laws did not apply to Gentiles—a point that would have helped the argument, if the epistle were addressed to Gentiles.

I also see reasons against a mixed audience. Chief among these is that circumcision is nowhere mentioned, although that would be a

---

49. Scott, *Hebrews*, 29–30.

50. Koester, *Hebrews*, 77.

51. Ibid., 48. He notes that the author assumes that there can be only one priesthood (p. 359), a point that Gentiles might not so readily assume. Similarly, the author asserts that humans cannot volunteer for priesthood (5:4), which would not necessarily be taken for granted by Gentiles.

52. Manson, *Hebrews*, 22.

relevant issue for a mixed audience.⁵³ Bruce notes that Hebrews (unlike Galatians) shows no evidence of "judaizing propaganda from outside."⁵⁴ If any of the readers were uncircumcised, they would have already believed what the author works so hard to prove, namely, that major elements of the old covenant are obsolete, at least for them. However, a discussion of circumcision would not be necessary for a Jewish audience, who were all circumcised at birth and were not facing any urgent decisions about it.

It is true that Gentiles who lost faith in Christ *could* retain respect for the Jewish Scriptures, as deSilva notes.⁵⁵ But they might also lose it, and the writer would be foolish to ignore the options available to a Gentile who was weary of persecution, weak in theology, and waning in loyalty. The best way for a Gentile to escape persecution, shame, and social pressure would be to return to paganism—but the author does not address such a possibility. He *assumes* that the readers will retain respect for the Scriptures, this is something that probably could not be safely assumed for Gentile readers.

Commentators who favor a Jewish audience often conclude that the readers were going back into Judaism⁵⁶—that is, they consider it an option available to the readers. But commentators who favor a Gentile audience usually do *not* consider the options. In the first century, could the readers avoid religion entirely?⁵⁷ Would they participate in the civic cult, or what excuse would they give for not participating? Would they attend a synagogue? Would they continue to believe that Jesus was at God's right hand? Which of these options would alleviate their lethargy,

---

53. A point mentioned by Dahms, "First Readers," 366. Similarly, Westcott wrote, "Nor does the letter touch on any of the topics of heathen controversy.... It is therefore scarcely possible that it could have been written to a mixed Church" (*Hebrews*, xxxvi). Schmithals writes, "an keiner Stelle deutet der Hebräerbrief an, daß sein Verfasser mal die eine, mal die andere Gruppe im Blick hat" ("Über Empfänger," 330, n. 44).

54. Bruce, "A Document of Roman Christianity?" 3502.

55. deSilva, *Perseverance*, 5.

56. They are not always clear on whether this would involve a rejection of Jesus.

57. Lane notes that some early second-century Christians neglected meeting together because of business pursuits (*Hebrews 9–13*, 290, citing the *Similitudes* of Hermas). This was motivated by secular interests, not persecution or social pressure. Although irreligion might have been an option for some lethargic Christians, social pressures might not be alleviated by it. Hebrews does not address irreligion (indeed, it assumes a desire to approach God), nor any other options that Gentiles might consider when weary of social pressures.

social pressure, or religious desires? These questions should be considered, but usually are not. For example, deSilva speaks of the readers "returning to a lifestyle of which the unbelieving neighbors would approve,"[58] but he does not consider whether the text gives clues about what sort of lifestyle the neighbors might be exhorting.

Nothing in the text proves that Gentiles were *not* among the readers, but the text does not address their background or the religious options Gentiles had if they left the community of people who believed in Jesus as the Christ. In effect, *even if Gentiles were in the original audience, the epistle is not written to them, for it does not address their particular needs.*[59] Thurén's comment about 1 Peter applies to Hebrews as well: "We can hope to distinguish not necessarily the real audience, but the type of audience and the type of situation *at which the text is aimed.*"[60]

Evidence for Jewish Readers

As discussed above, the superficial evidence for a Jewish audience is inconclusive, and the evidence cited for Gentile readers is also inconclusive. But is there any *additional* evidence in favor of Jewish readers? Bruce acknowledges:

> The whole argument is conducted against a background of Old Testament allusion; considerable familiarity with the Levitical ritual, and interest in it, are presupposed. Yet all this in itself does not require either the author or the people addressed to be Jewish; we have known Gentile Christians who were thoroughly familiar with the Old Testament, accepted it as sacred and

---

58. deSilva, *Perseverance*, 343. He gives no evidence for suggesting on p. 354 that readers might be tempted to participate "in idolatrous cults or ruler cult." In an earlier article, he wrote, "The author may be afraid that some of the members, desiring to reduce tension between them and the unbelieving society, are considering a return to engagement in the worship of idols" ("Exchanging Favor for Wrath," 111). But the text has no evidence that the author is concerned with such a possibility, which means that it was *not* a possibility *for the readers implied by the text.*

59. This is not to deny that Hebrews could be *helpful* for Gentiles (it has been helpful to many people in many cultures throughout the centuries), but it is to say that Hebrews was not written with their particular needs in mind. The Gentile theory may look plausible, in part, because modern interpreters have worked hard to show how this epistle can be relevant to modern Gentile audiences. However, the fact that it is useful for Gentiles today does not mean that it was originally written to Gentiles.

60. Thurén, *Rhetorical Strategy of 1 Peter*, 44.

authoritative Scripture, and manifested a lively interest in the details of the Mosaic tabernacle and the Levitical offerings.[61]

However, Bruce then adds this argument:

> His insistence that the old covenant has been antiquated is expressed with a moral earnestness and driven home repeatedly in a manner which would be pointless if his readers were not especially disposed to live under that covenant, but which would be very much to the point if they were still trying to live under it, or imagined that, having passed beyond it, they could revert to it.[62]

Bruce uses the rhetoric of the letter as evidence for a Jewish audience—why would the author be so focused on the old covenant if the readers were not?[63] The argument throughout Hebrews deals with Jewish institutions, using Jewish exegetical methods, presupposing an audience who assumes the validity of Jewish scriptures, and arguing about customs that would be of interest primarily to Jewish people. The book does not deal with priests and sacrifices in general, but only with Jewish priests and sacrifices. Although Gentile believers would have some familiarity with the Jewish Scriptures, no other book of the NT is so steeped in specifically Jewish *worship* traditions.

Hebrews 7:11 argues from a hypothetical situation: "Now if perfection had been attainable through the levitical priesthood . . . what further need would there have been to speak of another priest . . . ?" Bruce comments, "If they were Gentile converts, in danger of abandoning their Christian faith, their only response to these words would have been: 'We never thought there *was* perfection through the Levitical priesthood.'"[64] In other words, the rhetoric in that verse is not suited for a Gentile audience. Similarly, Lindars writes, "It is highly significant

---

61. Bruce, *Hebrews*, 5.

62. Ibid., 6. Hagner uses a similar argument when he writes, "The very thrust of the epistle's sustained argument seems rather clearly to suggest readers of Jewish background" ("Interpreting the Epistle," 221).

63. Salevao also gives a rhetorical argument: "Although there is no explicit statement by the author to the effect that the readers were on the verge of relapse to Judaism, the general tenor of the letter and the whole orientation of his argument gives rise to a strong inference that the danger of relapse was indeed a real threat" (*Legitimation*, 113).

64. Bruce, *Hebrews*, 166.

that the method of argument . . . takes the Jewish practice of atonement as the standard to which any exposition of the permanent effectiveness of the sacrifice of Christ must conform. It is because the readers are converts from Judaism, and this is the basis for their understanding of the issues."[65]

The epistle presupposes readers steeped in Judaism. The *simplest* explanation for this is that the readers were Jewish. It does not help us any to posit the presence of atypical Gentiles.[66]

Although we can never prove the ethnic identity of the readers, we can at least conclude that they are *culturally* Jewish. Lehne, for example, does not specify the readers' ethnicity, but she concludes that their "Jewish heritage can be taken for granted by the author as the common ground between him and his addressees."[67] Similarly, Guthrie, although saying that the readers were ethnically mixed, writes, "Prior to accepting Christ the worship orientation of these believers had been to the synagogue."[68] Bockmuehl also says that the readers might include Gentiles, but "on balance, the language of Hebrews will make sense to those who see themselves as part of Israel and understand its history to be their own."[69]

But does the Jewish-flavored argument simply tell us about the writer, rather than the readers? If we are to know anything about the audience, we must assume that the writer is addressing their real needs—he knows the audience better than we do. In Hebrews, he is addressing an audience that can be counted on to remain Jewish in orientation. The argument assumes that the only comparison needed, and the only other viable option for the readers, is the old covenant—and this suggests a completely Jewish audience. If we grant that the author

---

65. Lindars, "Rhetorical Structure," 395. "Converts from Judaism" could include Gentiles, but there is no evidence that there were Gentile converts in the audience.

66. "Gentile 'Judaizers' are known to us from other literature. . . . But this depiction of the addressees places them in substantially the same position as the more traditional view assigns to Jewish Christian readers, and there are no clear grounds for departing from tradition here"—i.e., no clear evidence for readers who are ethnically Gentile (Lincoln, *Hebrews*, 37).

67. Lehne, *New Covenant*, 16.

68. Guthrie, *Hebrews*, 20.

69. Bockmuehl, "Church in Hebrews," 136. He argues that the evidence for Jewish readers is inconclusive, but he does not offer any positive evidence in favor of Gentiles.

has an accurate view of the readers, we must conclude that the readers have a Jewish background.[70]

Why spend so much time proving that the old covenant is obsolete? Why climax the longest exposition with the conclusion that sacrifices are no longer necessary (10:18), unless the readers had a special interest in those sacrifices? Hebrews warns that the penalty for rejecting the new covenant is greater than the penalty for rejecting the old. The comparison could be helpful for others, but would have greatest relevance for readers who were worried about, or being accused of, rejecting the old. If there were Gentiles in the audience, the writer ignores their concerns and options. He is not writing to the needs of Gentiles—he has shaped his argument for a Jewish context.

Ellingworth, though favoring a mixed audience, presents evidence for Jewish readers: "The evidence is overwhelming that the author expected his readers to be thoroughly acquainted with OT persons, institutions (especially cultic institutions, e.g. 9:1–10), and texts, and with the Mosaic law, and to accept unquestioningly the divine authority of the OT."[71] Ellingworth also notes that statements such as Heb 9:22 "would be either contested or incomprehensible" in some non-Jewish traditions.[72] He notes that the readers are assumed to be "in continuity with Israel."[73]

Gordon favors a Jewish audience, though cautiously. "Alford is right insofar as there are surprising omissions in *Hebrews* if it is addressed to Gentile Christians."[74] He notes that Hebrews makes no effort

---

70. Lane seems reluctant to identify the ethnicity of the readers, but admits that 13:9 probably alludes "to the eating of prescribed foods within a Jewish cultic setting [e.g., a synagogue]. Those who framed their conduct by such ceremonial meals, then, are Jewish" (*Hebrews 9–13*, 535). This does not say that all the readers were Jewish, but implies that only Jews would be tempted to accept such teachings. Lane speaks favorably of the view that 13:13 addresses readers who felt "the pull of their Jewish heritage," were "tempted to turn back" and were exhorted to "sever the emotional and social ties with the Jewish community" (545–46). This could include proselytes as well as Jews.

71. Ellingworth, *Hebrews*, 23.

72. Ibid., 24. I suggest Heb 9:15 as an example: It argues that the eternal inheritance is given because "the sins committed under the first covenant" have been atoned. The argument assumes that sins defined by the old covenant are the barrier to salvation—an assumption that a Gentile would probably not make.

73. Ibid.

74. Gordon, *Hebrews*, 12. He quotes Alford: "Not a syllable is found of allusions to their conversion from the alienation of heathenism, such as frequently occur in St.

to show the readers that they are among the inheritors of the promises given to Abraham. "For people theologically weak in other respects they appear to have a remarkably strong grasp of the theology of participation with the Old Testament faithful."[75] Gordon notes that "Abraham's descendants" (2:16) could be spiritualized, but there is no evidence in the text that it *is* being spiritualized. He also suggests that Heb 11:15 supports a Jewish audience, for it says that the patriarchs did not seek to "return" to their previous land. For this comment to be relevant to the readers, it would refer to a religious return—and the letter does not address any Gentile option.[76]

Hagner notes that nothing in the book *requires* the readers to be Jewish, but he asks, "Which hypothesis is more successful in accounting for the phenomena of the book as a whole?"[77] The simplest hypothesis, the one that creates the fewest problems, is that the readers were Jewish. There may be "no overwhelming evidence" for Jewish readers,[78] but the hypothesis for which we have the *most* evidence is that of Jewish readership.[79] The Gentile hypothesis leads to viewing the otherwise highly skilled writer as essentially ignoring the background and religious options of some of the readers. Since Hebrews addresses only Jewish culture, it implies a Jewish readership.

The reason that the author does not discuss Sabbath and food laws in more detail (Koester's question)[80] is first, that these details were incidental to the particular crisis, and second, the author declares the entire old covenant obsolete and does not need to itemize every law within it, particularly since he focuses on the cult.

Koester writes, "Biblical interpretation is the art of asking questions of texts. The way questions are posed reflects the assumptions and

---

Paul's epistles" (*The Greek Testament*, IV.1.62). The other "surprising omissions" that Gordon mentions are apparently Gordon's own observations, for I could not find them in Alford.

75. Gordon, *Hebrews*, 13.
76. Ibid., 14.
77. Hagner, *Hebrews*, 3.
78. Gordon, *Hebrews*, 13.
79. Hagner, *Hebrews*, 3. He says that Jews, "far more than any others, would find pressing upon them the question of the relation between the old and new covenants, and they, more than any, might be attracted to their previous mode of life" (Hagner, *Encountering*, 23).
80. Koester, *Hebrews*, 48.

concerns of the interpreter and shapes the answers that are given."[81] Since the text of Hebrews is dominated by religious concerns, it is appropriate to include religious concerns among the questions: Why does the author give only Jewish rituals as a comparison for the superiority of Christ? Why does he ignore Jew-Gentile distinctions? How would the chapters on cultic details encourage people if they were not concerned with those very details?

The simplest explanation for these questions is that the readers were Jewish. Jewish concepts were important to them. If we are to hear Hebrews the way the original audience did, we must listen *as if Judaism is the only meaningful frame of reference.* If anyone in the audience had a pagan background, it is ignored in the epistle, and thus it does not help to posit such readers. The readers implied by the text are Jewish readers.

Were the readers in Palestine, or were they among the Diaspora?[82] Several elements of Hebrews argue against a Palestinian destination: it would be inappropriate to say that the Palestinian church had not yet resisted to the point of blood (12:4),[83] to use Septuagintal texts that had no parallels in the Hebrew or the Targums, or to say that they had given material support to other believers (10:34). Hebrews is written to people who relate to the cult through the Scriptures, not through Temple attendance. Ellingworth gives a concise response to this view; Bruce gives a longer analysis and response.[84] Hagner summarizes it well:

> Against this view, however, is the strongly Hellenistic character of the book, which does not fit well with, for example, a Jerusalem readership. It is further to be noted that the Jerusalem church was poverty-stricken and therefore hardly capable of the generosity for which the author compliments the readers (6:10, 10:34, 13:16).[85]

---

81. Ibid., 19.

82. For example, Hughes, *Hebrews*, 11. He is building on the view of Spicq (ibid., 12–14; see Spicq, *L'Épître*, 30). Bruce notes several others who advocate a Palestinian destination (*Hebrews*, 7–8). Among these are Buchanan, *To the Hebrews*, 256.

83. The phrase may be a metaphor from boxing, but it would be a particularly inappropriate metaphor to use for a group in which people *had* been killed for the faith.

84. Ellingworth, *Hebrews*, 29; and Bruce, "To the Essenes?" 217–32.

85. Hagner, *Hebrews*, 6. These points also argue against Essene readers. See Hurst, *Hebrews*, 43–66.

Summary on Ethnicity of the Readers

I conclude that the readers were most likely Jewish. I will repeat the primary reasons for this conclusion:

1) There is no evidence of Gentile terminology, concerns, or options. The readers are expected to agree without argument, for example, that there can be only one valid priesthood at a time. The only comparisons the readers need are Jewish ones.

2) There is no evidence of a mixed audience. There is no mention of circumcision nor any discussion of which old covenant laws apply to Gentiles. Numerous Jewish traditions are discussed, but non-Jewish traditions are ignored.

3) References to Gentiles are excluded when the Scriptures are quoted. This could insult Gentile readers, but for Jewish readers it would avoid a sensitive topic.

4) Hebrews presumes that readers view themselves as descendants of Abraham and Israel, with roots in the old covenant, with no need for reminders (unlike other NT writings that went to Gentiles) that this includes Gentiles, too.

5) The argument of Hebrews implies readers who can be assumed to unanimously respect the Scriptures and unanimously need no polemic (not even reminders) against paganism.

6) The readers need to be told that the old covenant and its laws are obsolete. It would praise Jesus too faintly to say that he is better than a law that everyone already knows is obsolete—that would amount to saying that he is better than nothing. For the comparison to be a valid form of praise, it must compare him with something that is respected.[86] The readers overvalue the Sinaitic law, and there is no evidence that they are proselytes.

---

86. Seid writes, "It is ridiculous to compare an obviously inferior subject to one which is clearly superior" ("Synkrisis in Hebrews 7," 347). This principle can be seen in rhetorical manuals by Aelius Theon, Aphthonius, and Nicolaus the Sophist (Kennedy, *Progymnasmata*, 53, 113, 163).

If the readers already considered the law obsolete, and the author wanted to compare Jesus with that law anyway, he would need to bolster the comparison by praising the law—e.g., "Even though the law is obsolete, it was the best thing anyone had, but now we have something much better in Jesus." But the author's persistent polemic against the law suggests that the readers had too high a view of the law.

7) Hebrews *implies* an exhortation to reject the old covenant. The argument in didactic sections could be characterized as "A is better than B" and in parenetic sections as "choose A." This argument *implies* "Do not choose B." The length of the argument and the vigor of the rhetoric imply that it is a real choice for the readers; 10:25 says that some have already gone astray. Hebrews does not accuse or warn the readers about reversion to Judaism because the boundary lines were not yet drawn in those terms. Hebrews warns the readers about a failure to listen as God speaks in a new way. It views faith in Jesus as a development, not a wholesale change in religion, as Gentiles might have seen it.

8) The argument assumes that the readers *will* worship, but paganism is not discussed as an option; the only option worth discussing is an attraction to Jewish rituals. The author does not discuss the options that would be available to readers who were being pressured by Gentile neighbors. The only basis of comparison the readers need is the old covenant. The readers are Jewish by culture and probably by ethnicity.[87]

9) Hebrews was probably written to one church in a city that had several churches. This suggests that it had doctrinal and hortatory needs that were different from the other churches, perhaps because it was different in ethnic composition.

10) The warnings about apostasy from God, repentance from dead works, and sexual morality are just as appropriate for Jews as for

---

87. These details do not *prove* that the readers were Jewish, or even that they had an attraction to the old covenant. These details do suggest, however, that the epistle was originally written for people who had a special need for and interest in such details—a people who (despite their acceptance of Jesus as Messiah) were attracted to the old covenant. To use a modern example, suppose we heard a sermon arguing that Christianity is better than animism. In most of the Western world, the sermon might be interesting in informing the audience about animism, but it would not motivate people to accept Christianity because the basis of comparison is only marginally relevant to the audience. However, the sermon would be very relevant in parts of Africa, where animism is practiced and animism is a viable option. An emotional appeal would be out of place in the Western church, but appropriate for the African setting. In the same way, the emotional appeals in Hebrews indicate that it is addressing options that are relevant to the readers.

Gentiles. These are mentioned in passing, and are not argued at any length, as they might have been for Gentiles.[88]

Since the text is the only information we have on the audience, we have to base our view of the audience on the text. The text of Hebrews indicates an audience that is concerned with Jewish Scriptures and Jewish worship rituals. It gives no indication of addressing Gentile concerns or options, and the simplest explanation for this is that the audience is Jewish. It does not help us any to speculate that the audience also included Gentiles when the text essentially ignores issues relevant to Gentiles.

---

88. Brown adds another argument based on the antiquity and unanimity of the title "to the Hebrews": "If the title arose as a scholarly deduction from the contents, when and how did this take place to account for such early unanimity? A counter-suggestion is that the title came from a tradition based on knowledge of the actual circumstances of composition and direction, i.e., that the letter was meant to correct Hebrew Christian views" (Brown and Meier, *Antioch and Rome*, 141).

2

The Occasion of Hebrews

COMMENTATORS OFFER SEVERAL REASONS FOR THE WRITING OF Hebrews. Most suggestions fall into one or more of three general categories, each describing the problem(s) the readers had: 1) spiritual lethargy; 2) external pressure; and 3) religious desires. These are not mutually exclusive, but some commentators emphasize one or two and exclude the others.

Lethargy

Wilson represents well the view that the main problem of the readers of the epistle was lethargy:

> This book is written for people who have lost their first enthusiasm, who have grown weary of well-doing, who have need of the admonition "Stiffen your drooping arms and shaking knees, and keep your steps from wavering" (12:12f. *NEB*). The danger is . . . a loss of hope and confidence, of abandoning the Christian faith in the face of pressures of one kind or another; and it is this that makes it relevant in the very different world of today.[1]

However, "loss of hope and confidence" is little more than a restatement of the problem; it is not an explanation for it. Attridge says that the readers had "a waning commitment."[2] Why were they lagging in commitment? He says that factors at work might include "persecution, the delay of the parousia, and general fatigue, doubt and lassitude."[3]

---

1. Wilson, *Hebrews*, 15–16. In some diagnoses of lethargy, I suspect that there is a desire to present the ancient problem in terms that are really more applicable to modern audiences.
2. Attridge, *Hebrews*, 13.
3. Ibid., 11.

Ellingworth blames it on a character deficiency: "Inner weakness may have been a chronic condition predisposing some of the readers to abandon, at some critical point, their faith in Christ."[4]

Kistemaker identifies it as complacency produced by peace: "Because of the peaceful times, religious backsliding had become a distinct threat."[5] Similarly, Schmidt writes, "a comparatively uneventful period in the history of the community was taking a toll on its members."[6] Koester suggests the problem may have come simply with the passage of time: "Those who favor a Gentile Christian readership generally argue that the listeners were . . . giving way to the fatigue and discouragement that was typical of second-generation Christians."[7] The argument is sometimes given in this way: The traditional view is that the readers were in danger of reverting to Judaism, but the real problem was that they were lethargic.[8] But this is a false dichotomy, since lethargy says nothing about the direction the readers were drifting. Lane writes that the audience had a "failure of nerve . . . because of an inadequate christology."[9] He says that the readers are lethargic, disheartened, and weary "in a social climate hostile to their presence."[10] But other than a defective Christology, Lane does not specify what the problem is:

> Whether the root of the problem was the delay of the Parousia (10:25, 35–39), social ostracism and impending persecution (12:4; 13:13–14), or a general waning of enthusiasm and erosion of confidence (3:14; 10:35) is a matter for debate. Whatever the case may be, one of the symptoms of a community in crisis was the faltering of hope.[11]

DeSilva, using insights from the social sciences, argues that the readers had less commitment because of a loss of honor; they had a

---

4. Ellingworth, *Hebrews*, 80.
5. Kistemaker, *Exposition*, 15.
6. Schmidt, "Moral Lethargy," 167.
7. Koester, *Hebrews*, 47.
8. This can be seen, for example, in Goppelt, *Theology of the New Testament*, 2:242.
9. Lane, *Hebrews 1–8*, cxxxviii.
10. Ibid., lxi.
11. Ibid., lxii. Delay of the Parousia and social pressures are reasonable explanations, but "a general waning of enthusiasm" is a merely a restatement. The real question is *why* the readers were losing enthusiasm, and how that might be manifested in their social circumstances.

slow erosion of loyalty because they were tired of being ridiculed and shamed:

> The danger of falling away stems from the lingering effects of the believers' loss of status and esteem in their neighbors' eyes, and their inability to regain a place in society, or approval from the outside world . . . . Neither the threat of violent persecution nor a new attraction to Judaism motivates this apostasy, but rather the more pedestrian inability to live within the lower status that Christian association had forced upon them.[12]

Similarly, Koester argues that the community, persecuted in the past, was growing weary of its burdens.[13] They had been promised glory with Christ, but had only dishonor in the community, and they were tired of the tension between the promise and the lack of possession.[14] So the author exhorts them to look to Jesus as evidence, to draw near to God through him, and have faith in the not-yet-visible. The author appeals to emotions such as confidence to encourage faithfulness, and he uses fear and shame "to create an aversion to unfaithfulness."[15] The readers are to fear God more than their social situation.

However, the doctrinal sections, particularly the cultic details, seem only vaguely related to "encouragement"—unless the readers needed encouragement in that precise area, or had a special interest in such details. The readers needed *reasons* to endure, and some of the reasons they are given in this epistle concern the old cult. We must assume that the highly skilled writer of Hebrews was addressing subjects of interest to the readers, subjects *relevant* to their lack of enthusiasm. They needed not only general encouragement, but in some way they also needed the argument about Jesus' ministry as high priest and the

---

12. deSilva, *Perseverance*, 18–19. In an earlier article, deSilva suggested that the readers were "no longer sure of the certainty of the message around which the group was formed . . . growing disillusioned with the sect's promise to provide" (deSilva, "Social-Scientific Perspective," 10). But he does not say what the sect had promised, nor how the epistle would have changed their expectations.

13. Koester, *Hebrews*, 71.

14. Ibid., 87. Although Koester views this as the primary problem of the readers, he also writes, "Reasons for the decline are never delineated and may not have been fully apparent to either the author or the listeners. Therefore, without pursuing the causes, the author defines the situation in a manner that the listeners would find plausible" (*Hebrews*, 208).

15. Ibid., 90.

obsolescence of the old covenant. As Dahms says, if they merely needed endurance, "the extent of the comparison with the Mosaic dispensation, the detail with which it is elaborated and the urgency with which it is argued would be unwarranted."[16] The repeated emphasis that Jesus is better than the old order would be "quite overdone if the only concern is for the steadfastness and maturation of the readers."[17] Kim puts it more boldly:

> If the author's real interest was simply to persuade apathetic Jewish-Christians [or any other Christians, for that matter] to get serious about their faith, he did not have to: 1) choose to reflect on texts that imply discontinuity with Judaism; or 2) make pejorative statements about the Levitical priesthood and law, Mosaic covenant, and Levitical sacrifices. Encouraging apathetic Jewish-Christians does not have to come at the cost of deprecating specific Jewish institutions.[18]

Attridge classifies Hebrews as epideictic rhetoric, designed to reinforce existing values rather than persuade action.[19] Like an oration, the epistle "celebrates the ongoing significance of a person and certain events connected with him . . . . The oration as a whole appeals for continued and renewed commitment to the Jesus tradition in a situation uncomfortable for that tradition."[20] In other words, it attempts to reinvigorate people who are lethargic but who are not being asked to change anything. In support of this, Attridge notes that the hortatory sections of Hebrews are not polemic: "If it is the work's aim to wean the addressees from Judaism, it is remarkable how small a role an appeal

---

16. Dahms, "First Readers," 365.

17. Ibid., 366. For example, there would be little need to say that not only was the old covenant obsolete, but that it would soon disappear (8:13), or to point out the obvious, that the offerings were made according to the law (10:8).

18. Kim, *Polemic*, 61.

19. Attridge, "Paraenesis in a Homily," 211–26. Some commentators prefer to describe Hebrews as deliberative, urging a particular decision, and some conclude that Hebrews has elements of both types of rhetoric. Epideictic and deliberative speeches could be mixed and overlap, and there is little value in attaching a particular label to the epistle, as I argue in Appendix B.

20. Attridge, "Paraenesis," 214, 221. Übelacker argues that most of the exhortations in Hebrews should be classified as paraclesis rather than parenesis ("Paraenesis or Paraclesis"), but this label is attached after we ascertain the function; it does not help us determine what the function of the exhortations is.

to keep free from the Israel of the flesh plays in the explicit hortatory segments of the text."[21] Perhaps Attridge would see the readers saying, "Yes, I've always believed that . . . Yes, I want to do that; yes, you have given me more reasons for my conviction."

However, we must ask, *What is wrong with lethargy?* What were the readers tired of doing, in danger of not doing, and what did they want to do instead? What external behavior gave evidence that the readers were lethargic? An attempt to correct lethargy needs to include an exhortation to do something positive. Further, Hebrews suggests urgency. It suggests that the readers were in danger of slipping away, and indeed some already had (10:25). The readers were not just waning in commitment—they were in danger of dropping out, and if we want to understand the occasion, we need to ask, What would they do instead?

In their lethargy or timidity, what were they tempted to do? This is not a typical "reinforce traditional values" speech. Rather, Hebrews has a corrective tone. Its stern warnings indicate that the readers are facing a serious choice and imply that some of them would make the wrong choice if this message is not heeded. One of the last exhortations (13:13) is an appeal for movement, for *change*, not just reinforcing a previous pattern.

The fact that hortatory sections of Hebrews are not overtly polemical is a valid observation.[22] With the exception of 13:13, they identify what the readers were to do, not what they should avoid. Nevertheless, there is an *implied* polemic. When the expository section emphasizes that A is better than B, and the subsequent exhortation is, "Choose A," the implied exhortation is "as opposed to B." Hebrews presents two options: access to God through Christ on one hand, and an ineffective attempt to have access through ritual on the other. When the hortatory sections urge faith in Christ, they are de facto arguing against ritual. The absence of explicit polemic in the hortatory sections is a matter of rhetorical strategy, not proof that the author was not asking the

---

21. Ibid., 220. The observation is an important one, even if not stated well. Simply staying away from "Israel of the flesh" (if that were possible for Jewish readers) would not in itself wean anyone away from an attraction to the old covenant.

22. Gench observes that "the comparisons and statements of superiority appear in the expository sections of Hebrews rather than in the exhortations. In the exhortations . . . there appears to be no differentiation between the two faiths and no efforts to dissuade people of the attractions of Judaism" (*Hebrews and James*, 9).

readers to make choices. The author is not polemical even when discussing persecutions of the past—his polemics are confined almost entirely to the law.

Reasons suggested for lethargy include delay of the Parousia,[23] passage of time, inner weakness, and social shame. All these may well be involved, but they do not account for the character of most of Hebrews. For example, if the primary problem of the readers was low social status due to their unorthodox belief in a messiah, then the best way to raise their social status would be for them to abandon that belief and embrace a more accepted form of Judaism or polytheism. But the author assumes throughout Hebrews that the readers have beliefs about Christ that can be counted on. For example, Koester writes:

> It seems clear, however, that the listeners had not actually fallen away, since the author can assume that they still affirmed basic Christian beliefs. For example, he does not try to convince the listeners that Jesus died and was exalted to God's right hand, but assumes that they will grant these points as the basis for his argument (1:1-4). Moreover, the exhortations to "hold fast" and not to abandon the Christian hope and confession of faith (3:5; 4:14; 10:23, 35) assume that the listeners have not yet relinquished their beliefs altogether.[24]

In other words, the author can assume that the readers retain a belief not only in the Jewish Scriptures, but also in Jesus as the Messiah. The readers believe that he is the Son of God, exalted to God's right hand. The exposition of him as high priest builds on this foundation, but the foundation itself is not argued. (I will say more about the readers' beliefs in the next chapter.)

However, if the readers are not in immediate danger of renouncing Christ, what option do they have for alleviating their low social status, or minimizing the negative consequences? It is important to consider the options the readers have; this will help us test hypotheses about the

---

23. The delay of the Parousia is mentioned by many, including Attridge, *Hebrews*, 11; Gordon, *Hebrews*, 15; and Lehne, *New Covenant*, 120. "Three times the writer stresses the need for eagerly awaiting the parousia of Christ" (Lincoln, *Hebrews*, 57).

24. Koester, *Hebrews*, 71. See also Dahms, "First Readers," 366–69. DeSilva points out that it would be "bad rhetorical form" to correct the readers early in the message (*Perseverance*, 95), which implies that the author assumes that the readers agree with the high Christology of 1:1–4.

situation they are in. Something other than shame and low social status must also be involved.

External Pressure

Most commentators suggest that, in addition to lethargy, another factor is at work among the readers: external pressure, which might range from subtle social pressures for conformity, to an overt threat of bodily harm or death. As Lehne says, "Internal explanations alone are not sufficient to diagnose the predicament of the addressees, nor to explain the author's mode of reply . . . . The text furnishes hints of suffering and abuse, impounding of property and imprisonment, which point to official (state) persecutions (10.32–34)."[25]

Lindars speaks of the "urgency and anxiety which characterise the letter from end to end."[26] The readers are not just suffering a slow erosion of confidence—there is an external threat as well. Texts such as 10:35–36, the "yet" of 12:4, and 13:3 imply a renewed threat of persecution. Gordon writes, "There is one factor that calls for attention more than most, and that is the effect of hardships and persecution."[27] He cites several examples of the letter's "remarkable preoccupation with the idea of avoiding, or at any rate surmounting, death."[28] Murray writes that the author "sees the Hebrews' naïve and undeveloped view of Jesus as too incoherent to sustain their faith in [a time of] persecution (by Jews?); they have got dangerously isolated and if they stay where they are they will find they are no longer with Christ."[29] Cockerill puts it this way:

> Apparently they had become lax and were in danger of sinking into a state of spiritual immaturity, of stunted growth (5:11–14). At the same time, their Christian distinctiveness had brought them shame from the outside world (13:12–13).

---

25. Lehne, *New Covenant*, 121, 120.
26. Lindars, *Theology of the Letter*, 5.
27. Gordon, *Hebrews*, 16.
28. Ibid. His examples include 2:14–15; 5:7; much of chapter 11; and 12:4. Similarly, Bulley writes, "What further needs to be noted is the very definite cast given to *pistis* in chapter 11, particularly its relationship to suffering and death, and to see how frequently suffering appears in the remainder of the document . . . . The author of Hebrews is concerned with faithful action in the face of suffering and/or death" ("Death and Rhetoric," 410, 414).
29. Murray, "Jews, Hebrews and Christians," 205.

They were suffering (12:4–11) and may have been facing another round of persecution that would require them to give their lives (11:35–38). This combination of spiritual lethargy, external pressure, and impending trials exposed them to the danger of apostasy.[30]

Lane also mentions trials: "loss of their property, their freedom, and perhaps even of their lives.... They had become weary with the constant struggle they faced as Christians."[31] They are afraid of persecution and might be tempted to deny Christ.[32] Guthrie writes that "their experience of persecution and an increasingly blurred picture of Jesus and the Christian faith had led to a further drifting from right thinking and right living."[33] Hewitt suggests that "they had become grieved at, and absorbed with, their sufferings.... It is also possible that the Jewish nation was facing a serious crisis and was making a strong appeal to all Jews for their help and loyalty."[34] Lincoln writes that it is likely that "the writer believes that a renewed threat of persecution is imminent and is aware that the prospect of death for some is a realistic one."[35]

Some commentators suggest that Judaism's legal status was a factor. Some conclude that "the addressees are ... attracted to the safe status of a *religio licita* enjoyed by Judaism."[36] Bruce writes, "Probably they were reluctant to sever their last ties with a religion which enjoyed the protection of Roman law and face the risks of irrevocable commitment to the Christian way."[37] Cockerill says, "If they had Jewish roots, they may have been tempted to blend back into the general Jewish environment.... By participating in these activities, they would ... have been protected from persecution by non-Jews, since the Roman government recognized Judaism as an accepted religion."[38]

---

30. Cockerill, *Hebrews*, 15.

31. Lane, *Hebrews: A Call to Commitment*, 21.

32. Ibid.

33. Guthrie, *Hebrews*, 22.

34. Hewitt, *Epistle to the Hebrews*, 39–40. For speculation about what that "serious crisis" may have been, see Appendix C.

35. Lincoln, *Hebrews*, 55.

36. Attridge, *Hebrews*, 11.

37. Bruce, *Hebrews*, 8.

38. Cockerill, *Hebrews*, 17. Similarly, Witherington writes, "It is thus very believable that in Rome in the late 60s our author might have to stave off defections of Jewish

However, Koester writes, "It seems unlikely that legality was a factor.... Roman policy toward non-Roman religions was one of broad tolerance as long as there was no threat to the state."[39] Further, Judaism was not a fully "safe" religion. He observes that many Gentiles treated Jews with contempt, and "it is not clear that Christians would have perceived Judaism as a refuge."[40] The status of Judaism as a legal religion would not guarantee safety, but it may have provided *some* increase in security. However, for people who really wanted to avoid persecution and were willing to give up some religious beliefs, polytheism would be the best refuge.

What are the readers' critics pressuring them to do? I will say more about that in the next chapter. Before that, I want to discuss the religious interests that the text implies that the readers have. People who accepted the Scriptures as authoritative would be likely to have certain religious beliefs as well—beliefs that limit their social options.

Religious Interests

Numerous commentators recognize that the text implies certain religious interests among the readers, but only a few explore this in detail. Ellingworth says that "a recurring theme in Hebrews is that of true worship," but he interprets this as merely pointing "to a cultic setting similar to that of the synagogue homily."[41] In other words, the interest in worship occurs simply because the epistle would be read in a worship meeting. But not all homilies include this theme; this one seems to reflect a special interest. Lane says that the readers were attracted to "traditions"[42]—probably Jewish traditions. "This attraction appears to have been the source of unresolved tension between the community and their current leadership (13:1, 17–18)."[43]

Christians, who were feeling the heat and thought it less problematic and safer to just be Jews—not Jewish Christians—since Judaism was a recognized ancient and licit religion, not a new superstition" (*Letters and Homilies*, 55–56).

39. Koester, *Hebrews*, 71.

40. Ibid., 71 n. 155. Nor is it clear that Roman authorities would have attempted to define when a Jewish person left the *religio licita*.

41. Ellingworth, *Hebrews*, 25.

42. Lane, *Hebrews 1–8*, lxi.

43. Ibid.

Johnson narrows the focus considerably: "The number of synonyms used by the author and the frequency of his usage suggest a significant concern with the problem of sin."[44] Hewitt notes that the author wants to make this point: "If [a person] is to draw near to God, mediation of some kind is absolutely essential.... The main object of the priesthood was, therefore, to bring [people] into abiding fellowship with God."[45] This implies that the readers have an interest in approaching God, or feel a need for a mediator. Donelson hints at a religious interest when he writes, "Jesus gives us access to a fearful God"[46]—the audience is assumed to be interested in approaching God, yet realizing a difficulty, a difficulty that is resolved by Jesus. DeSilva writes that the author "assumes that 'pleasing God' is a goal firmly in place" in the readers' minds.[47]

Gordon says that the author "sets out to demonstrate the uniqueness of Christ as divine Son and as heavenly priest, and the sufficiency of his self-offering to deal with the problem of human sinfulness.... It is suggested that the author is addressing a problem of perceived 'cultic deprivation' on the part of the 'Hebrews.'"[48] That is, the readers feel that new covenant worship lacks substance and is ineffective in dealing with their feelings of guilt. Moule argues that "the whole burden of the Epistle can ... be epitomized in two resounding ἔχομευs: we *have* a high priest, we *have* an altar."[49] The stress in Hebrews on what "we have" suggests that the readers felt a need for having these aspects of religion. Outsiders accused them of lacking religious necessities, and Hebrews gives them an answer.

Johnson writes, "With references to sanctuaries, to the presence of God, and to repetitive actions, the author revealed a concern with

---

44. Johnson, *Going Outside the Camp*, 99.

45. Hewitt, *Hebrews*, 41–42. Lincoln points out that the author assumes that the readers *want* access to God: "Qualification for access to a holy God is the goal of salvation" (*Hebrews*, 91).

46. Donelson, *From Hebrews to Revelation*, 21.

47. deSilva, *Perseverance*, 174

48. Gordon, *Hebrews*, 19–20. However, if the readers participated in the Eucharist on a regular basis, they would have a worship just as tangible as synagogue meals were, and thus no "cultic deprivation."

49. Moule, "Sanctuary and Sacrifice," 37.

ritual."⁵⁰ Lane writes, "The writer interpreted the worship of God as the central directive of the apostolic parenesis."⁵¹ The entire Christian life is described as worship in 13:15–16. Colijn concludes, "For the author of Hebrews the essence of salvation is worship. Hebrews calls us to draw near to God in fellowship with one another as we journey to the city that is to come."⁵²

Casey also posits a religious yearning among the readers:

> Members of the community were Jewish Christians imbued with knowledge of and love for their Judaic heritage . . . . The "Hebrews" are a discouraged people who have grown weary with the life that is theirs . . . . The homilist is addressing people whose lives were deeply involved in and influenced by these institutions [cult and sacrifice], and . . . he is telling them they must not return to them . . . .
>
> [The readers] are asked to turn from their own rich and mysterious cultic heritage and to remain faithful to a new way, a way less satisfying and much less secure. The new way no longer entails sacrifices, high priests, or external ritual seen to effect purification over and over again. Instead, the homilist says, christian [sic] life demands conversion, confidence and—above all—faith.⁵³

Davies notes that "the entire letter is an argument that Christianity supersedes Judaism,"⁵⁴ and he concludes that the readers (Gentile, in his view) are "under pressure to embrace Judaism . . . . This would perhaps be the best explanation of the extraordinary harshness of the writer's warnings about the consequences of infidelity."⁵⁵ He presents the problem as primarily a doctrinal one—the readers are attracted to the old covenant. He gives little comment on *why* the old covenant would be attractive the readers:

> The readers may be dismayed at the idea that Christianity means the abandonment of Judaism. Those who valued the Old Covenant most positively would need to be assured that the New

50. Johnson, *Going Outside*, 109.
51. Lane, *Hebrews 9–13*, 572.
52. Colijn, "Let Us Approach," 586.
53. Casey, *Hebrews*, xii, xiv, 64–65.
54. Davies, *Hebrews*, 3.
55. Ibid., 5–6.

Covenant contained all that the Old did, and, even more, was its true fulfillment. Such assurance our letter seeks to provide.[56]

Why does Hebrews have a lengthy expository section dealing with cultic details? Although other explanations are possible, the simplest explanation is that the readers have an interest in these details—they have religious beliefs that include an ideological (not just a cultural) attraction to the Levitical cult.[57] The abundance of worship-related words and concepts indicates an audience for whom worship is important. In a well-crafted epistle designed to address a problem that the author perceives as a life-and-death threat for the spiritual life and salvation of the readers, he deals with the options they are struggling with, not a tangential point in hopes that readers might catch a hint.[58] Lincoln writes, "The negative comments on Judaism within the theological exposition do give the impression that Judaism is in some way an immediate threat."[59] Would he compare Christ with something that the readers had no desire for? Such a comparison might be academically interesting, but it is not suited to the urgency implied in the emotion-laden exhortations of Hebrews.

The problem for some readers may be apathy, but the only *religious* option considered in the text is the old covenant cult. This suggests that

---

56. Ibid., 4–5. Koester, although he takes no position about the ethnicity of the readers, also argues that they had some attraction to either the Jewish community or Judaism's priestly traditions. "It seems likely that Heb 7:11–19 deals with live issues" (*Hebrews*, 357; similar thoughts on 406).

57. One point against this argument is that 5:11, shortly before the long section about cultic details, says that the readers have become dull in hearing, perhaps indicating that they were not interested in hearing about this subject. However, if they were not interested, I would expect more calls for attentiveness in this section. Instead, as I argue in the next chapter, the arguments seem to assume that the readers already have an interest in approaching God, and the arguments assume that if they do not approach by Christ, they are attempting to approach by ritual. That is, the author assumes that they have an interest in ritual as a possible means of approaching God.

58. "Hebrews is pervaded by the comparison and contrast between two dispensations of revelation, the old covenant and the new covenant, stressing the superiority of the latter.... In theory this could just be theologizing which does not necessarily have a direct relevance to the audience's situation. But it makes much more sense in this pastoral word of exhortation that such a massive interest in the relationship of the two dispensations does in fact have a bearing on the concrete situation" (Lincoln, *Hebrews*, 58).

59. Lincoln, *Hebrews*, 37.

it is the only choice relevant to the readers. I find it hard to imagine that the longest expository section of the epistle draws a comparison with something that is only marginally relevant to the situation. The argument implies that at least some of the readers want the old covenant rituals. *They* do not view it as apostasy, but the author argues that it *is* apostasy. Witherington writes, "There can be no doubt that the audience of this sermon is in some social distress and under some pressure to renege on their commitments to Christ and his community . . . . It is an argument directed to Jewish Christians to make clear that going back to non-Christian Judaism is not an option for them any more than going forward into paganism is."[60]

Religious beliefs are a crucial component of the social world of the readers. The author does not try to prove *that* they should worship; the primary concern seems to be *how* they may approach God. If the readers retain respect for the Jewish Scriptures, as the author of Hebrews assumes, they will also have biblically based religious beliefs that affect their options. People who accept the Scriptures as authoritative (especially if they do not understand that the old covenant is obsolete) might also accept its worship regulations as authoritative. They could easily think that they should worship God in the way God had commanded. They might feel that they have a religious duty to continue to support the Levitical cult. As Manson writes, Jews "would not all, when they became Christians, readily feel themselves immediately dispensed from all further obligations to the ritual and the ordinances."[61]

Pfitzner writes:

> The contrast between old covenant and new is no mere rhetorical device, but points to a real problem: the relationship between Christianity and Judaism . . . . The passionate appeal of Hebrews to hold on to the new surely hints at the temptation to move back, in some sense, to the old . . . . Without wanting to give up their confession, the readers are possibly tempted to seek security under the cover of Judaism.
>
> Neglect of worship (10:25) is symptomatic of external pressure and inner fatigue. That helps to explain why the Letter . . . is full of cultic language taken from Old Testament texts that must

---

60. Witherington, *Letters and Homilies*, 26.

61. Manson, *Hebrews*, 43. They would not necessarily think that Gentile believers had the same obligation.

have played a role in the community's worship. Hebrews asserts the certainty of faith in the context of the Christian cultus.[62]

Pfitzner says that the author's central appeal is "to hold fast to the confession and to claim priestly access into God's presence.... Neither christological heresy nor failure to come to grips with sin and guilt (Lindars 1991) is the problem."[63] The real issue, Pfitzner argues, is "neglect of worship.... Every climactic point in the Letter is a statement about worship."[64] Pfitzner concludes, "This reading of Hebrews as a call to worship (10:25) provides us with a framework for understanding both the eschatology and the parenesis of Hebrews."[65] I will analyze the argument of Hebrews in more detail in the next chapter, and that analysis will reveal that the author assumed that the readers have certain religious beliefs. But first, I will survey what other scholars have said about the religious interests of the readers.

Chester says that the author tries to "counter the strong attraction of the cult."[66] Spicq argues that the readers (former priests, in his view) want the elaborate liturgy of Judaism.[67] But could readers be involved in the liturgy if they were not in Jerusalem? Lindars offers this suggestion: "If, as seems more likely, the readers are far away in the Dispersion, the reference is probably to synagogue meals, held especially at festival time to give the worshippers a stronger sense of solidarity with the worship of the temple in Jerusalem."[68] He asks, "Why is it that the readers have lost confidence in the power of the sacrifice of Christ to deal with their consciousness of sins?"[69] He hypothesizes that the gospel they heard spoke only of forgiveness of past sins, but "some of them at least began to be oppressed by renewed consciousness of sin."[70] The readers are "deeply troubled in conscience."[71] The solution to the problem, Lindars

---

62. Pfitzner, *Hebrews*, 29, 20.
63. Ibid., 24, 28.
64. Ibid., 27, 28.
65. Ibid., 43.
66. Chester, "Hebrews: The Final Sacrifice," 64.
67. Spicq, *Hébreux*, 30.
68. Lindars, *Theology*, 10.
69. Ibid., 12.
70. Ibid., 13.
71. Ibid., 43.

says, is worship: "What the readers need is renewed confidence in the value of the Christian liturgy.... The sacrifice of Christ is proclaimed in every meeting of Christians for worship.... The readers then should not be frequenting synagogue worship in order to feel the benefit of the sacrificial system."[72]

Lindars highlights the readers' desire for forgiveness, and he suggests a possible reason. However, he does not explain how deeply troubled people would be comforted by this letter, which, as he admits, "has caused misery to readers of a tender conscience all through the centuries."[73] If their main need is the new liturgy, why is the author so vague about what that liturgy *is*? In contrast to its concern with old covenant details, Hebrews shows little concern with the details of worship or liturgy in the new covenant. Instead, the question is framed in broad categories: Do we approach God through the details of the old covenant, or simply through Christ? The desire to approach is assumed; the question is *how*—and no "method" is prescribed for approaching God through Christ. Instead, there is a lengthy call for faith in the unseen. If there are allusions in Hebrews to the Eucharist, as various scholars suggest, they are too vague to be responses to an urgent problem.

The author argues that forgiveness is available through Christ; he does not argue for forgiveness through a new covenant liturgy—not through rituals that must be repeated. The author does not offer a replacement liturgy—he calls for faith in the invisible, faith in what Christ has done. The author urges the readers to meet together not for liturgy, but for mutual encouragement (10:25). The sacrifices of the old covenant have been replaced not by liturgy, but by praise and good works (13:15-16). The readers want forgiveness, but Lindars overestimates their anxiety. Their problem is not hypersensitivity, but in some respects, the opposite: dullness of hearing.[74] They are not hearing the

---

72. Ibid., 11.

73. Ibid., 2. Koester responds to this view when he notes, "The author does not simply assume that people have troubled consciences and are looking for relief. Writing to a dull and sluggish audience (Heb 5:11; 6:12), the author has attempted to *disturb* the consciences of his readers, making them uneasy before God" (*Hebrews*, 405, emphasis added).

74. The author warns, "Do not harden your hearts" (3:8). He writes to people who are drifting away without being aware (2:1). "We do not want you to become lazy" (6:12). The shaming language in 5:12 is *not* what a guilt-ridden reader would need. The stern warnings 6:4-6; 10:26 and 12:15-25 would accentuate, rather than alleviate,

implications of the message about Jesus Christ. Lindars characterizes the readers' needs as "practical,"[75] but Hebrews exhorts them based on *doctrinal* expositions. The readers may be attracted to the Levitical cult, but the more important factor seems to be that *they believe it has validity*. Since they think it is better to worship in the way that God commanded through Moses, Hebrews argues that Christ is the better way.

Lehne offers an insightful picture of the problem:

> Judging from the author's manner of argumentation and exhortation, we can detect on the part of the readers a kind of longing for some form of Jewish cultic observance that they seem to be missing in their new faith-community . . . . Possibly they are attempting to maintain a dual allegiance, as it were, by continuing their association with a local Synagogue of (non-Christian) Jews and simultaneously believing in Jesus . . . .
>
> . . . The writer of Heb. faces several kinds of problems in the congregation which he addresses. Along with the concrete predicament of abuse and suffering, and a nostalgia for their Jewish heritage (a diagnosis prevalent in the English-speaking world of scholarship), the recipients display a lack of enthusiasm in their faith and hope (the preferred German diagnosis)."[76]

She offers an attractive hypothesis: "It is plausible that in 9.8 the author is referring, not so much to the situation of contemporary Jews, but to the yearnings of *some of* his addressees for a conservative form of *Jewish-Christianity* that included some kind of concrete replacement of Levitical worship."[77] This view is similar to that of Hagner, who writes that the readers may have been "attempting somehow to remain within Judaism by emphasizing items held in common between Judaism and Christianity. They may have been trying to survive with a minimal Christianity in order to avoid alienating their Jewish friends or

---

the problem of a hypersensitive conscience. This leads me to believe that the readers' attraction to the old covenant cult was due more to ideological conviction than to personal anxiety.

75. "If the readers are tempted to resort to such teachings, it is for practical reasons, because they feel the need for them" (Lindars, "Rhetorical," 388). But they would feel a need for these specific practices only if they believe that they are efficacious for the guilt they feel. Their doctrinal beliefs are an essential part of their situation. As Lindars says, "The law provides the standard which his readers accept" (ibid., 403).

76. Lehne, *New Covenant*, 16–17.

77. Ibid., 100.

relatives."[78] Chester writes, "The writer deliberately polarizes the positions and drives a wedge between the nascent Christian and Jewish movements."[79] The author argues not just that Christ is better, but that he is the *only* effective means of atonement. Manson writes,

> The danger to their faith lay not in a return to Judaism as such, but in a retardation of their Christian progress . . . by an undue assertion of their Jewish-Christian inheritance . . . . The sin of the 'Hebrews' group was not that of abandoning Christianity for Judaism, but rather of remaining as Christians under the covert [sic] of the Jewish religion, living too much in the Jewish part of their Christianity.[80]

The hybridizing approach was causing the readers to *drift* away from faith in Christ. The threat of apostasy seems to be subtle—more in worship practices than in an explicit renunciation of Jesus. The readers were in danger of denying Christ in their actions, not in their words. Dahms presents the following points to argue that the readers, although Jewish, are not in danger of overtly renouncing Christ: 1) The text presents Jesus as the Christ without any argument about it. 2) It presents Jesus as the Son of God without any attempt to support the assertion. 3) Jesus is called Lord "without any explanation or elaboration."[81] 4) "If the readers were really in danger of lapsing into Judaism . . . it would be useless to describe Christ's sufferings as the endurance of the hostility of sinners against himself. If they had been really in danger of lapsing into Judaism they would have been tempted to think that Jesus was the sinner who deserved to be destroyed."[82] Dahms concludes that "the readers are in danger of becoming a sect for which Christ is important but for

---

78. Hagner, *Hebrews*, 87. They were "holding to a minimalist Christianity that also could pass as a form of Judaism (and thereby avoid persecution)" (Hagner, *Encountering*, 86).

79. Chester, "Hebrews," 64.

80. Manson, *Hebrews*, 15–16, 24. He suggests that "a group of Jewish Christians . . . was . . . giving up its Christian meetings and virtually dissolving back into the general life of the Jewish community" (69)—but he cautions that 10:25 does not prove this hypothesis. He suggests that the group was "tempted to accentuate one-sidedly the Jewish element in their inheritance, and were living so entirely on the sub-Christian level of their religion, that . . . they seemed to be turning from Christ" (168).

81. Dahms, "First Readers," 366–69.

82. Ibid., 372–73.

which his death has no soteriological significance."[83] "The readers were evidently . . . holding that priestly and sacrificial significance is to be found in the levitical priests and offerings."[84]

How could the readers participate in the old covenant? There is no evidence that they are involved in the temple. Instead, the argument is about the tabernacle. The readers know the sacrifices through the law of Moses, which mentions only the tabernacle. However, it is possible that they participated in the sacrifices vicariously—through the temple tax, synagogue attendance, Torah readings, rituals, and fellowship meals.[85] Scriptures about Yom Kippur, for example, could easily be used to support a claim that sins are forgiven only through this ceremony (Lev 16:30), and that the atonement is effective for all Jews who are faithful to the old covenant, and that this faithfulness is demonstrated in the Diaspora by participation in synagogue traditions.[86]

---

83. Ibid., 371. Similarly, deSilva writes, "It is not that the hearers have been thinking 'wrong' things about Jesus—it is, rather, that some of them are not thinking enough of Jesus, the benefactions he has brought, and the promises that have been made" (*Perseverance*, 108–9).

84. Dahms, "First Readers," 373. As evidence that this approach is plausible, Dahms notes that "many Jewish Christians in the earliest days of the Church apparently considered participation in the Jewish ceremonies essential (cf. Acts 3:1; 21:20–26; cf. 10:14)" (ibid.). Bénétreau also suggests a composite environment in which believers, primarily of Jewish origin, were tempted to go backwards, without assuming that this was to majority Judaism. "L'aboutissement éventuel du processus n'est pas clairement désigne" (*Hébreux*, 1:28). In his view, the weakening of Christian convictions came from the attractiveness of temple rituals, fear of persecution, and laziness (ibid., 28–29).

85. "The Jews had their own festivals and sacred days, most of which centered on the Temple in Jerusalem. Since these typically involved sacrifice, Jews not able to attend the festivals in Jerusalem—particularly those in the diaspora—could only have limited participation in these sacred days. Nevertheless, there is evidence that Jews gathered locally to observe these days and participated through prayer, fasting, hymn singing and banqueting. . . . The evidence in most cases points to the synagogue as the place where Jews came together to observe these national festivals. . . . The synagogues of the Second Temple period functioned de facto, if not necessarily by design, as vehicles that transported the ancient worshipers closer to the center; that they served in effect as distant courts of the Temple, wherein a congregation had some sense of being near to the *axis mundi*" (Binder, *Into the Temple Courts*, 416, 478). It should be noted that vicarious participation in temple rituals through synagogue worship does not necessitate a pre-70 date. Even after 70, Jews could claim that synagogue rituals were sufficient substitutes for the atonement rituals. However, there is no evidence in Hebrews that anyone viewed the sacrifices as replaceable. For more on the date of the epistle, see Appendix C.

86 This is speculation, not a point I consider proven.

Conclusion

There is evidence in Hebrews that the readers are affected by lethargy, external pressure, *and* religious beliefs and desires. Hebrews addresses their various needs. For example, chapters 7–10 address the readers' doctrinal deficiencies, Heb 11 is targeted more on their need for faith in time of trial, and Heb 12 addresses their lethargy. Each section is relevant to the readers, and it is not necessary to choose one at the expense of the others. Lehne comments that "Brown rightly insists on the (often neglected!) possibility of *different outlooks* among the addressees."[87] Some may have been more affected by lethargy, some more by fear of persecution, some by attraction to the old covenant, and some by two or all three factors. She writes:

> The internal longing for some kind of concrete replacement for the Levitical cult may have been occasioned in part by the external charge of atheism, based on the absence of visible cultic institutions, officials and symbols, and in part by the campaigning of conservative Jewish-Christians. In this writer's view these factors are by no means mutually exclusive . . . .
>
> The combined weight of these factors, perhaps coupled with a disappointment over the delay of the *parousia*, seems to have produced spiritual lethargy and a lack of concrete acts of love and fellowship among the readers.[88]

Attridge also says that the problem may have been "a rather complex situation, with a variety of factors at work."[89] Koester acknowledges diversity when he writes, "For listeners who remain committed to God and Christ, Hebrews . . . maintains the values they already hold. For those tending to drift away from the faith, Hebrews . . . seeks to dissuade them from apostasy and move them toward a clearer faith commitment."[90] Gordon mentions several problems the readers faced, but concludes: "There is one factor that calls for attention more than most, and that is the effect of hardships and persecution."[91]

---

87. Lehne, *New Covenant*, 152, n. 60. She is referring to Brown and Meier, *Antioch and Rome*.

88. Lehne, *New Covenant*, 120.

89. Attridge, *Hebrews*, 12–13.

90. Koester, *Hebrews*, 82.

91. Gordon, *Hebrews*, 14–16. The other problems he notes are: "spiritual torpor . . . tensions between the leadership and certain of the flock," strange teachings (probably

Not all readers would be equally affected by each factor, although some might be affected by them all: tired of waiting, weary of persecution, wistful for worship, feeling alienated from their old communities, therefore attracted to teachings that might help them resolve their social isolation, avoid persecution, and assure them of forgiveness.

Since people are different, it is likely that some are more pressured by external circumstances and others more by internal desires. The external pressures may be social pressure and persecution, both of which might be reduced by moving toward a more traditional religion. The internal pressures may include fatigue from trials, being tired of waiting for Christ's return, and desire for more traditional worship practices. Hazy concepts of Christ and the new covenant, as well as allegiance to the Jewish Scriptures, could encourage the readers to look to the old covenant for atonement and worship.

For many readers, these factors are interrelated—they are lethargic not just due to the passage of time, but also because they are tired of the social pressures, and because of the pressures, they feel alienated from God and hence tempted to look for more concrete evidence of his approval. Religious beliefs are an important aspect of the community, and of the text. If the readers retain respect for the Scriptures, as the author assumes, then they have religious scruples that limit their options. The readers are not simply bowing to social pressure, but doing so *within limits circumscribed by their religious beliefs*.

The author never considers polytheism as a viable option, and as I argued in chapter 1, the readers are probably Jewish. However, as I will argue in chapter 3, we must also read as if certain beliefs now labeled Christian may be taken for granted—that Jesus is the Messiah, the Son of God, exalted at God's right hand, and that the Scriptures are to be interpreted in this light. The readers are Jews who believe that Jesus is the Christ, tempted not to abandon that belief, but socially and religiously pressured to participate in Jewish rituals and to pull away from the messianic community. The main attraction of old covenant worship is not its beauty or tangibility, but simply that it is commanded in the Scriptures.

The social pressures, weariness, and doctrinal pressure work together to create an urgent situation. To encourage the readers to go for-

---

associated with Jewish food laws), weakening commitment to the original confession, and the delayed Parousia.

ward in the faith, the author must address their underlying concerns, such as fear, interest in the cult, and weariness. So he begins with teachings familiar to the readers—the greatness of Christ. Then he moves to the implications: Christ is a priest, which means that the old covenant is obsolete and forgiveness is obtained only through Christ. Therefore the readers should look to him and have faith in him, rather than looking to the old cult. I will argue this in more detail in the next chapter as I examine the arguments in Hebrews, noting especially ideas that the author assumes the readers already hold, and ideas on which resistance seems to be expected.

3

Religious Beliefs of the Readers

THE AUTHOR OF HEBREWS ASSUMES THAT THE ORIGINAL RECIPIENTS of the epistle share certain beliefs with him. These can be taken for granted, stated without apology, and given without supporting reasons. These include a belief that Jesus is the Christ, and that he has been exalted into heaven and seated at the right hand of God. Corollary with that is the belief that Ps 110:1 describes his heavenly session: "The LORD says to my lord, 'Sit at my right hand until I make your enemies your footstool.'" Hebrews quotes or alludes to this verse six times. The priesthood of Christ, which is crucial to the central theological argument of the epistle, is predicated on the belief that Ps 110, including v. 4, is about Jesus, without any attempt to argue that this psalm actually applies to Jesus.

However, on some other points the author provides extensive supporting argumentation, as if the topics *were* in question, and certain beliefs could *not* be taken for granted. Chief among these is the old covenant law. Here the author does not assume that the readers share his opinions: he goes out of his way to make his points, and he supports them with several lines of reasoning. This suggests that the readers, although firm believers in Jesus Christ, were also attracted to old covenant worship laws.

Modern readers may feel that this is an odd combination of beliefs, since one is now characteristic of Christianity and the other is characteristic of Second Temple Judaism. However, the evidence in Hebrews is strong for both beliefs, and a realistic thesis about the readers' situation should include both beliefs. In this chapter, I will survey the epistle, paying special attention to the arguments, since the arguments often imply that the readers already have certain beliefs, and that certain other beliefs may be in question.¹ Although the conclusions could be grouped by topic, I have chosen to survey the epistle according to the sequence of the text, in an inductive manner. The evidence shows that the readers 1) had a firm belief in Jesus as the Son of God and Messiah and 2) were attracted to the old covenant. I will describe the social situation in which this combination was plausible.

Assumed Beliefs About Jesus as the Christ (Heb 1)

Hebrews begins with a number of assertions, most of which are not argued—they are simply stated: God spoke to our ancestors and has now spoken by a Son, the creator, sustainer, and heir of everything, who is like God in glory and being, and he is now at God's right hand (1:1–3). The credibility of the entire epistle hangs on this latter concept, which is never defended. It would be foolish for an author to begin with several points that the readers would question,² and assuming that the author of Hebrews is not foolish, I conclude that he believes that his audience already believes these ideas.³ From the opening statement (the exordium) alone, I conclude that the implied readers believe the following:

1. There is an inevitable amount of subjectivity involved in "mirror-reading" the epistle to see the beliefs of the readers, since the author's rhetorical strategy might sometimes call for a subtle approach, and other times merit a blunt correction. In general, my methodological strategy is that if the author states ideas without providing substantiation, I conclude that he did not expect resistance on these points and the readers probably already agreed with him. But when he provides supporting argumentation, it suggests that he expected resistance and was dealing with a topic in dispute. The more argumentation that he provides, the more disputed the point.

2. Although a writer might theoretically begin with a point of contention if it were to be substantiated with further argumentation, this would be contrary to normal rhetorical style, since it would weaken the author's *ethos* right at the start. Montefiore writes, "It is improbable that any epistle would open with controversial or unfamiliar Christological statements" (*Hebrews*, 37). DeSilva says that an introductory polemic would be "bad rhetorical form, running the risk of alienating the hearers by 'correcting' them too quickly (before trust has been fully established within the speech)" (*Perseverance*, 95). Koester writes, "Rhetorically, it was good practice to establish common ground with the audience by reinforcing what they already knew to be true" (*Hebrews*, 182). Reed summarizes the advice given in ancient rhetorical manuals: "The *exordium* serves to generate a positive relationship of trust and compliance between the speaker and the listener, that is, to build *ethos*" ("The Epistle," 181).

3. The author's use of the word "restore" in 13:19 indicates that he was formerly part of the community and he would therefore be familiar with its beliefs.

- Some Jewish books are authoritative.[4]
- The Son of God appeared on earth, initiated a new age in history, and is now seated in heaven. Later verses assume without argument that the Son is named Jesus.
- The Son was the means of creation, has authority over all and sustains all things.
- The Son is like God in glory, being, and authority.

In short, the readers had a high Christology.[5]

However, two phrases within the exordium are defended later in the epistle: 1) He "made purification for sins"—a point elaborated and defended in detail in chapters 8–10, yet stated here as idea that presumably would be accepted. 2) He became "as much superior to angels as the name[6] he has inherited is more excellent than theirs" (1:4). Although his superiority over angels is supported in the remainder of chapter 1, it also seems to be an area of previous agreement. Anyone who believes that the Son has authority over all things and is seated at the right hand of God, would *already* believe that he was superior to angels.

The author supports his point with a catena of biblical quotes, but he does not attempt to prove that any of the scriptures are actually about Jesus. Rather, he *implies* that they are, and assumes that the readers will agree.[7] It would be poor rhetorical strategy to confront the readers with

---

4. The author uses the LXX, but we cannot be sure about the boundaries of his canon.

5. Attridge says, "Hebrews does not introduce a high christology to its audience but develops and deepens affirmations that they already have" (*Hebrews*, 164). In doing so, he applies elements of the wisdom tradition to Jesus. Lindars writes, "The author is careful to begin with propositions which are not in dispute" ("Rhetorical Structure," 390). He names three doctrinal positions that are not in dispute: "the messiahship of Jesus . . . his human sufferings and death . . . the eschatological plan of God" (ibid., 394).

6. The author does not say what "name" he is talking about, which again suggests that he did not expect serious opposition to his statement. He is concerned about status, not a specific name, and his argument in 1:4 assumes that the readers already believe Jesus has inherited a superior status. "The prominent υἱός/πατήρ terminology and familial imagery in 1.5 strongly suggest that the unspecified name of 1.4 is 'Son'" (Mackie, "Confession of the Son of God," 116).

7. "The writer, especially at this early stage in his argument, is not trying to prove theses which his readers were likely to question . . . . The messianic interpretation of the text, and more specifically its application to Christ . . . are presupposed in Hebrews

points of contention so soon in the epistle, especially without support; it would be wiser to establish rapport with the readers by giving points of agreement. The author is not attempting to argue a case here. Rather, he is rehearsing material that the readers already believe—material that the author will soon use as a foundation for another argument.

Some scholars have posited that the author is either combating an angel-Christology (Qumran had angelic messianic figures) or an exalted view of angels as mediators (perhaps including the worship of angels).[8] Although some Jews did have a very high view of angels,[9] I do not think that Hebrews is addressing that problem. My reasons include:

1) It could be rhetorically risky to attack the readers' beliefs in the beginning, yet the comparison with angels is the first subject addressed after the exordium.

2) The quoted scriptures in Heb 1 are given minimal explanation. Although questions could easily be raised about several passages, the author does not attempt to argue that these passages apply to Christ, which implies that he did not expect the readers to dispute these passages. He does not expect resistance on this point.

3) The recipients apparently agree that Christ has been raised to the right hand of God (mentioned in the exordium), which already implies that he is superior to the angels.

4) The author continues the contrast between angels and Christ in 2:5–18, but they are no longer the main point of comparison. In 2:16, they are clearly a literary foil, and their role in the epistle is for the most part done.

5) Heb 12:22 and 13:2 mention angels in a positive way, without the qualifications that might be needed if the readers were tempted to hold too high a view of angels.

. . . . He is building on beliefs which he appears to assume that his readers will readily accept" (Ellingworth, *Hebrews*, 109, 130, 137). France writes, "The breath-taking boldness of assuming, without argument, that the 'Lord' described in Ps. 102:25–27 is the Son could surely have been attempted so confidently only in circles where this novel 'exegesis' was already agreed" ("Writer of Hebrews," 255 n. 22).

8. DeSilva has a good discussion of the views and a concise response (*Perseverance*, 92–94).

9. Goldin writes, "The simple man . . . turns to these angels and spirits for assistance. He has been reassured many times that the Lord is nigh; but angels and ministers of grace, and demons, are nigher" ("The Magic of Magic," 131).

I conclude that the comparison with angels serves two purposes. First, it provides an introductory encomium of praise for Jesus, the focus of the epistle. Second, it forms a rhetorical foil leading to the exhortation in 2:1–3. As deSilva says, the warning against drifting away from the message is the real goal of Heb 1:4–14.[10] The author begins the epistle with a point on which his readers are already in agreement: Christ is superior to the angels. He reinforces this point with a review of prooftexts that he assumes the readers are already familiar with. By the time he gets to 1:14, the readers may be thinking, "Yes, we know that. What is your point?"

The First Exhortation and the Purpose of the Epistle (Heb 2–6)

The author reveals his point in the hortatory conclusion: "Therefore we must pay greater attention to what we have heard." This exhortation is the rhetorical purpose of Heb 1:5–14.[11] Indeed, it is a preliminary

---

10. "The logical connector Διὰ τοῦτο . . . suggests that this warning against 'drifting away' from the message, and so 'neglecting so great a salvation,' is the goal of the preceding section" (deSilva, "Exchanging Favor for Wrath," 110).

11. Other scholars who support this view include:
- Schenck: "The contrast between Christ and the angels is a part of the contrast between the two covenants . . . . It is very relevant to the author's contrast between the two covenants, even if this contrast is not made very explicit in Heb 1" (*Understanding the Book of Hebrews*, 75, 43).
- Koester: "Angels are important because they were associated with the giving of the Law" (*Hebrews*, 200). The epistle repeatedly contrasts Christ and the law of Moses.
- Johnson: "The point of the previous exposition, in short, is precisely this exhortation" (*Hebrews*, 86).
- Larsson: "The whole comparison in Heb 1–2 is to be understood as a demonstration of the superiority of the new revelation over the old. The relationship between the angels and the Old Testament is the very reason why the author discusses their position at all ("How Mighty Was the Mighty Minority?" 103).
- Barrett: "There seems to be no evidence for such an angel-christology in the first century . . . . The heavily underlined contrast in Hebrews 1 must have an internal explanation, and there is no need to look further than Hebrews 2:2–4" ("Christology of Hebrews," 116).
- Hahn: "These verses actually serve to reveal the author's main purpose in arguing for Christ's superiority to the angels in the preceding chapter . . . . He is really intent on showing that Christ is a superior mediator of a new and better covenant, over and against those who mediated the 'old covenant' (8:6, 13): the angels (chs. 1–2), Moses and Joshua (chs. 3–4), Aaron and the Levites (chs. 5–7)" ("Kinship by Covenant," 508–9).

statement of the main exhortation of the epistle.¹² Son notes that "the hortatory units in Hebrews do not develop in a logical way but constantly repeat the same exhortation, 'do not reject God's word but hold fast.'"¹³ Subsequent exhortations will describe *the way* in which readers should be attentive—not to neglect salvation, to consider Jesus, not to harden their hearts, to enter the rest Jesus offers, to hold fast to a confession about him, to draw near to God through him, to fix their eyes on him, etc.

The author calls for "greater attention"—but greater than what? Here are three possible points of comparison:

1) Be more attentive than the ancient Israelites were.¹⁴ This comparison would be appropriate for ch. 3, but it is not suggested by the context here.
2) Be more attentive than you have been, or than you currently are.¹⁵ The word "drift" in Heb 2:1 suggests that the readers have been paying less attention than they used to, and their attention needs to increase, perhaps to its previous levels. This is a viable option, and the author sometimes encourages the readers to return to their previous level of commitment.
3) Be more attentive to the message about Christ than to "the message declared through angels"—that is, more attentive to Christ than to the law of Moses. This contrast is also in the context. It gains additional support when we see that the author repeatedly

---

12. In an epistle that consistently drives toward exhortation, it is appropriate to allow an exhortation to express the main theme of the work. On the Rhetoric L forum, Fred Long notes that "the first imperatives ... function as thesis statements" in several epistles—see Phil 1:27; Col 2:4–7; 2 Thess 2:1–2; 1 Pet 1:13–16; 2 Pet 1:10–11; and Jas 1:26–27 (Online: http://groups.yahoo.com/ group/rhetoric-l/message/821; accessed 13 July 2005). Mitchell argues that the exhortation in 1 Cor 1:10 is the thesis of the epistle (*Paul and the Rhetoric*, 1). Koester argues that 2:5–9 is the propositio of the epistle (*Hebrews*, 219); Übelacker argues for 2:17–18 (*Der Hebräerbrief*, 193–96). But calling an indicative statement a propositio seems to imply, erroneously, that the epistle's exhortations are digressions away from the main purpose. I suggest that 2:1 also be given serious consideration as a possible propositio. Witherington argues that "it was not necessary to have a narratio or propositio" (*Letters and Homilies*, 44–45). I agree that it is not *necessary* to have either one, but I believe that 2:1 is an adequate indication of what the epistle is about.

13. Son, *Zion Symbolism*, 22.

14. Suggested by Ellingworth, *Hebrews*, 135.

15. Ibid.

compares Christ to the old covenant. In the context of these comparisons, the readers are encouraged to choose Christ—which implies by context that they should not choose the old covenant. The author wants the readers to be more attentive to the message of salvation through Christ than to the law, which was the traditional focus of Second Temple Judaism. Although I believe that the author would agree with this third possibility, and it is a consistent theme of the expository sections, he does not normally include the contrast with the old covenant *in his exhortations*.[16]

By exhorting readers to be attentive to the recent message of salvation, the author implies that his epistle is on this very topic, and hence he is asking for attentiveness for his own message as well. He has begun not by challenging their beliefs and creating resistance, but as a good orator, he is using an area of agreement to draw them toward what he wants to say. The readers were probably already willing to hear a message about Christ, but the logic reinforces the importance of doing so. The author has created a bridge from a point of agreement to a call for attentiveness. He does not say anything negative about the law (he does not even mention it by name) but by mentioning its penalties (2:2), he subtly anticipates his more polemical discussion of the law later in the epistle (e.g., 12:19–21).

Most of ch. 2 supports this theme of attentiveness. People should listen to Christ because the world to come will be ruled by Christ (2:5–9). The eschatological hope depends on Christ, not angels. Since Ps 8 promises that humanity[17] will have authority over all things, it is to be expected that the "lord" seated at God's right hand (i.e., second only to God) was a human and therefore mortal before his exaltation (2:14). People should listen to Jesus because he is "the pioneer of their salvation" (2:10), blazing the trail that the readers should follow. Most of this chapter is a review for the readers—they would already know that Jesus died before he was raised into heaven. But the chapter bolsters the plausibility of the message about Christ by using scriptures to explain

---

16. See the table in chapter 6, pages 153–54. When a warning is included in the exhortation, it is generally a comparison with the readers' own behavior; that is probably the meaning in 2:1 as well.

17. The LXX of Ps 8 speaks of ἄνθρωπος and υἱὸς ἀνθρώπου. The author may have interpreted this respectively as humanity in general and a specific individual; he sees the promise fulfilled by Christ and yet still applicable to others.

the rationale for the Savior's death, which was psychologically a difficult part of the message to embrace and a likely point of attack by people who were pressuring the readers to leave the Christ community.

However, the author does mention in passing points that may be new, points that he will later build on: the Savior tasted death "for everyone" (2:9), through his death he freed others from the power of death (2:14–15), and he was a "high priest" who made "a sacrifice of atonement for the sins of the people" (2:17). It is difficult to ascertain from the text whether the author is mentioning concepts the readers already know, or whether he is casually introducing points that he will soon develop and support. The epistle later argues in great detail for the points mentioned in v. 17, implying that even if the readers know of these concepts, they did not know them as well as the author wants them to.

In verse 10, the author introduces two words that play an important role in the epistle: Christ was *made perfect* through *sufferings*. With these words and their cognates, the author will appeal to the readers' desire for being made complete (i.e., salvation[18]) and their natural concern about sufferings. Christ's offer of salvation is credible because he already has the desired reward, but the less-pleasant part of the message is that he had to suffer in the process, which hints that his followers will, too. In the last part of v. 17, the author says that Jesus "is able to help those who are being tested"—probably appealing to a desire that the readers already have: They want help in their difficulties.

The author argues that since Jesus can help people in time of trial, the readers should "consider" (κατανοήσατε, which invites the readers to think carefully[19]) that he was faithful (3:1). The author then compares Jesus to Moses, and in keeping with Greek rhetorical conventions of praise by comparison (*synkrisis*), he does not denigrate the lesser

---

18. The author uses a variety of terms for salvation without explicitly saying that they refer to the same thing: purification for sins, the coming world, sanctification, freed from the fear of death, the house of God, the Sabbath rest of God, resurrection of the dead, the age to come, the promised eternal inheritance, perfection, entering the heavenly sanctuary, the city with foundations, a heavenly country, Mt. Zion, the heavenly Jerusalem, the firstborn enrolled in heaven, a kingdom that cannot be shaken, etc. These are not synonyms, but are used (usually without explanation) for eschatological rewards.

19. Danker, BDAG, 522. The author is again calling for attentiveness—he is not asking the audience to put the epistle aside to think about Jesus in the abstract. Rather, he will specify what they should think about.

person.[20] The argument could have been simple: A son is better than a servant, so Jesus the son is better than Moses the servant. However, the author includes the theme of being faithful (πίστος) as the point of comparison—probably because the question revolves not just around Moses, but also around faithfulness. The author appeals to readers who value faithfulness and view Moses as a good example of faithfulness. He offers Christ as a better example, and urges the readers to follow that example.

Verse 12 includes a direct exhortation with strong, emotionally charged words: "Take care . . . that none of you may have an evil, unbelieving [ἀπιστίας] heart that turns away from the living God."[21] These words, immediately following a description of disobedience and punishment, make the warning here much stronger than the warning in 2:1–3. The second-person imperative in 3:12 is more direct than the first-person plural indicative and hypothetical question of 2:1–3. However, the author is still vague about what the threat actually is. The implication is that the readers will provoke God if they do not hold on to their confidence (3:6) and assurance (3:14). How do they hold firm? So far, the epistle has described faithfulness in two ways: paying attention to the message of Christ (2:1), and remembering that he is worthy of more honor than Moses (3:1–3). The author will give additional descriptions as the epistle proceeds.

Chapter 4 begins with another exhortation: "Let us take care . . ." [φοβηθῶμεν, let us fear] and uses the metaphor of "rest" to encourage the readers to "make every effort" (4:11). This concludes the discussion of "rest" that begins in 3:7. In this passage, the author does not attempt to explain the meaning of the word "rest"—his primary purpose is to

---

20. As Smith observes, "It would have undermined his proportional comparison to point to any flaws in the character or work of Moses" (*Hebrews*, 57). However, the author does give a subtly negative role for Moses in 3:17. He asks, Who were the people who disobeyed? He answers: "All those who left Egypt . . . " He could have stopped there, but he adds the words διὰ Μωϋσέως. In 3:16–18, the author asks: Who was it . . . who was it . . . who was it? The answer is: The people led by Moses . . . those who sinned . . . who were disobedient. Through parallelism, Moses is put in bad company. There is an obvious response to the problem of disobedience, but what is the alternative to the "problem" of following Moses? The rhetorical questions suggest that it is not enough to follow Moses. Eisenbaum observes that "Moses is held at least partly responsible for the people's failures" ("Heroes and History," 388).

21. "Rather than 'unbelief,' then, *apistia* here means the 'faithlessness' that is the opposite of 'faithfulness'" (Johnson, *Hebrews*, 117).

show that the offer of rest *is still valid*. God has an offer that extends beyond Moses and beyond Joshua. That is the point the author wants to emphasize for the readers.

Why would this point need to be argued? An audience attracted to the old covenant might think that the "rest" is the weekly Sabbath. The author says "on the seventh day" as part of the quote from Gen 2:2—that is to be expected—but he also prefaces the quote with a reminder that God is talking "about the seventh day." He is drawing extra attention to the seventh day, including it in the comparison.[22] He is implying not only that the "rest" that God offers in Ps 95 is not the entry into Canaan, it is not the weekly Sabbath, either. Just as Moses is not directly denigrated but is presented as less than Jesus, the Sabbath is not directly criticized, but it is not the rest that God exhorts his people to enter.

At the end of chapter 4, the author says that Jesus[23] is a source of "mercy and . . . help in time of need" (4:16), again suggesting that the readers were desirous of such help, and they will not receive help if they ignore Jesus. Since disobedience will be punished (4:11) and God judges all people (4:13), people need both mercy and help. The author then elaborates on the function of a high priest, and quotes Ps 110:4 in support of Jesus being a priest "according to the order of Melchizedek" (5:6, 10). There is little argumentation here, as if the point will not be disputed. He mentions in passing that Jesus "learned obedience through what he suffered" (5:8)—a veiled hint for readers to likewise view their trials in a positive way (Heb 12 has a more overt exhortation).[24] Verses 9–10 associate Jesus' role as Savior and his role as priest. Then the author pauses, warning that the subject needs sustained attention

---

22. The logic used in 4:8 could easily be applied to the Sabbath: If the weekly Sabbath had given them rest, then God would not have spoken in Ps 95 of another *day* (the word "rest" would have been sufficient; the word "day" hints that the author is talking about the Sabbath).

23. People should approach the throne of grace *as a result of* (οὖν) the fact that Jesus is a high priest who sympathizes with weakness (4:15–16) and because (γάρ) the function of a high priest is to help people (5:1). In both cases, the logic suggests that the high priest occupies the "throne of grace."

24. "Jesus provides a model here for what the audience is being called to do . . . . The pattern of enduring hardship and calling upon the Lord for help is affirmed as the 'normal' condition" (deSilva, *Perseverance*, 191–92). Heb 5:9 encourages readers to be obedient, as Christ was.

(5:11)²⁵ and is essential for salvation (6:4-8). He balances his threat with assurance (6:9-10), pleads for diligence (6:11-12), and emphasizes that God's promise gives steadfast hope (6:13-19).

With this forceful warning and reassurance, the author seems to shift from areas of general agreement and prepares to address new ideas, on which he expects some resistance, perhaps even to argue against ideas of the readers.²⁶ His criticisms of the law have heretofore been subtle; they will soon become blunt. He exhorts the readers to press "toward perfection" (6:1-2).²⁷ He states that people are saved "through faith and patience" (6:12), hinting that the readers need such, and he gives Abraham as an example of patience (6:15). However, there is something odd about Abraham's example: Due to God's oath, the promise was certain whether or not Abraham was patient—and he had no choice *but* to wait. The author uses Abraham as an example of patience because he wants the *readers* to be patient, and Abraham is an example they respect.²⁸ His purpose here is hortatory, not expository.

In 6:17-18, the author makes a transition toward God's promise *to the readers*: God gave an oath to stress the certainty of this promise to "the heirs of the promise"²⁹ so that "*we . . .* might be strongly encouraged to seize the hope set before *us.*" He does not say what the promise is—presumably the readers already believe that they are heirs of a

---

25. The passage criticizes the readers, but then affirms their ability to go forward. It also appeals: If you want to grow, if you value righteousness, if you want to know what is good, then listen to what I have to say.

26. The warnings and reassurance come right after the author mentions Jesus' role in salvation and as high priest (5:9-10). Although both ideas may be superficially acceptable to the readers, the author will soon develop the connection between them with argumentation that implies that he expects resistance.

27. The "basic teachings about Christ" may refer to what he has said thus far. The author wants them to move forward from those teachings to something new. Rather than going back to the foundation (the six points that are not specifically about Christ), he will go forward. The rhetorical effect is to assure the readers: "I will not treat you like babies." A more subtle result is that the readers will complain about the conclusion only at the risk of categorizing themselves as babies who could not comprehend the argument.

28. The "patience" he exhorts is functionally equivalent to faithfulness. The passage may hint that the readers were giving up hope on a promise associated with Christ.

29. The only oath God swore to Abraham was in Gen 22:15-18, the promise to give him many descendants. The readers of Hebrews were among the heirs that God promised.

promise of salvation given to Abraham.³⁰ The passage serves to assure the readers of success, but in passing it also gives two principles that the author will soon use in his doctrinal argument: 1) the blessing is given by a superior (6:14; 7:7), and 2) God's oath is doubly sure (6:18; 7:21).

With a promise of salvation on one side and a threat of permanent rejection on the other, the stakes are high. After this extended call for the readers to be attentive, the author is ready to resume his discussion of Christ being a high priest—the topic that is "hard to explain" (5:11).

A New Priesthood Implies Abrogation of the Law (Heb 7–8)

At the end of ch. 6, the author again mentions Melchizedek, and in ch. 7 he begins to develop the topic. First he shows that Melchizedek is greater than Abraham. The author normally states a conclusion and gives a reason; here he breaks the pattern by giving major and minor premises and forcing the readers to come to the conclusion.³¹ This is only one step toward his real goal, which is to argue that Christ is superior to the Levitical priests. In 7:9, "Levi" really refers to the Levites and priests, for Levi himself never received tithes.³²

The author begins to approach the subject from another angle in 7:11, showing that the Levitical priesthood was inadequate. He begins, not by citing inadequacies (that could make him sound like a complainer), but by showing that *Scripture* implied an inadequacy: "Now if perfection had been attainable through the Levitical priesthood—for the people received the law under this priesthood—what further need would there have been to speak of another priest arising according to the order of Melchizedek?" (7:11). An assumption hidden in the logic here is that there can be only one priesthood—that the Melchizedek

---

30. As I will show in the next chapter, the promises in Genesis do not explicitly include salvation, but first-century Jews assumed that they did, based on their concept of what a covenant entailed.

31. A direct statement may have offended some readers.

32. "Dans l'épître, la comparaison-contraste de base est entre le sacerdoce lévitique et Jésus (cf. 5.1–10); après 7.17, Melchisédek va disparaître définitivement de la scène" (Bénétreau, *Hébreux*, 2:29). After Christ is shown to be superior to the Levitical priests, the role of Melchizedek is done. "The final paragraph of chap. 7 leaves Melchizedek entirely behind, to the extent of omitting the last line of Ps. 110:4. The focus is now on Jesus" (Ellingworth, *Hebrews*, 382).

priesthood necessarily *replaced* rather than supplemented the Levitical priesthood.[33]

Verse 11 implies a logical connection between salvation, priesthood, and law. The author asks whether the priesthood can bring τελείωσις—i.e., salvation. He then gives the reason for his question: "For [γάρ] the people received the *law* under this priesthood." The reason he bridges from the priesthood to the law is because he wants to explore whether *the law* brings salvation.[34] Verse 12 makes the connection more obvious: A change in priesthood implies a change[35] *in the law*; they stand or fall together. So the author first shows that the priesthood has been changed, concludes that the commandment about priesthood has changed (7:18), and he broadens that conclusion to argue that the entire law has changed (7:19). The author argues that if God did something forbidden by the law (appoint a non-Levitical priest, contrary to Num 18:7), it means not just an abrogation of one specific commandment, but a negation of a much broader category.[36]

He concludes the section by saying that the law did not bring anything to completion (7:19)—that is, did not give salvation.[37] The

---

33. The author does not consider the possibility that one priesthood could be in heaven while the other worked on earth. Spicq (*Hébreux*, 137) and Westcott (*Hebrews*, 216) make the same observation. It suggests that the readers came from a Jewish background, since Gentiles would be aware of a multiplicity of priesthoods and might question this assumption. DeSilva observes another assumption: "Another 'given' within the institution of priesthood is that individuals may not volunteer their services or select themselves for the honored office" (*Perseverance*, 188). Again, Gentiles would be less likely to assume this.

34. In other words, We want to know whether the *law* brings salvation, so we ask first about the priesthood, because the law was given under the priesthood, and if one fails, the other does as well.

35. In 7:12 the word "change" is vague—it could mean a slight revision or a major overhaul. The author will soon argue for the latter (the law is "changed" as thoroughly as the priesthood is), but he initially uses a less offensive term.

36. It might be possible for the readers to go through Heb 7 with a narrow definition of "the law" (perhaps only the commandment restricting the priesthood to Levi), but the author implies in v. 11 that it is a broader category, and it becomes inescapably clear in 8:13 that a very broad category is intended. Jews would normally understand "the law" to refer to a large category, whereas "laws" would refer to specific commandments.

37. Heb 7:11 had said only that the priesthood did not bring perfection; the author expands the scope of his criticism in v. 19 to the entire law. "On note dans cette section un décalage, ou plutôt un élargissement: le non-accomplissement mis au compte

author could have argued more simply that God changed the priesthood, showing that the priesthood did not bring salvation. But he expands the discussion to the law in 7:12-19, then goes back to the priesthood in 7:20 *without building anything on his conclusion about the law.*[38] This was not a step in a larger argument—it was a point that the author went out of his way to make. Apparently the readers needed to know not just that the Levitical priesthood was obsolete, but also that the law of Moses could not give salvation and was no longer valid. This is further shown by the author's use of pejorative words for the law—even though it was contrary to normal rhetorical methods of comparison to denigrate the point of comparison.[39] If the readers already believed that the law was "weak and ineffectual," there would be little need to say that the covenant of Christ was better. But if the readers were attracted to the law in *opposition* to Christ, then it would be quite appropriate for the author to criticize one and urge the other.

The cessation of the law is noted again in 8:13 and at a crucial junction in the flow of the epistle: Right after the author says that offerings are unnecessary (10:18), he moves to an exhortation for faithfulness (10:19-25) and gives another strong warning (10:26-31). The author states bluntly that the law is obsolete; he makes its termination the conclusion of his longest doctrinal exposition, and he makes it the launching point for his most vigorous exhortation. The author does not merely advocate faith in Christ—*he advocates Christ over against the law.* The comparison is always against the law, and the exhortations for the new over against the old are the focus of the final contrast in Heb 12:18-24. This was the key doctrinal question the readers needed.

The argument in 7:10-20 is tightly connected—γάρ is used nine times, suggesting that the author is trying to prove a case on which he expects opposition. He takes the unusual step of repeating himself in 7:13-14, even though the facts were common knowledge: Jesus was

---

du sacerdoce lévitique au départ (v. 11), est référé à toute la loi (v. 19)" (Bénétreau, *Hébreux*, 2:41). The author views priesthood and law as two sides of the same coin, but begins with priesthood and moves toward the law as a whole, suggesting that the point about priesthood was more palatable to the readers; the law was a more sensitive topic.

38. That is, he does not base further conclusions on the word "law." When the author states that cleansing rituals were imposed for a limited time (9:10), he *may* be basing that conclusion on the belief that the law was ineffective (7:19), but more likely, on the belief that the old covenant is terminated (8:13). The rationale is not made explicit.

39. See note 86 near the end of chapter 1.

descended from Judah, and Moses never authorized anyone from Judah to be a priest. Verse 12 uses the word "necessarily"; 7:14 begins with "it is evident" and 7:15 with "it is even more obvious"; these words are "rhetorical devices intended to enhance the persuasiveness of the argument."[40] The rhetoric suggests that the author expected opposition to what he was saying. The readers were tempted to look to the old covenant law as a means of being in a right relationship with God. This was likely due to external pressures and arguments coming from outside the community of believers.[41] The readers were being pressured with doctrinal arguments to look to the law, and they were tempted to accept those arguments, so the author responds with doctrinal arguments to exhort them to keep their faith in Christ, and to explain why the alternative is inadequate.

However, the author does not take away something without also offering something better as a replacement. In 7:18–19, the criticism of the law is sandwiched by a μέν . . . δέ construction: On one hand, the law is abrogated; on the other, a better hope is offered, through which readers may approach God (this "approach," it is implied, gives the τελείωσις that the law and priesthood could not bring). This better hope is to be found in the "better covenant" (7:22). The author assumes here that the readers want to approach God *by means of a covenant*. This is a Jewish idea, since διαθήκη meant "last will and testament" in non-Jewish Greek.[42]

Jesus can save people, the author argues, because he lives forever and holds his priesthood forever (7:24–25). The Levitical priests could not save people because they were themselves in need of salvation. It is appropriate that an effective high priest would be one who had been "exalted above the heavens" (7:26); he is able to deliver the goods because he *has* them. Jesus has reached the goal that the readers want. In verse 28 the author reminds the readers that *the law* appoints priests who are weak, but it is by an *oath* that God appointed a priest who has

---

40. Ellingworth, *Hebrews*, 371.

41. Since the author used to be part of the community, it is likely that he is addressing recently introduced ideas, not longstanding beliefs, and those new ideas were associated with recently intensified pressures.

42. Danker, BDAG, 228, and Behm, "The Greek Term διαθήκη," 124–26. Westcott writes, "The idea of a 'testament' was indeed foreign to the Jews till the time of the Herods" (*Hebrews*, 299). The author assumes a Jewish meaning of διαθήκη.

already "been made perfect forever." As Kistemaker says, "A law can be annulled; an oath lasts forever."[43]

The author calls attention to his main point[44] in 8:1—"We have such a high priest"—that is, one described in 7:26 as sinless and in heaven, able to save those who approach God through him. Hebrews 8:2–6 presents a number of ideas that are later developed in more detail: Jesus must offer something, he serves at a true sanctuary in heaven, and the Levitical sanctuary is a copy. It seems that the author expects less opposition on these points, for he feels free to mention them without extensive argumentation.[45] But when he mentions the "better covenant" and "better promises"[46] in v. 6, he pauses to give substantial support from Scripture.

The author will highlight one benefit of the new covenant in 10:17, but in chapter 8 his purpose is not so much to describe the new covenant, but simply to argue that it has rendered the old one obsolete.[47] The readers need to be convinced that the old covenant is obsolete before they are willing to consider any benefits of the new. The author claims in 8:6 that the new covenant is better [κρείττων], but he does not follow that with arguments supporting the word "better." The conclusion of the passage is simply that the old covenant is obsolete, implying that

---

43. Kistemaker, *Exposition*, 200.

44. Heb 8:1 serves not just as a summary of the preceding paragraph, but also describes the main doctrinal point of the epistle. Yet the author's purpose is not simply to convey this information—he has a hortatory goal: that the readers remain loyal to this high priest.

45. His argument in 8:4 is based on the old covenant, even though he will soon argue that it is obsolete. He says that Christ could not be a priest if he were on earth, because the priesthood was restricted to Levi. But logically, if the old covenant is obsolete, its restriction would no longer apply, and it would be permissible for Jesus to be a priest on earth. Stanley resolves the problem by assuming that Jesus would remain on earth only if he had not died: "The meaning of this phrase is that if Jesus were *still* on earth, *if he had not died*, then he could not be a priest" ("New Covenant Hermeneutic," 72, italics added). But the fact that the author did not have to specify this suggests an audience that assumed the validity of the old covenant.

46. The author does not say what the better promises are. They are probably equated with salvation and the promises of Abraham (6:17–18).

47. Grässer remarks that the author "zitiert Jer 31,31–34 mit dem *einen* Ziel, die Aussage von V 13 als Quintessenz des Ganzen zu erreichen: Weil die zweite Diatheke »neu« heisst, muss die erste veraltet sein" (*An die Hebräer*, 2:101, italics in original).

the new covenant is now operative.⁴⁸ The author begins by arguing that the old covenant had a defect (8:7).⁴⁹

The author does not argue that Jesus brought the covenant that Jer 31 described—he does not show a correspondence between prediction and fulfillment. The primary argument in *favor* of the new covenant is simply that the old is obsolete. It is sufficient for the author's purpose to simply note that a new covenant was predicted, and that God therefore deemed the old one inadequate. If the readers accept that, then it is assumed that they will accept that the new covenant has been put into effect through Jesus Christ.⁵⁰ The author offers no comment on the vast majority of the quote. As Grässer comments, the disproportion between the quote and the terse commentary points out the main goal of the argumentation: "Der zweite Bund ist nicht die restitutio des ersten, sondern seine substitutio."⁵¹

The author does not do anything with the details of Jer 31—he says nothing about law in the heart, God being their God, or everyone knowing the Lord (he even omits most of those details when he quotes Jer 31 again in Heb 10:16–17). In verse 13, he highlights the point he wants to make from this citation: "In speaking of 'a new covenant' he

---

48. Bénétreau writes, "On s'attendrait à ce que soient explicitées les *meilleures promesses* qui fondent la nouvelle alliance annoncées en 8.6. Au contraire, c'est le sort de l'ancienne alliance qui retient l'attention" (*Hébreux*, 2:59). Ellingworth observes, "At this stage of the argument, the author's main concern is with the supersession of the old covenant and thus with the negative part of the prophecy (v. 9), rather than with its stronger positive aspect (vv. 10–12), which is explored later (especially in 10:15–18)" (*Hebrews*, 413).

49. His criticism is indirect in two ways: 1) the word "covenant" is not in the text, so readers must supply it, and 2) he pairs the old covenant with the word "faultless," but argues against that pairing, forcing readers to supply the conclusion.

50. If the readers used eucharistic words similar to Luke 22:20 or 1 Cor 11:25, they would already be favorably disposed to the idea that Jesus instituted a new covenant; they just had not realized that this implied the end of the Mosaic covenant. Gordon observes, "That 'the days' (v. 8) of Jer. 31.31 had now come would not have been doubted by a writer who could claim in the first sentence of his letter that the Christian era belonged in the 'last days' (1.2)" (*Hebrews*, 93). The only thing that the author argues *against*—implying that it is the only thing vying for the readers' attention—is the Mosaic covenant.

51. "Das »Missverhältnis« zwischen dem ausführlichen Zitat und dieser lapidaren Feststellung fällt natürlich auf, stellt aber das eigentliche Argumentationsziel um so deutlicher heraus" (Grässer, *Hebräer*, 2:103).

has made the first one obsolete." He reiterates the point by saying, "And what is obsolete and growing old will soon disappear."

Again, it would be faint praise to say that Christ was better than an arrangement that everyone knew did not work — that is, better than nothing. For a comparison to be an effective form of praise, it must compare with something still respected. The author never says, "The law is good but Christ is better." Rather, he argues that the law, although valid, was never effective.[52] He is not just presenting Jesus as the better of two alternatives — he is saying that Jesus is effective, whereas the law is not. He goes beyond the rhetoric of comparison — he is arguing *against* the law, arguing for supersession. As Manson says, if the author simply wanted to highlight the superiority of Christ,

> he could have dispensed with the so-often repeated reminder to his readers that the order, the rites and the sacrifices of Judaism *were ended*. It would have been enough to show that Christianity transcended Judaism, the noblest religion of the past, without insisting *pari passu* and all the time that it abrogated and superseded it. But the latter insistence would be of the very essence of the matter if he were writing to Jewish Christians on whom the hand of the past still lay very heavily.... The character of his particular emphases all gain in intelligibility and point if we suppose the group to be conservatively Jewish-Christian in sentiment and tendency.[53]

To praise the sacrifice of Jesus, it would have been sufficient to comment about sacrifices, but the author goes further, to the law as a whole, to the covenant, apparently because it is also a subject of concern. Throughout chs. 8–10 he weaves the theme of covenant, expanding the significance of his conclusions beyond the superiority of Christ over the old priesthood, sacrifices and sanctuary, although his point could have been made without mentioning covenant at all. The argument implies that the readers were tempted to view the old covenant as still valid.

---

52. Stylianopoulos writes, "The author throughout the epistle clearly intends to separate and reject the Mosaic cult as completely valueless. He shows little interest in establishing unity and continuity between the Old and New Covenants" ("Shadow and Reality," 218). He concludes, "The Epistle to the Hebrews, except in the case of the interpretation of Old Testament 'prophetic' quotations, never suggests fulfillment of the one covenant by the other, but μετάθεσις, ἀναίρεσις, σάλευσις, and ἀθέτησις of the former" (ibid., 230).

53. Manson, *Hebrews*, 147, 157.

The Only Effective Atonement (Heb 9:1—10:18)

The author then describes the tabernacle and its furnishings (9:1–5). These are reported, not argued, for they were probably common knowledge, and the author does nothing with most of the details. But they help the author build rapport with the audience, and provide a pause in the intensity of the argumentation.[54]

Based on the fact that the Levitical high priest could enter the Holiest Place only once a year,[55] the author argues that the way into the true sanctuary (i.e., the way to salvation) was then hidden (9:8). He writes, "gifts and sacrifices are offered that cannot perfect the conscience of the worshiper" (9:9).[56] Presumably the readers will accept the logic that external rituals cannot affect the internal conscience. He notes in passing that the rituals were temporary commands, "imposed until the time comes to set things right" (9:10).[57] He does not offer supporting reasons for the assertions in vv. 8–10; they seem to be based on the belief that the law and old covenant are obsolete—points that the author may consider already sufficiently proven. The remainder of the chapter provides further support for the idea that the sacrifices symbolized something for "the present time."

In Heb 9:11, the author begins to describe the ministry of Christ, who entered the sanctuary in heaven (the presence of God) by means

---

54. "The author follows his usual practice of giving, first, a favourable or at least neutral description of circumstances under the old dispensation, and next, mentioning their negative aspects, thus opening the way for positive statements about Christ" (Ellingworth, *Hebrews*, 419). Heb 9:4–5 (like 7:2b–c) is a summary of information from Scripture, but information that plays no part in the author's argument.

55. He had to enter several times on the same day: to offer incense, to sprinkle blood, and to retrieve the censer. Although Yom Kippur is important because the high priest was allowed to enter the Holy of Holies only on that day, the day does not have a privileged role in the author's argumentation. Rather, he paints a *composite* picture of the sacrifices and rituals, whether they are daily, yearly, with blood, with water, for covenant inauguration or covenant maintenance. On 9:13, Ellingworth writes, "The author is moving away from specific reference to the Day of Atonement liturgy to the underlying principles of OT sacrifice" (*Hebrews*, 454).

56. Τελειόω is apparently a word that the author thought would appeal to the readers; here he points out that the effect is in the conscience, not the body.

57. This verse "contains one of the author's most negative judgments on the levitical order, comparable with 8:13" (Ellingworth, *Hebrews*, 442). The author does not *explicitly* state that the rituals are obsolete (ibid., 444), but if the covenant is obsolete, the regulations are as well.

of his own blood, obtaining eternal redemption—a redemption that purifies the conscience of believers (9:14). Since he was perfect in conscience, he can help others become perfect in conscience. Levitical priests, who were "without blemish" only on the outside, could be effective only on the outside. They could not perfect themselves, much less anyone else. The author then draws a conclusion from Christ's efficacy in providing salvation: "for this reason [διὰ τοῦτο] he is the mediator of a new covenant" (9:15). This assumes that *salvation must be given in the context of a covenant*[58]—an idea that also is reflected in 9:15b when the author states that the *purpose* of the new covenant is "that those who have been called may receive the promised eternal inheritance." A covenant brings salvation.

Why can people be saved through the covenant Christ brought? Heb 9:15 gives this reason: "because a death has occurred that redeems them from the transgressions *under the first covenant*."[59] It is surprising that the author is concerned about transgressions under a covenant that is now obsolete. However, if the readers were being pressured to conform to that covenant, they would be very interested in this redemption.[60] The author is saying that transgressions were atoned not by the rituals of Yom Kippur (contra Lev 16:30), but by the death of Christ. The first covenant required death as the penalty for transgressions, and Jesus has supplied a death effective for all.

---

58. Jewett notes, "That the mediation of a covenant is an aspect of *priestly* ministry is a completely unprecedented claim on the part of our author, for the term mediator was normally linked with juristic procedure, or in Judaism, with the role of Moses and the angels" (*Letter to Pilgrims,* 134, italics added). The author assumes that salvation is not only linked to covenant, but also to priesthood; therefore priesthood and covenant are linked; salvation must be obtained by a priestly act and the covenant must be inaugurated by priestly ministry.

59. The author apparently believes that the death of Christ redeemed people who transgress the *new* covenant as well as those who transgress the old (once is enough for all time), but he does not have occasion to say this because the focal point of the controversy is the old covenant.

60. It is also possible that the author is commenting on the way that the *patriarchs* can be saved. He uses the perfect tense participle κεκλημένοι rather than a present tense participle, and he has moved from the first person "our" of 9:14 to the third person of 9:15. However, there is nothing in the context to indicate that anyone is concerned about the salvation of the patriarchs.

To substantiate that the first covenant was enacted with blood, the author summarizes the events of Exod 24 (with a few additions).[61] This story was probably common knowledge, so the author's effort to *prove* the point may suggest that he is strengthening the case for a conclusion that might be resisted: Just as the old covenant was inaugurated with blood and everything was purified by blood, so also the new covenant was inaugurated and people are purified by the blood of Christ (9:23).

He summarizes: "under the law almost everything is purified with blood, and without the shedding of blood there is no forgiveness" (9:22). It was *necessary*, 9:23 says, for the tabernacle and other things to be "cleansed" (dedicated for sacred purposes[62]) with blood, apparently because that blood showed the penalty of covenant transgressions. Since the earthly copies were dedicated with blood, the author reasons that the heavenly things needed to be dedicated with better blood.[63] The penalty of transgressing the old covenant was death, and the transgressors could not be redeemed with lesser substitutes (animals), but only with a life more valuable than their own.

How do we know that this better sacrifice was necessary? Because (γάρ) "Christ . . . entered into heaven itself" (9:24). The author reasons from what actually happened to conclude that such was necessary.[64]

---

61. Exod 24 says nothing about water, wool and hyssop, and in the story-flow of Exodus, the tabernacle and vessels did not yet exist. Morris surmises, "Perhaps we are meant to see the dedication of the tabernacle as a kind of renewal of the covenant" ("Hebrews," 12:89). As with the offerings, the author is creating a composite picture based on the entire law. This improves the analogy with the new covenant, in which the covenant was inaugurated and the heavenly sanctuary dedicated by means of the same offering. In 9:19, the author again mentions "law" without any need to do so.

62. Ellingworth argues for this meaning for "purifying" the heavenly things: "The explanation which best accords with the context is well expressed in the *New Jerusalem Bible* note: 'The "purification" of the sanctuary, whether the earthly or the heavenly one, does not necessarily imply any previous "impurity": it is a consecratory and inaugural rite'" (*Hebrews*, 477). Spicq has the same view: "Le ciel n'a pas besoin d'être purifié (le verbe *katharizesthai* n'est pas répété), mais d'être consacré pour devenir un sanctuaire, apte à la liturgie dont le nouveau grand prêtre sera l'officiant; c'est une « dédicace »" (*Hébreux* 159–60). See also Hurst, *Hebrews*, 38–39.

63. An argument from lesser to greater could have gone the other way: Since heavenly realities are better than earthly copies, they do not need rituals to dedicate them.

64. Ellingworth comments on 7:26, "Such statements are consequences drawn from what he believes God has in fact done" (*Hebrews*, 393). Kim says, "The author of Hebrews seems to begin with the eschatological revelation of Jesus as the perfect sacrifice and then work back from there to conclude that the Levitical sacrifices were

The fact that God sent Christ shows that the previous arrangement was ineffective—animal sacrifices offered by priests who have sins of their own could only illustrate redemption, not give it. Everything in the epistle flows from the belief that Christ is now at the right hand of God.[65] He was "offered once to bear the sins of many,"[66] and so the author concludes that once was enough.[67]

Just as judgment follows death, Christ will return and bring salvation (the positive counterpart of judgment) to "those who are eagerly waiting for him" (9:27–28). Here the author indirectly exhorts the readers to wait for the Parousia, but he does not focus on it.[68]

In chapter 10, the author explains *why* Jesus' death was effective. The law was a shadow and could not remove sins (10:1–4). Consequently (Διο) "Christ came into the world" (10:5).[69] If salvation cannot come by the law, the author reasons, it must come by Christ. This contrast—either the law or Christ—is found repeatedly in the epistle,[70] suggesting that this was the choice the readers faced. Although they accepted the ascension of Christ into heaven, they were tempted to

---

inadequate . . . . Instead of going from problem to solution, he likely started with the solution and then identified the problem" (*Polemic*, 175).

65. "The starting-point is not, at least not directly, the historical fact that Jesus was crucified only once, but the conviction that his death and enthronement do not need to be repeated, because the enthronement shows the permanent efficacy of the death" (Ellingworth, "Old Testament in Hebrews," 192).

66. This seems to be an allusion to Isa 53:4–6. The author states several times that Christ's death atoned *for everyone*, but he does not attempt to prove the extent of the atonement; it seems to be based on Isa 53. The argument assumes that if Jesus' death was effective for anyone, it was effective for everyone.

67. Kim, *Polemic*, 185.

68. Perhaps this was a sensitive subject for the readers. On the other hand, many NT documents mention the Parousia, but we cannot conclude that every allusion indicates an audience tired of waiting.

69. The text has "he"—Christ is not named until 10:10—the author assumes that the readers will accept without question that the psalm is messianic. "There is no attempt at argument or justification . . . . It is probable that this Christ-centered understanding of Scripture was generally accepted in the community to which Hebrews was originally addressed" (Ellingworth, *Hebrews*, 499).

70. As discussed above, the first section of the epistle has only subtle comparisons. Hebrews 11 is the primary exception, but that chapter is notable for *not* mentioning the law for any of the OT heroes.

look to the law for worship, atonement, and salvation.[71] Although they accepted Jesus as the Messiah and Son of God, he was in danger of being a figure without a function.[72] So the author argues that Jesus is not just sitting in heaven, he is the source of help and salvation, and his death, rather than being an embarrassment, is the means by which he brought salvation.

In general, although the author sometimes give supporting reasons when he says that Christ is effective, he tends to give *more* reasons when he says that the old covenant is ineffective, suggesting that he expects more resistance on that point, that it is the focal point of the current controversy. This indicates that the biggest problem that the readers had was not objections to the new, but an attraction to the old. Since the readers had only two choices, it was enough to disprove one, and the readers' already positive view of Christ meant that they would accept him as the only rational alternative.[73] The author never attempts to prove that only two possibilities exist—he simply assumes that salvation is either by the law, or else it is by Christ. He assumes that the readers will accept Christ's death as efficacious if the Levitical rituals are shown to be inadequate.

The author quotes Ps 40:6–8 as words of Christ: "Sacrifices and offerings you have not desired, but a body you have prepared for me." He regroups the quote into two parts: First, "You have neither desired nor taken pleasure in sacrifices and offerings and burnt offerings and sin

---

71. Schenck concludes that many of the readers "believed that the Levitical system not only provided legitimate means of atonement in addition to that provided by Christ but perhaps even that it was essential for complete and continuous atonement . . . . The Levitical system in some way stands as the audience's main alternative to Christ" (*Understanding the Book,* 102, 107). Similarly, Grelot writes, "l'accent est mis sur l'alliance . . . comme si les destinataires de la lettre n'avaient pas eu une confiance suffisante dans la mort du Christ en croix comme sacrifice propitiatoire qui avait obtenu le pardon de tous les péchés humains. . . . Ici l'auteur s'adresse à des judéo-chrétiens qui ont longtemps attaché leur espérance de salut au *culte du Temple* et aux *rites de purification* destinés à les absoudre de leurs péchés" (*Une lecture,* 91, 95, italics in original).

72. "The main concern of our author is about defection from the high Christology that the community in Rome had already embraced" (Witherington, *Letters and Homilies,* 97).

73. If the readers were troubled by an experience of guilt feelings about post-baptismal sin (as Lindars suggests in *Theology of the Letter to the Hebrews,* 10–14), a verse such as 10:2 could be counterproductive. Such people might conclude from v. 10 that since they still had "consciousness of sin," they were therefore not cleansed, and the old covenant sacrifices should therefore still be offered.

offerings"—after which the author inserts the reminder that "these are offered according to the law," thereby indicating again that he is dealing with the law as a whole, not just the sacrifices.[74] The author resumes the quote by saying, "Then he added, 'See, I have come to do your will'" (10:9).[75] After this regrouping, the author asserts: "He abolishes the first in order to establish the second." In context, "the first" is the first part of the quote—the sacrifices—but by implication, it implies that the law as a whole has been abolished.[76] In its stead, Christ has established "the second"—in context, doing the will of God, but by implication, the new covenant and new priesthood, effective access to the presence of God, and eternal salvation.[77]

In 10:11–14, the author repeats the thoughts of 9:25–26. In contrast to the repetitious sacrifices of the old covenant, which "can never take away sins," Christ made one sacrifice effective for all time. The stress on frequency suggests that the readers may have viewed the repetitive nature of the Levitical rituals in a positive way, and the author responds by arguing that repetitions indicate ineffectiveness. As a conclusion to the doctrinal section that began at 7:1, the author repeats two points from Jer 31. God promised to make another covenant, and he promised to forgive their sins. The longest doctrinal exposition of the epistle ends with these words: "Where there is forgiveness of these, there is no longer any offering for sin" (10:18). The climax of the argument is about sin offerings, not thank offerings, peace offerings or other rituals. Although some verses in Hebrews indicate that all rituals are equally obsolete, the focus in the epistle is on sin offerings, suggesting that they were the primary concern of the readers. The grand finale of the longest doctrinal

---

74. Cockerill writes, "By affirming in v. 8 that 'the law required' these sacrifices 'to be made' . . . the author of Hebrews reminds his readers that the sacrifices are part of a covenant or legal system that stands or falls together" ("Structure and Interpretation," 195 n. 58).

75. The author stops the quote just before Ps 40:8b, which says, "your law is within my heart." Although this clause would have tied in well with the quote from Jer 31:33, it would make it more difficult for the author to contrast the law with the new covenant (Heb 10:8–9).

76. The author has earlier used "the first" as a substantive for the old covenant, and as a substantive for the tabernacle. The entire Levitical cluster—priesthood, law, covenant, tabernacle, sacrifices and rituals—is abolished.

77. The author does not develop a new law or new rituals. He does not describe the content of the new covenant as well as he does the old; the connections between covenant, law, and priesthood are explicit for the old but not described for the new.

passage in the epistle is that sacrifices are obsolete—suggesting that the readers had been especially interested in those sacrifices.[78]

It is not difficult to imagine Jewish readers attracted to the old covenant, but it is more difficult to imagine readers with a high Christology (implied in Heb 1 and throughout Hebrews) looking to the old covenant for atonement. Could they accept Jesus as an exalted person, but not as the Savior? The readers did not necessarily *have* such a view—but the rhetoric suggests that that they were being pressured to accept such a view, and the author combats that view. The readers' more traditional Jewish neighbors may have been saying, "You can believe that Jesus is in heaven if you want to, but in order to be faithful to the Scriptures and to our covenant with God, you should participate in the Levitical rituals for atonement, for being right with God. Your belief about Jesus is harmless as long as you show solidarity with the covenant people by participating in our synagogue traditions. You don't have to give up your belief about Jesus, as long as you do what God's people are supposed to do." The readers may have been tempted to think that this was an acceptable compromise, a position that would avoid persecution, but the author is saying that it amounts to apostasy, tantamount to a rejection of the salvific efficacy of Jesus, and it is based on an obsolete law that can never provide access to God.

---

78. Westcott writes, "This is the last—the decisive—word of the argument" (*Hebrews*, 317). Übelacker says that we should go to the end of the argument (i.e., 10:18) to see the purpose of the central section. "Da der Vf. grundsätzlich immer zusammenfasst, erwarten wir uns auch hier einen Leitfaden" (*Hebräerbrief*, 226). He concludes that the main purpose of the central section has to do with forgiveness and sacrifices to achieve forgiveness (ibid.).

Strobel writes, "Dieser Lehrsatz, der die umfangreiche theologische Erörterung des Hohenpriestertums Jesu 4,14—10,18 abschliesst, betont die Abschaffung der Opfer, weil Christus eine vollkommene Vergebung ermöglicht hat. Das Gesamtergebnis der überaus vielfältigen Überlegungen wird in schlichtester Weise noch einmal zusammengefasst. Man hört heraus, dass mit solcher Grundsatzerklärung eine judenchristliche Hörerschaft zu jener Gewissheit gebracht werden soll, die sie die Bindung an das Alte endgültig aufgeben lässt" (*Brief an die Hebräer*, 124).

The context implies that the readers desired sacrifices. However, this does not in itself indicate when the epistle was written. People could want sacrifices and rituals *after* the temple was destroyed just as well as they could before. Sensitivities about the temple (fears of impending destruction, or angst about a recent destruction) may be one reason that the author never mentions it—he keeps the argument more objective by dealing with the tabernacle. And since the tabernacle was a temporary place of worship, it may have subtly supported the author's argument that the rituals were temporary. See Appendix C for a discussion of the date of the epistle.

Exhortations for Faithfulness (10:19—13:25)

The third major section of the epistle is primarily hortatory.[79] The author begins by reasoning, "Therefore, my friends, since we have confidence to enter . . . and a great priest over the house of God, let us approach with a true heart . . . . Let us hold fast to the confession" (10:19-22, echoing key words from 4:14-16). Since sacrifices are not needed, and since people can enter by Christ, the readers are exhorted to keep their confession. The readers apparently want to approach God, and the author argues that they cannot do it with Levitical rituals, but they can with Christ, because he has opened a new path and has provided a means of cleansing the conscience. On that basis, the readers are urged to hold fast to their confession—and to hold fast to all that goes with the confession.

The author gives more exhortations in 10:23-25, with the implication that these also logically follow from faith in Christ. When the readers "hold fast to the confession," they will also continue meeting together and encouraging one another. However, why is the existence of a high priest reason to meet together to encourage one another (10:25)? Is there a connection between sacrifice being unnecessary and meeting being necessary? The author assumes without argument that *assembling together is an inseparable part of what it means to confess Christ*. He is thinking in terms of a package, a constellation of beliefs that the readers are already familiar with—one religious approach as opposed to another. The author argues for this package by claiming that 1) the alternative is inadequate, 2) Christ is sufficient, and 3) faith is commendable.

The author argues that it is necessary for the readers to confess Christ. But the readers cannot logically conclude *necessity* unless all relevant alternatives are addressed. The author is assuming an audience for which the only viable religious options are those he mentions—namely, the old covenant cultus on one hand, and faith in Christ on the other.

In Heb 10:24-27, the author argues the following: Do not abandon the assembly, because deliberate sin will be punished. This argument

---

79. Even chapter 11, although not directly hortatory, supports the author's exhortation: He wants the auditors to imitate those who have faith. "Although the section is expository in form, it is parenetic in function, inviting Christians to emulate the example of those who responded to God with active faith" (Lane, *Hebrews 9-13*, 316). Hagner writes, "The author is less concerned with providing information than with motivating his readers" (*Encountering*, 144).

assumes that dropping out *is* a deliberate sin. The rhetoric uses a strong emotional appeal (the warning passage) without articulating the premise. It is a rhetorical strategy, not a logical theological explanation. The readers may have been facing threats such as, "If you are not faithful to the covenant of Moses, you will suffer the covenant curses." The author responds with equally severe threats: "Those covenant curses are irrelevant because of Christ; what you really want to avoid is being unfaithful to the *new* covenant. If you go back on it, there is no salvation. Don't abandon the only effective approach to God."[80] The author does not elaborate on the punishment that is worse than death—the rhetorical question leaves that to the imagination of the readers—but if the readers were afraid of being killed for allegiance to the Christ community, then it would be rhetorically appropriate in that situation to tell them that apostasy had a punishment *worse* than death. The verse also implies that neglecting to meet together is equivalent to despising Christ, counting his sacrifice as unholy, and insulting the Spirit of grace.[81] The author may avoid saying these things directly as a matter of rhetorical strategy. He assures the readers in 10:39 that such things are not appropriate for them. Verse 32 also argues by implication rather than statement. The implication is that if they continue in their earlier behavior, they will not be punished.

The style of the argumentation has changed—whereas the logic was tightly connected in the central doctrinal section, it is now more allusive. Motivational rhetoric appeals more to emotion than it does to

---

80. DeSilva writes, "The potential apostate is warned that leaving the group does not mean getting out from being under hostility and danger—it means exposing oneself to the greatest danger and loss . . . . They are led to consider [apostasy] not as a movement toward what their neighbors would consider just and pious but as a movement toward the utmost injustice and impiety toward one who had gone to the most extreme lengths (death itself) to bring them the benefits that they now so carelessly spurned" (*Perseverance*, 355, 239).

81. "Simply leaving the voluntary association called the 'church' becomes an active assault on the honor of one's divine benefactor and mediator" (ibid., 238). Montefiore acknowledges the implication when he writes, "Persistent absenteeism . . . may have been almost tantamount to apostasy," but then he draws back from that conclusion: "but it is not to be equated with it" (*Hebrews*, 177). Stanley notes that Ps 40 and Hab 2 both "speak of the coming one . . . . Both passages also speak of God's displeasure, which is directed in vv. 5, 6 toward levitical sacrifice and in v. 38 to those who shrink back. On the basis of these links, it seems that for our author shrinking back is equivalent to relying on levitical sacrifices, since both are linked to God's displeasure" (Stanley, "New Covenant," 178, 205).

logic, and the author does that by praising the readers' past performance, promising unspecified rewards, playing down the cost, and expressing confidence for the future. His indicative sentences imply exhortations.

Verses 32–35 also give us the most concrete description of the readers: They endured a time of persecution shortly after they became believers. Some were imprisoned; others were plundered. The persecutions are not completely over (13:3), but no one has been killed (12:4).[82] But the readers feel threatened with more severe persecutions. The author implies that they have confidence (10:35) and faith in Christ, but he believes that his epistle is needed to strengthen them in the faith, to prevent an erosion of their confidence. He encourages them by saying that their faith will soon be rewarded.

Hebrews 11 is an encomium on faith, which is preparatory to a renewed call for perseverance—that is, faithfulness and patience (12:1). Among the examples of the faithful is Abraham. Gordon suggests a way in which his example would be relevant to the readers: "The example of Abraham's abandoning of the assured and the familiar for the uncertainties of life in Canaan could help to stiffen the resolve of those who had stepped out in faith without having received any tangible fulfillment of the promises that had inspired them in the first place."[83] Similarly, Thompson writes, "The author describes the faith of Abraham (11:8) and Moses as a 'going out' or abandonment of security. His reason for presenting these heroes in such terms is demonstrated at 13:13 where the author wants to encourage his readers to 'go out' or abandon their security for the sake of Christ."[84]

The author's purpose here is not to analyze Abraham objectively, but to exhort the readers; he therefore describes the circumstances of Abraham in such a way as to provide a model relevant to the readers.[85] For example, no one would have thought that Abraham considered returning to Mesopotamia (11:15)—the argument has a rhetorical purpose. The idea of "return" would be significant for believers who were

---

82. Heb 12:4 may allude to a boxing match rather than martyrdom—but it would be in poor taste to use that metaphor if anyone in the recipient community had been killed for the faith.

83. Gordon, *Hebrews*, 133.

84. Thompson, *Hebrews*, 157.

85. "The author has fastened onto aspects of the ways in which the patriarchs' 'faith' was enacted that correspond most nearly to the condition of the audience" (deSilva, *Perseverance*, 401).

being urged to return to their former practices.[86] The author is arguing that the patriarchs did not feel "at home" in Canaan, and did not want to return to their original home, therefore they must have wanted a heavenly land instead of some other earthly territory (11:16). His real point is that he wants the readers to similarly look to a heavenly reward rather than trying to be "at home" on earth. Although the author exhorts the readers to have beliefs about the past (e.g., the atonement and enthronement of Christ) and the present (his intercession), this passage focuses on faith in future rewards as the motivation for *behavior* in the present. For the author, faith is not just belief in the invisible—it also means obedience. "For Hebrews, faith is faithfulness."[87]

The arguments in this chapter are not as logical as those in earlier chapters (e.g., 7:1—10:18). The author is not trying to prove his points—they are not in dispute. He has a different rhetorical purpose in this chapter: By presenting positive examples, he is trying to encourage the readers to have faith.[88] He is not trying to prove that Moses acted in faith—the readers already *know* that Moses had faith, and they already know that they should have faith, too. However, the author wants to draw exemplary lessons from the life of Moses. He is saying, "Even if you have to give up enormous treasures, or if you are persecuted with the people of God because of your belief in Christ, do not give up.[89] The reward is worth the sacrifice. If you want to follow Moses, follow him in this regard—do not be dissuaded by external pressures." Verse 27 presents another point of imitation: Moses left Egypt in faith, not fearing

---

86. "The implication can hardly be missed that our author does not want his readers to return to their previous Judaism" (Hagner, *Encountering*, 149).

87. Thompson, *Hebrews*, 146. "The primary dimension of faith for Hebrews is that of endurance, faith*fulness*" (Schenck, *Understanding*, 65). "Faith for our author . . . is practically interchangeable with obedience" (Hagner, *Hebrews*, 72). When the author argues for obedience (in ch. 3, for example), he is appealing to a value that the readers already hold (building rapport, or *ethos*). Although the epistle has some miscellaneous imperatives in ch. 13, the primary "obedience" advocated is being faithful to the confession of Christ.

88. Croy notes that *Rhetorica ad Herrennium* 4.3.5 advises orators "that *exempla* be placed *after* enthymemes if possible . . . . This strategy corresponds to the overall structure of the Epistle to the Hebrews. The author has reasoned in chapters 1–10 with what might be called enthymematic arguments . . . . The exempla of 11.4—12.3, culminating in Jesus, would not have had the same persuasive force if they had stood alone" (*Endurance in Suffering*, 72).

89. "Vv. 35b and 36 are linked by the theme, directly relevant to the readers' situation (10:32–39; 12:4), of endurance under persecution" (Ellingworth, *Hebrews*, 627).

the king.⁹⁰ Lincoln writes, "Moses stands out for the way in which his depiction in 11.24–27 is so explicitly adapted to speak to the situation of the readers."⁹¹

Verses 35b–39 give a rapid series of unpleasant outcomes, implying that the difficulties were endured by choice, and that the people who suffered had faith in a future reward—something that was "promised" (11:39). Rhetorically, this brings the readers into the tension of people who look for a reward even as they are persecuted. It reminds the readers that they also have something better waiting for them—better than this world—but their belief in that promise requires a willingness to endure various difficulties.⁹²

Hebrews 12 draws a conclusion from the exemplars of faith. The exhortation is couched in athletic imagery; the basic claim implied is that people should persevere in their loyalty to Jesus, getting rid of distractions and keeping their eyes on Jesus, who set a perfect example of faith/fulness. The people mentioned in Heb 11 show that faith is needed—and that it is possible—for spiritual success. The logic again implies that the situation of the readers is in some way analogous to the situations reviewed in Heb 11. The author does not highlight examples of people who had faith despite boredom, or faith despite lethargy. Rather, the examples are faith in a time of crisis, suggesting that the reluctance of the readers is due to external pressures.

Verse 2 gives an example from Jesus. He willingly endured the cross, counting its shame as unimportant, being assured of future joy.⁹³

---

90. Commentators puzzle over this point, noting that Moses initially fled in fear, but in the exodus he left in faith. Heb 11 includes several items slightly out of chronological order—the incident in 11:17 came before 11:13, 11:21b came before 11:21a, and the names in 11:32 are not in order. Chronological or not, the author probably included this point (and the similar point in 11:23c) because the readers were threatened with a governmental edict. The author's main concern, deSilva suggests, is to point out that "Moses left his earthly homeland, status, and heritage behind" (*Perseverance*, 412). This was not merely historical data—the purpose is to exhort readers to be willing to do the same.

91. Lincoln, *Hebrews*, 105.

92. Attridge observes that, on the surface, "imprisonment seems to be a rather anticlimactic conclusion" (v. 36). However, he suggests that "the prominence of the reference to imprisonment here is not accidental" (*Hebrews*, 350), implying it was a threat the readers already faced (cf. 13:2).

93. Although the grammar of the verse might permit the meaning, "Jesus endured the cross instead of keeping the joy he already had," such would give no reason for *why*

Because of his example, the readers are exhorted to be steadfast (v. 3).[94] The logical connector (γάρ) suggests that the experience of Jesus is comparable in some way to the situation of the readers—that the readers might also have to endure some difficulties and despise some shame in order to gain the reward set before them.[95] (Verses 5–11 also indicate that some unpleasant circumstances were affecting the readers—although not as unpleasant as what Jesus faced.) They are to consider his example because it has similarities to their own. The fact that he succeeded in more difficult trials should encourage them to persevere in their own trials.

The verb in 12:7a may be imperative or indicative; either way, it implies that the readers are experiencing difficulties. The author quotes Scripture and encourages them to view their difficulties as divine training. The author uses simple logic: If children, then discipline. If no discipline, then not children. It would seem that the point has been sufficiently proven, but the author adds another argument: We respected our parents who disciplined us, so we should respect God even more, since his discipline has better results. The author draws the conclusion in 12:12: Be strong and continue on the right path. The length of the argumentation suggests that this was not a hypothetical situation—it was of immediate relevance to the readers.

Jesus accepted pain instead of pleasure, and the context suggests that a reason is being given. Further, 12:3 implies that the example of Jesus is relevant to the readers—and pre-existent joy is not. They are to endure their difficulties for the hope "set before them" (6:18, using the same Greek word and form). Third, it would be odd to say that joy was "*set* before" Jesus if he already had it. Since chapter 11 ends with the promise of reward, 12:2 should most likely be understood as another example of that. See the extensive discussion by Croy in *Endurance*, 177–85. The joy for Jesus "is not something for himself alone, but something to be shared with those for whom he died" (Bruce, *Hebrews*, 339).

94. Verse 3 has γάρ with an imperative—an unusual construction, apparently supporting the exhortation of 12:1–2. "Γάρ marks a strong affirmation, 'by all means consider' . . . and indicates the close link with v. 2" (Ellingworth, *Hebrews*, 643).

95. "The addressees are asked to see society's hostility against them as a token of society's unworthiness [cf. 11:38a], not a mark of the believers' lack of value or honor . . . . We, too, are called to look ahead to the 'joy' that God 'set before us' as an incentive to endure in costly discipleship" (deSilva, *Perseverance*, 425, 438). The crucifixion *could* provide motivational support for readers who were merely lethargic, but in such a case we might expect the author to use an argument from lesser to greater: If people can be faithful even in difficult times, how much more should we find it easy to be faithful in times of peace!

In verse 18, the author begins a striking comparison between the old covenant and the new. The passage is "the rhetorical climax of the epistle"; "vielleicht der theologisch bedeutsamste Abschnitt im ganzen Mahnschreiben."[96] However, it does not argue a case in the way that previous expository sections do. Rather, it builds on what previous passages have developed. The logic is allusive—the first location is not even named, nor is the "voice" named.[97] A contrast is presented between fear and joy, with the *implication* that the readers will enjoy the good only if they follow the author's previous exhortations. The place of fear is the location of the old covenant; the place of joy and community is found with Jesus, the mediator of the new covenant. This is the choice the readers faced: between old and new covenants. There was no other option worth discussing.

Verses 25–29 conclude with a warning: The Israelites did not escape when they refused; we will not escape if we refuse.[98] There is a promise of an unshakeable kingdom to come, but this promise comes with a threat[99]—which is yet another reason that the readers should not abandon the new covenant: We have been given a great gift, so we should be thankful.[100] The author includes another veiled threat: "Our

---

96. Ellingworth, *Hebrews*, 669, and Grässer, *Hebräer*, 3:302; cf. Lane, *Hebrews 9–13*, 448.

97. Vanhoye observes that the author does not include God in this picture, although Deut 4–5 identifies the speaker as the Lord. In several ways, the author distances God from the old covenant ("Le Dieu de la nouvelle alliance," 321). Koester writes, "God remains hidden. The physical phenomena . . . do more to conceal God than reveal him" (*Hebrews*, 549).

98. The author gives warnings, but he has not described any warnings spoken from heaven regarding the new covenant. He leaves punishment up to the imagination of the readers.

99. "The use of ἐπαγγέλλομαι in a warning context is at first puzzling" (Ellingworth, *Hebrews*, 686). "This final catastrophe of the world, however awful in itself, is a 'promise'" (Westcott, *Hebrews*, 419).

100. DeSilva notes the cultural expectation of showing gratitude: "Those who receive benefits from a patron should not be reticent about publicizing that benefit . . . . The client who insults rather than honors his or her benefactor and who responds with disloyalty rather than reliable service will be excluded from future benefits . . . . The horror and baseness of offending the divine patron should outweigh the temporary disadvantages of offending society through continued Christian commitment" (*Perseverance*, 340, 350, 354).

God is a consuming fire" (12:29).[101] This warning is surprising, for the author has just associated fire and dire threats with the *old* covenant, and a threat seems to be an odd way to motivate gratitude. However, it is more understandable if the readers were tempted to adopt rival approaches to worship. Their relatives may have been threatening them with divine punishment for abandoning the old covenant; the author responds with threats for abandoning the new.[102]

Chapter 13 presents another dramatic change in writing style: a series of imperatives and several veiled hints about the situation of the readers. Verse 7 exhorts the readers to imitate the faith of the community's previous leaders, who have apparently died, presumably natural deaths. Verse 9 tells the readers: "Do not be carried away by all kinds of strange teachings; for it is well for the heart to be strengthened by grace, not by regulations about food, which have not benefited [spiritually, that is] those who observe them." The strange teachings apparently concern foods.[103] "Strengthening the heart" has no previous parallel in Hebrews, and may be a slogan of the opponents—that observing certain food laws would strengthen the heart (probably meaning a person's loyalty for or standing with God).[104] The strange teachings may have had something to do with eating from the altar (13:10), perhaps in a vicarious way

---

101. Grässer notes, "Καὶ γάρ *denn* (Vg.: etenim wie 5,12) zeigt an, dass jetzt das Verhalten der Dankbarkeit V 28 begründet wird, und zwar durch Hinweis auf den strengen Richtergott" (*Hebräer*, 3:338).

102. Grässer says that each major section in Hebrews ends with a warning about God's judgment (ibid.). On 3:340, he quotes Barth: "Grace would not be *grace*, the serious and effective address of God to man, the effective establishment of fellowship with him, if God did not oppose man's opposition to Himself, if He left man to go his own way unaccused and uncondemned and unpunished, if He ignored the miserable pride of man, if the man of sin had nothing to fear from Him, if it were not a fearful thing to fall into His hands (Heb. 1229)" (*Church Dogmatics*, IV.1: 490). The warnings may also help the readers feel the *need* for a sacrifice that averts the wrath of God.

103. "The verse strongly suggests that the false teachings have something to do with foodstuffs" (Ellingworth, *Hebrews*, 707). Jewett notes that the earlier mention of food in 9:10 is odd: "What do regulations concerned with foods and drinks and various baptisms have to do with the author's previous description of the gifts and sacrifices of the old cult?" (*Letter to Pilgrims*, 146). He suggests that these regulations were mentioned because they were significant to the readers; 13:9 indicates that "foods" did have contemporary relevance.

104. "It was alleged that the competing teachings concerning food will strengthen the heart and keep it from defection" (Lane, *Hebrews 9–13*, 531).

through synagogue meals.[105] So the author responds that a person's heart will be strengthened more by grace than by special foods. Those serving the tabernacle[106] (another negative reference to Levitical worship) do not have a right to partake of the altar that believers have.[107] The logic is allusive, not precise. The author shifts in mid-sentence from what "we" have to what "they" have—perhaps meaning, "We have an altar, that is, a source of forgiveness,[108] but the Levitical priests cannot even receive

---

105. Logical connectors such as γάρ tie 13:9–15 together, showing that the strange teachings are associated with the Levitical altar. "The allusion is to the consumption of foods in some way connected with Jewish sacrificial meals" (ibid., 532). "The sphere of grace is contrasted with a cultus in which salvation, or at least 'strengthening,' is offered through ritual meals" (Ellingworth, *Hebrews*, 707). Isaacs concludes that grace is "contrasted . . . over against Judaism's sacrificial offerings (see 9:9–10), which were ineffectual" (*Hebrews and James*, 157).

On synagogue meals, see chapter 2, note 85. Josephus speaks of "common suppers" in the synagogues (*Antiquities* 14.10.8). Lane reports that Thurén has collected material showing "that eating, joy, and the praise of God at cultic meals, especially the fellowship meal, were associated with the thought of being supported by the grace of God" (*Hebrews 9–13*, 533, referring to Thurén, *Das Lobopfer*, 188–96).

If the "strange teachings" involved Levitical rituals, they may have been "strange" in three ways: 1) If the readers were in the Diaspora, they could participate in Levitical sacrifices only vicariously, through synagogue meals, and that is alien to the Scriptures. 2) This idea may have been a recent innovation, at least for the readers. 3) It may be "strange" to what the readers had previously done in the Christ community.

106. Montefiore observes the irony that the people are said to serve the tabernacle rather than God (*Hebrews*, 244). Gordon observes the irony that "it is the adherents of temple and sacrifice who are now cultically debarred" (*Hebrews*, 167). DeSilva notes that the author is "inverting the normal Jewish discourse about priests' rights to eat at certain tables in the temple, from which nonpriests cannot eat" (*Perseverance*, 498).

107. Literally, this would mean that priests were not allowed to believe in Jesus and participate in the new covenant, but that is probably not what the author intended to say. Young says that the author probably meant an extended definition of "those who serve the tent"—not just priests, but also laity who look to the old covenant rituals as necessary. "Although the language in 13.10 is specific to priests, it refers to anyone whose worship is still conditioned by the system of Levitical law" ("'Bearing His Reproach,'" 247). The point is that "the old order and the new are mutually exclusive; those who serve the tent, that is, the Levitical system, cannot at the same time adhere to the new order in Christ" (ibid., 246). Similarly, on an earlier verse Peterson argues, "Those commentators who argue that τόν λατρεύοντα refers to 'the priest in the act of sacrifice' (cf. 9:6), are making an unwarranted restriction of our writer's meaning" (*Hebrews and Perfection*, 134).

108. The logic suggests that the "altar" may be the cross. It could be argued that people "eat" from the cross by means of the Eucharist. But to be precise, the author does not say that believers eat at all. An altar is a place of sacrifice, not of eating, and believers are to offer praise and good works (13:15–16). Just as the author uses "offer"

benefits from their own worship, as illustrated by the fact that they cannot eat from their sacrifices." Verse 11 notes that Scripture specifies that the bodies of sin offerings had to be burned outside the camp. (The main concern seems to be about sin offerings, not other rituals.)

As the author draws to a close, he includes one more analogy based on the fact that Jesus suffered outside the city of Jerusalem. The logic of the analogy is inconsistent,[109] but rhetorically it serves as a transition to the exhortation to leave the religious system that was centered in Jerusalem: "Let us go to him *outside the camp* and bear the abuse he endured" (13:13). In the author's view, a person relying on involvement in Levitical rituals is *ipso facto* not relying on the only effective atonement, the death of Jesus. He therefore exhorts the readers to put those rituals behind them[110]—in effect, to leave the religious community that relies

---

as a metaphor, he also uses "eat" as a metaphor meaning "receive benefits." Johnson paraphrases it as "share in the worship consisting in praise and thanksgiving to God" (*Hebrews*, 348).

109. Koester writes that this section is an "allusive passage that engages listeners more by images that stimulate the imagination than by a logical argument" (*Hebrews*, 575). Ellingworth observes, "Problems arise when attempts are made . . . to specify in greater detail the logical steps in the argument" (*Hebrews*, 716). Many exegetes have even greater struggles with the implications about the Christ community's break with Judaism. It should be noted that the Levitical rituals that the author rejects as useless are not a part of Judaism as it is known today. Isaacs rightly notes that "the 'camp' here that our author exhorts his readers to abandon . . . is not therefore Judaism per se but the Mosaic cult and its shrine" (*Hebrews and James*, 159). As Ellingworth notes, the author views the *people* of the old covenant in continuity with those of the new covenant (*Hebrews*, 716)—but he views the approaches to worship as dramatically different. He emphasizes that the old covenant is obsolete and urges the readers to embrace the new. In short, he advocates continuity in the people, but change in the worship.

110. Westcott says, "Hitherto he has shewn that the Christian can dispense with the consolations of the Jewish ritual: he now prepares to draw the conclusion that if he is a Christian he *ought* to give them up" (*Hebrews*, 437, emphasis added). Thompson says that the author encourages the readers "to take the risk of a total break with the synagogue. Jesus, in dying outside the camp, is the great example of one who renounced old loyalties and old securities for the sake of faith" (*Hebrews*, 181). Although the sentence might imply that the readers are currently inside the "camp" of old covenant worship, the author's use of a first-person plural exhortation indicates that the words cannot be pressed too tightly.

Walker explains the rhetorical strategy: "Not only must he do everything he can to establish rapport with his audience and build up his argument from shared presuppositions; *he must also understate his applications.* If he had opened his sermon with the bald statement that they should have nothing further to do with the synagogue, he would have lost his audience immediately. He had to tread with incredible care. The

on the old covenant—and accept the social consequences of allegiance to Jesus Christ.

Verse 15 concludes by exhorting the readers to offer "a sacrifice of praise" by confessing the name of Jesus (13:15).[111] Those who want the reward should give allegiance to Jesus, and be faithful to his community (13:16)—or in the words of the initial exhortation (2:1), to pay more attention to Jesus than to the alternative.

Summary

The readers implied by the text:

1) view the Jewish scriptures as authoritative;
2) view those scriptures from the perspective that Jesus fulfilled various messianic prophecies and allusions, and ascended to heaven at the right hand of God;
3) are tempted to view those scriptures as authoritative revelation on how people should worship and be found acceptable by God;
4) face threats of persecution that are weakening their zeal for Jesus; and
5) have the old covenant worship system as the only relevant alternative that the author needs to address.

The people most likely to fit this profile are Jews who believe that Jesus is the Messiah. Although the readers were at first persecuted for this belief, they were eventually tolerated. But more recently, renewed pressure, even the threat of death, was being used to pry the readers away from the Christ community so that they would conform to the older traditions. The demand for conformity was not done by threat

---

critique had to be set within a positive context (concerning Jesus) and some of the practical implications must be left for the audience to draw out for themselves.... This then adequately explains the otherwise puzzling fact that the contrast with Judaism comes only in the exegetical passages, not explicitly in the sections of exhortation and application" ("A Place for Hebrews?" 239).

111. The "confession" throughout Hebrews involves Jesus; God is not in question. In other words, people praise God by accepting the Savior he sent, doing good, and sharing. These actions please God (13:16), and God rewards those who please him (11:6). The author would say that doing good without confessing Christ was not enough. Praise was not done in private, but in the communal meetings that should not be neglected. The primary reason given for the assemblies is mutual exhortation, rather than worship (10:25), but the worship function of those meetings was probably taken for granted.

alone—as might be expected for this audience, it was also done through arguments based on the Jewish scriptures. The author's opponents could easily argue that "on *this* day [Yom Kippur] atonement shall be made for you, to cleanse you . . . from all your sins" (Lev 16:30).[112] The arguments in Hebrews center not on whether Jesus is the Christ, but on whether he is a means of atonement. The opponents were not attacking beliefs about Jesus being in heaven, but about him being the means of salvation. The readers were being pressured to observe the laws of Moses for an assurance of divine acceptance (and salvation) rather than see salvation in Jesus alone. The pressure is not for a rejection of Jesus as the Christ, but merely for participation in the old covenant worship. Cockerill suggests the way they might participate:

> Hebrews 13:9–16 suggests that they were tempted to participate in certain ceremonial meals that were celebrated by Jews throughout the Roman world and were associated with the sacrificial rites in the Jerusalem Temple. By participating in these activities, they would have been shielded from the ire of their fellow Jews who looked askance at Christianity.[113]

However, the author believes that if they look to the cult for forgiveness, they are relegating Jesus to irrelevance[114]—denying him by actions instead of words.[115] They would continue to believe in him as a great teacher exalted into heaven as the son of God, but he is irrelevant to their practical needs—he is an inconsequential belief, a figure without a function. So the author argues that the old covenant is obsolete and that Christ is integral to true worship. Stanley summarizes the message in this way: "Our writer means to persuade his readers to place their trust

---

112. Barclay notes the importance of the Day of Atonement and the temple tax (*Mediterranean Diaspora*, 415–18). Lindars writes, "Every Jew, however far away from the temple, could feel part of the [Day of Atonement] act, because rest from work, fasting and special prayers were enjoined on everyone. It gave a sense of solidarity with the temple ceremonial, in which reconciliation with God was effected, and also of fellowship with Jews everywhere, because of the high level of local observance" (*Theology*, 85).

113. Cockerill, *Hebrews*, 17.

114. As Lindars writes, "By adopting behaviour which belongs to their former life within Judaism, they are denying the continuing efficacy of atonement through the sacrifice of Jesus, thus repudiating the very thing [atonement] that they want" (Lindars, "Rhetorical," 397).

115. "They did not necessarily regard themselves as apostates. But for their leaders and the author their behaviour strikes at the root of the Christian faith" (ibid., 405).

in the priestly ministry of Christ when they are accustomed to placing it, at least to some degree, in the ministry of the Mosaic covenant."[116]

So the author responds to these recent arguments and threats by 1) addressing the doctrinal questions and 2) exhorting the readers to be steadfast in time of persecution. He begins with an uncontested point—that Jesus is exalted into the heavens (ch. 1). His exaltation already implies that he is greater than the angels and that his message is more important than the greatest message of angels—the law of Moses. Since Jesus has reached the situation the readers want for their eternal future, he is the pioneer of salvation, and his death as a human is seen as an appropriate and necessary part of his trailblazing role in the salvation of humans (ch. 2). The author urges the readers to be faithful and to see Jesus as the means by which they are accepted by God (chs. 3–4). So far he has built a positive case for Christ—that what Jesus did was part of God's purpose—without addressing competing views. He then prepares the readers for more difficult argumentation and warns them about the penalties of apostasy (chs. 5–6).

The "difficult" topic is the priesthood of Christ, which is shown to be superior to the Levitical priesthood (ch. 7). The holy place of Christ, in heaven, is superior to the Levitical sanctuary, and the ministry that he performed is superior to the Levitical ministry. Due to the readers' allegiance to the Scriptures, the author bases the argument on passages of Scripture, and Jer 31 provides proof that the Scriptures themselves indicate the need for a new covenant, thereby showing that the old covenant was temporary (ch. 8). Although Greek rhetoric normally gave praise through a comparison with other respected entities without denigrating the point of comparison, the author of Hebrews goes out of his way to denigrate the old covenant law and its associated ministries. This deviation from normal rhetorical style shows that the author expected opposition on this point.

The readers' primary questions had to do with the validity of the old covenant, not the content of the new. The author works harder to prove the ineffectiveness of the old, than he does to prove the effectiveness of the new. He acts as if the readers have only two alternatives: to approach God through the Levitical rituals or to approach through Christ. If the old way is discredited, it is assumed that the new way will be accepted

---

116. Stanley, "Structure of Hebrews," 263.

with little resistance. Minor details in the argument also suggest that the readers think the old covenant to be still valid (e.g., 8:4; 9:15).

The goal of the epistle is to exhort allegiance to Christ *and his community*. It calls for fidelity not just to beliefs about Christ, but to continued association with the community of believers. Community loyalty is part of the package being advocated, over against the old covenant package. The author calls the readers to see Jesus as the crucial link they need in their relationship with God, and he again warns them of the dire results of apostasy (ch. 10). He reminds them of the value of being faithful in times of trial, and sketches the readers' situation as a choice between old covenant fear and new covenant joy (chs. 11–12). After a few more exhortations, he encourages the readers to leave elements associated with the old covenant (foods, animals, city, and camp/community) and embrace by faith the elements of the Christ community (mutual assistance and confessional loyalty) despite the persecutions that will likely come (ch. 13).[117]

The epistle carries a tone of urgency—some have already turned away from the community, and the author is afraid that others will follow them into irreversible apostasy. In this life-and-death situation, the author deals with subjects that are directly relevant to their waning allegiance, and he spends a large portion of his letter on the old and new covenants because that is a crucial component of the readers' crisis. Throughout the epistle, the author takes various arguments that *might* have been used in favor of the old covenant and turns them around to argue for the new covenant:

> Your relatives and neighbors urge you to be faithful to the living God? So do we. They talk about how important the voice of God is? We have an even *more* important message in Christ. They urge you to look to God's anointed representative, the high priest? So do we, but we have a better high priest. They urge you to enter a weekly rest? We urge you to enter an eternal rest. They urge obedience? So do we. They say that God will reject you if you go to the Christ community? We say that God will reject you if you leave. They offer numerous rituals of cleansing and atonement? The repetitions are actually an indication of ineffectiveness, but we offer the reality that was effective the

---

117. "His use of new covenant rhetoric did indeed seek to create boundaries between his community and the larger Jewish society from which he came" (Kim, *Polemic*, 146).

very first time. They offer an impressive line of priests? We offer an impressive priest, one who has actually reached the salvation that we want. They offer a covenant relationship with God? We have one, too, only it is better and eternal.

Whether the opponents actually argued these things cannot be proved, but such arguments are plausible for the situation, and the author addresses them. By exhorting the readers to leave behind the old covenant system of worship and to embrace a worship pattern centered on Jesus, he is implying that the Christ-confession is a religion distinct from and separate from Second-Temple Judaism. He is calling for a separation.

4

"Covenant" in Jewish Literature

SINCE MY RESEARCH GOAL IS TO EXPLORE THE FUNCTION OF THE covenant motif in the argument of Hebrews, it is appropriate to investigate the meaning this word would have for the readers. Jewish writings of the Second Temple period, including Greek translations of the Scriptures, would shape the range of meanings possible for this word; the text of Hebrews itself can then be used to see which of these possible meanings seems to be intended. Since the readers of Hebrews apparently knew the Scriptures only in Greek, I will analyze the use of διαθήκη in the LXX. Although there is a large volume of material, my analysis will be brief at most points.

Of special interest is whether the concept of covenant focused on obligations or on promises. Weinfeld, for example, argues that *covenant* refers primarily to an obligation imposed by a superior power; it is sometimes used as a synonym of commandment or law.[1] Other scholars argue that it has the more general meaning of "agreement."

Covenants Not Involving God

Although my primary interest is in covenants between God and people, I will begin by analyzing other covenants. This reduces any tendency to make all covenants, and the concept of covenant itself, fit into the pattern of divine covenants, and minimizes the tendency for theological conclusions to *a priori* influence the definition of covenant.[2] Moreover,

---

1. Weinfeld, *TDOT* 2:255. Most of the literature about covenants in the Jewish scriptures is based on the MT and the Hebrew word בְּרִית, but the observations generally apply to διαθήκη as well, since there are only minor differences in the use of בְּרִית in the MT and διαθήκη in the LXX—see Appendix D for exceptions.

2. Quell begins in a similar way: "To understand the legal character of the covenant

the concept was used for social relationships before it was used analogously for a relationship with God; the theological uses imported and adapted the meaning already established through social uses. First-century Jews would see διαθήκη used in the LXX for social relationships as well as for relationships with God.

A covenant could be made between individuals, between leaders of nations, between a leader and the people, or between nations. The word could be used for "many different types of oath-bound promises and relationships . . . . These phenomena may be roughly classified as 'treaties,' 'loyalty oaths,' and 'charters.'"[3] Jacob and Laban made a covenant of nonaggression (Gen 31:44).[4] David and Jonathan made a covenant of friendship (1 Sam 18:3; 20:8, 16; 22:8; 23:18). It did not specify any future actions; it was a relationship of personal loyalty rather than a legal contract. In these covenants, the parties were nearly equal; the relationship was not imposed by superior force.

Abner made a covenant with David (2 Sam 3:12–13). Although David had superiority, Abner initiated the covenant. Psalm 55:20 refers to a covenant between friends, presumably equals. Διαθήκη is also used to refer to a marriage agreement (Prov 2:17; Mal 2:14; cf. Ezek 16:8).[5] Hosea 10:4 mentions a διαθήκη in which violations are resolved by lawsuits—perhaps a business contract. Job uses the term figuratively, as an agreement with nature, with Job's eyes, or with Leviathan (Job 5:23; 31:1; 41:4). None of these describe an imposed obligation.

Διαθήκη is also used for an agreement or alliance between roughly equal leaders: Abraham made a treaty with Abimelech (Gen 21:27, 32); and Abimelech made one with Isaac (Gen 26:26–31).[6] Solomon and

---

relationship, we may begin by concentrating on examples in which human participants alone enter into בְּרִית status" (*TDNT* 2:111).

3. Mendenhall and Herion, "Covenant," 1179.

4. For studying first-century Jewish attitudes about covenant, it is appropriate to assume the historicity of all covenants described in Scripture. For first-century Jews, it would not matter when the various documents were written; all were part of the canonical writings and semantic background that first-century Jews would have had for the term.

5. "Parents do not covenant to look after their children; it is built instinctually into parenthood. But when the family relationship is extended to someone outside it, specifically when someone marries and brings a new person into the family, a covenant is involved. Covenants establish relationship where there was no relationship before" (Goldingay, "Covenant," 768).

6. "Covenant" and "oath" are used in synonymous parallelism in Ps 105:9–10 and 1 Chron 16:15–17. Weinfeld notes: "Instead of 'cutting a covenant' (*karath berith*),

Hiram had an alliance (1 Kgs 5:12); Asa proposed one with Ben-Hadad, referring to an earlier alliance (1 Kgs 15:19; 2 Chr 16:3).[7] All these were voluntary agreements; none were imposed. Several other treaties were made among near-equals—e.g., several nations had an agreement with one another to attack Israel (Ps 83:5). Tyre had a treaty of brotherhood with someone, perhaps Israel (Amos 1:9). Edom had covenant partners that would later attack Edom (Obad 1:7). Zedekiah made a covenant with the people to free their Hebrew slaves (Jer 34:8–9). After they changed their minds (34:11), Jeremiah condemned the people for violating not only their own covenant but also the Mosaic covenant.[8]

Based on this evidence, I cannot agree when Hegermann says that *covenant* "is used almost without exception for a one-sided obligation, albeit one that has a pledge attached."[9] A covenant *can* be a one-sided obligation, but that does not mean obligation is part of the standard meaning. The indications of unilaterality or obligation are given by the context; they cannot be assumed simply because the word διαθήκη is used. Otherwise, the above uses would be puzzling, and readers would not know who imposed what on whom. Nicholson correctly says, "The semantic content of the word was such that it could be used indifferently for unilateral and bilateral arrangements."[10] Kutsch offers three categories of covenant: 1) a self-imposed obligation or promise; 2) an obligation or requirement imposed on a weaker party; and 3) mutual obligations.[11] These categories, though they may be useful for analysis, are not mutually exclusive, since a covenant that emphasizes requirements could

---

one could use 'cutting an oath' (*karath 'alah*, Dt. 29:11[12]), and instead of 'entering a covenant' (*'abhar/ba' babberith*), one could say 'entering an oath'" (*TDOT* 2:256).

7. Asa apparently refers to the agreement between Ahab and Ben-Hadad (1 Kgs 20:34).

8. "Those who transgressed my covenant and did not keep the terms of the covenant that they made before me, I will make like the calf when they cut it in two and passed between its parts" (Jer 34:18). Here Jeremiah alludes to details of a covenant-making ceremony: walking between slaughtered animals, presumably in a self-maledictory oath. This was not part of the Mosaic covenant, but was apparently a common custom.

9. Hegermann, *EDNT* 1:299.

10. Nicholson, *God and His People*, 105.

11. Kutsch, *TLOT* 1:256–59, 261. He emphasizes the concept of covenant as an obligation. The English word "covenant" is an adequate translation, particularly since it (unlike the German *Bund*) is not in common secular use, and therefore readers are more likely to look to the context to see what sort of relationship is meant.

also include some minor promises in return, and a promissory covenant could include minor obligations.

Some of the treaties did involve a relationship between a weaker power and a stronger one. The Gibeonites tricked the Israelites into making a covenant (Josh 9:6–16), and even though this treaty was made by fraud, it was honored—the Israelites were obligated to protect the Gibeonites from other Canaanites (Josh 9:19–10:7). If readers did not already know it, they would see from the context that a διαθήκη was a treaty between nations, and that it obligated the stronger nation to protect the weaker. This covenant between unequals does not fit into a theory of imposed obligation, for it was the *weaker* party that initiated the treaty,[12] and it was the stronger party that had to comply with the obligations it entailed. A treaty normally involved *mutual* obligations. Goldingay writes, "Hosea overtly critiques Ephraim for making a berith with Assyria (Hos 11:12—12:1). And when Judah makes a covenant with neighbors in order to be able to resist Assyria, Isa 28:15, 18 declares that it has made a covenant with death."[13]

Much later, Babylon imposed a διαθήκη on Judah (Ezek 17:12-14). A suzerain-vassal treaty like this, found also in Hittite and Assyrian history, is the model that some scholars say is normative for covenants in general. But even this treaty was not completely one-sided. McConville writes, "Nebuchadnezzar's covenant with Zedekiah implied an undertaking on the part of the former to keep the Jewish kingdom intact as long as its puppet king remained a loyal vassal (Ezek 17:14)."[14]

In summary, διαθήκη denotes an agreement between two or more parties, equals or unequals, usually involving an oath,[15] often stating

12. Similarly, the people of Jabesh-Gilead proposed a covenant of servitude when they were besieged by Nahash the Ammonite (1 Sam 11:1-2); here the weaker party took the initiative.

13. Goldingay, "Covenant," 770.

14. McConville, *NIDOTTE* 1:748. If Egypt invaded a Babylonian vassal, Babylon was expected to assist the vassal; otherwise Egypt would take the tribute money and Babylon would lose a source of revenue. The vassal was part of the empire, and Babylon would simply be defending its own property. Such economic realities would create an assumption of protection, even if protection was not an explicit part of the treaty (cf. Josh 9). Knoppers writes, "The Great King was to protect the vassal's dynastic claims, to provide military protection, and to be loyal to the vassal, just as the vassal was to be loyal to the suzerain" ("Ancient Near Eastern," 694).

15. For a similar definition, see Christiansen, *Covenant in Judaism and Paul*, 6–7; Knoppers, "Ancient Near Eastern," 696; or Goldingay, "Covenant," 767.

and usually assuming permanence.¹⁶ The covenant of imposed obligation is only one type of covenant; διαθήκη includes a variety of other relationships. Obligations may be specified or assumed for one or both parties. Therefore, when διαθήκη is applied to a relationship with God, the obligations of the agreement need to be demonstrated from the text; we cannot assume that the obligations are unilateral simply by the use of the word διαθήκη.

God's Covenants With Noah and Abraham

Scripture describes a variety of covenants that God made with people. Gen 6:18 and 9:9–17 describe a covenant in which God promised not to destroy all life in a flood. Although God had given Noah some commands (9:1–7), the promise is not said to be conditioned on obedience. Indeed, if the promise had been conditional on human compliance, the situation would be no different than before, and the promise would have been rather pointless.

The covenant with Abraham is of much greater importance for Jewish self-understanding and for NT studies. God promised to make Abram a great nation and to bless the world through him (Gen 12:1–7). Years later, God again promised to bless him with uncountable descendants. Abram asked for evidence (Gen 15:1–8), so in a dream, God reaffirmed the promises, and "a smoking fire pot and a flaming torch¹⁷ passed between" slaughtered animals (15:9–17). The meaning of this dream is given in 15:18: "On that day the LORD made a covenant with Abram." Abram asked for evidence; he was given a covenant. No obligations for Abram were stated; God obligated only himself (15:18–21).¹⁸ This covenant is dominated by promise.

---

16. Barr observes that if a duration is mentioned, it is "always *ʿōlām*, 'forever'—no one, it seems, ever made a *bᵉrît* for a limited period, or if they did so no instances of it found their way into the biblical text" ("Some Semantic Notes," 33).

17. Most commentators see the firepot and torch as representing God, and the movement between the dead animals as part of a self-maledictory ritual (cf. Jer. 34:18–19; Goldingay, "Covenant," 768). They find it significant that Abraham is not pictured as passing between the animals and he is given no obligations.

18. Freedman and Miano note that God's commands to Abraham "are not officially part of the covenant agreement, but they illustrate the mutual relationship implicit in the pact" ("People of the New Covenant," 9).

Many years later, God again gave a covenant to Abraham. Gen 17 includes two details that Gen 15 does not: First, God promised not only that there would be numerous descendants, but that God would also establish his covenant with them[19] and be their God (Gen 17:1–7). The phrase "to be your God" will be seen in subsequent covenants,[20] and in its historical context it probably meant provider and protector (the benefits people wanted from deities) and ruler (people understood that if they wanted the benefits they had to obey the deities).

Second, God commanded circumcision. Circumcision is not only called "my covenant," it is also called "a sign of the covenant" (Gen 17:10–11). It is not a meritorious act, but it indicates acceptance of the divine favor. Although God had given an unconditional covenant to Abraham (a promise of land and descendants), the covenant with his descendants (offering to be their God) was formally conditioned on circumcision.[21] The combination of conditional and unconditional works in this way: If a descendant rejected circumcision, the covenant with Abraham would still be valid in that he had many descendants, but the covenant with that particular descendant would not be valid; God would not be that person's God.[22] In effect, circumcision became an acceptance ritual of a perpetually open offer of a covenant relationship.

Does Gen 17 describe a second Abrahamic covenant, or a modification of the first one? Williamson notes that many scholars view Gen 17 as "either a renewal of the previously established covenant or the next phase of its development," but he argues that there are two distinct

---

19. Lev 26:42 refers to a covenant with Abraham, one with Isaac, and one with Jacob. Although this verse makes it sound like separate covenants were involved, they were considered a single covenant (Exod 2:24; 6:4–5; 2 Kgs 13:23; Acts 3:25).

20. The full "*Bundesformel*" is "I will be their God and they will be my people." Such a formula may have originated in marriage or adoption—see Sohn, "'I Will Be Your God,'" 357. Similarly, Weinfeld, *TDOT* 1:278, and Cross, *From Epic to Canon*, 3–21. Hahn develops the concept in his dissertation "Kinship by Covenant." Sociologically, it would be easier for a term of friendship to be used euphemistically for oppression, than for a term of oppression to then be used for friendship among near-equals.

21. Hillers says this is not a conditional covenant, but as he admits, those who lack the sign do not share in the covenant (*Covenant*, 104). It is therefore a condition, albeit a simple one.

22. We will see a similar mixture of promise and contingency in the covenant with David.

covenants.²³ Granted, there are important differences, but subsequent scriptures (and first-century Jews, the focus of this study) refer to only one patriarchal covenant. Functionally, the descendants of Abraham *had* to focus on the covenant involving circumcision, since *they* could participate in the promises only if they were counted among Abraham's descendants by being circumcised. For *their* purposes, Gen 15 and 17 were amalgamated into a single covenant. If covenant is viewed as a contract that specifies obligations, then Gen 15 and 17 describe different covenants, for the details are different. However, if a covenant is a *relationship* emphasizing loyalty, then Gen 17 is better seen as a development of the Gen 15 covenant—Abraham and God have only one relationship.

Mosaic Covenants

Exodus tells us that God "remembered" (that is, he took action to uphold²⁴) his covenant with the patriarchs and brought the Israelites out of slavery in Egypt (Exod 2:24).²⁵ God made a covenant with them at Mt. Sinai, which detailed for them *how* he would be their God (the promise of Gen 17:7). Thus the Sinai covenant, although distinct, is also a development of the Abrahamic covenant.²⁶ As ruler of the people, God

---

23. Williamson, "Covenant," 146. He cites the time gap and the differences. Hahn argues for *three* covenants: Gen 15, 17, and 22 ("Kinship by Covenant," 185–86). Goldingay calls Gen 17 "God's second covenant with Abraham" ("Covenant," 768), but he stresses continuity between all the covenants from Abraham to Jesus. "The Jesus covenant is thus a reworking of the covenant, analogous to the several reworkings that have preceded it"; he refers to "previous versions of *the* covenant" (ibid., 776, italics added).

24. "When God 'remembers,' the word carries a sense of obligation on God's part to do something for someone or for Israel as a whole" (Mitchell, *Hebrews*, 64).

25. Robertson notes that since the people were descendants of Abraham, "the nation of Israel already was in a covenantal relationship with the Lord through Abraham" (*Christ of the Covenants*, 171).

26. Anderson puts the relationship between these covenants in this way: "In the final form of the Pentateuch . . . the Abrahamic covenant, which guarantees the promise of land and prosperity, is the overarching theme within which the Mosaic covenant of law is embraced" (*Old Testament Theology*, 137). Goldingay calls the Sinai covenant a "nuancing of the Abraham covenant" that involves "a more wide-ranging response on the people's part and a mutual relationship" ("Covenant," 770). "Exodus is clear that Yahweh and Israel are already in covenant relationship. What happens at Sinai reconfirms the covenant, specifically in light of the expectations of Israel and the undertakings that Yahweh makes to take the people to the land and care for them there" (ibid.).

promised to bless them if they kept his laws, and they promised to obey (Exod 19:5–8). The Sinai covenant placed obligations on the Israelites, like a suzerain-vassal treaty. However, God also obligated himself—he agreed to treasure the people as a special nation if they obeyed. In effect, he promised to provide for and protect the people as their overlord. However, in length of text, obligations far outweigh the promises.[27]

God gave numerous regulations (Exod 20:1—23:19) and promised to give the people the land of Canaan (23:20–31). Moses built an altar, animals were sacrificed, Moses read "the book of the covenant"[28] and the people agreed to obey (24:3–7). "Moses took the blood and dashed it on the people, and said, 'See the blood of the covenant that the LORD has made with you in accordance with all these words'" (24:8). It is not stated what the blood symbolized,[29] but it would have given solemnity to the event.

The Decalogue formed the introductory basis of the covenant; Exod 34:28 equates the Decalogue with the "words of the covenant."[30] But the covenant included more than the Decalogue, and more than Exod 20–23. For example, it would have included the pre-Sinai commandments about Passover (Exod 12–13). And the tabernacle instructions that immediately followed Sinai would have been understood to be part of the covenant (Exod 25–31; Heb 9:1). This shows that the covenant was a relationship, not a contract that specified every detail in advance.[31]

27. "In the context of the Old Testament as a whole the Sinai covenant overshadows other covenant establishments both in length and reception, and in that promises and blessings are subordinate to obligations" (Christiansen, *Covenant*, 48).

28. In this context, the book of the covenant would be Exod 20–23.

29. The role of blood "never yields to a developed and normative conception of the blood ritual in the OT tradition of the covenant.... There is no clue to its significance" (Quell, *TDNT* 2:115). Kutsch notes that it was normal for blood to be sprinkled on the altar, but when blood was sprinkled on the people, something unusual was signified—a curse for disobedience. It was "einen Verpflichtungsritus" ("Bund," 400). "Both Yahweh (represented by the altar) and the people are spattered with blood, sealing their commitment and bringing home the solemn undertaking that this meeting on Sinai represents. It is as if either will be torn apart for failure to keep their undertaking" (Goldingay, "Covenant," 771, alluding to the self-maledictory curse).

30. Deut 4:13 also equates the Ten Words with the covenant, as if the entire covenant had been written on the stone tablets. The Decalogue was considered to be the core of the covenant.

31. This fluidity can make it difficult to determine when a covenant is genuinely new, or a development of a previous covenant, as I will illustrate below. Although some Jews stressed continuity between all the covenants, they could also make distinctions

The people accepted God as their overlord, which implies his right to issue new laws—indeed, his obligation to give new instructions when the Israelites encountered new situations. Even the people could initiate changes in the laws, as the daughters of Zelophehad show (Num 27).[32]

Although law dominated, this covenant also included promises. God promised to be their God, which in that culture would imply that he would give health, wealth, land, and military strength. As their lord, he would also provide regulations for civic and religious well-being. Since the Israelites were entering new environments, they would look to God for instructions on how to prosper in the new locales. "Covenant cannot be defined by law," McNamara writes. It "has reference to a living God . . . . The covenant is not a term that describes a static religion. The covenant looks backward and forward: backward to the covenant with God and to God's promises, to what God has done; forward to what God will do again."[33]

After Israel fell into idolatry and Moses broke the first tablets, God reissued the covenant, and repeated many of the commands (Exod 34).[34] God commanded obedience and promised to give the nation military success (vv. 10–11); the link between obedience and favor is not explicit, but implied.

Although the weekly Sabbath was part of the Ten Commandments (Exod 20:8–11) and repeated in the book of the covenant (23:12), it was called a covenant in Exod 31:16. It was also declared as a "sign" between God and the people (31:12, 17); this suggests that it was a sign not of itself, but of the Mosaic covenant. The people were obligated to keep the Sabbath; God's role was to sanctify the people (31:13). Although the text might permit treating this as a distinct covenant, there is no evidence

---

among them. There can be development within a covenant, and separate covenants can have similarities.

32. Contra Freedman and Miano, who say, "The initiative rests solely with the Divine Suzerain . . . . In none of the biblical examples does the human party propose the covenant or any of the terms" ("People," 8). Other examples of human initiative in the covenant relationship are the beginning of the monarchy and the construction of a temple.

33. McNamara, "Some Targum Themes," 355.

34. Some might see this as a separate and distinct covenant, for the first covenant was broken, and the covenant in Exod 34 had slightly different laws and promises. However, it seems best to view this as a renewal, and the minor variations show that a covenant is a living relationship, not a contract.

that the Jews ever did so; it is given in the context of the Mosaic covenant, and it is called a covenant in the sense of a decree, not to make it distinct from the larger covenant. A similar use of διαθήκη to mean a decree can be seen in the "covenant" of showbread (Lev 24:8) and the "covenant of salt" in the offerings (Lev 2:13; Num 18:19). These are not separate covenants, but decrees within the Mosaic covenant.

Similarly, God made a διαθήκη with the Levites that they would receive meat from sacrifices (Num 18:19). There was no covenant ritual, and no obligations were mentioned. It was a gift, functioning as part of the cultic system of the Mosaic covenant. The word διαθήκη simply stresses the permanence of the promise. The promise to Phineas that his family would always be priests is also called a covenant (Num 25:12–13).[35] These "covenants" are simply declarations or promises from God.[36]

Deuteronomy describes a covenant when the Israelites were gathered in Moab, about to enter Canaan. Even though they were the *children* of the Sinai generation, Moses said that God had made the Sinai covenant with *them*, not their ancestors (Deut 5:2–3). This covenant is distinct from the Abrahamic covenant, although it was a fulfillment of the promise in Gen 17:8 (Deut 4:13; 29:13; Lev 26:42, 45), and it incorporates the main elements of the Abrahamic covenant—the promise of land, numerous descendants, circumcision, and the promise to be the people's God (Deut 28:1–14; Lev 12:3). Just as God had promised to bless the world through Abraham, Israel would become a blessing to other nations if the people obeyed (Deut 4:6–8).

This covenant in Moab included laws that the Sinaitic covenant did not have, and it is also called a distinct covenant: "*in addition to* the covenant he had made with them at Horeb" (Deut 5:1; 29:1). Perhaps the meaning is that the Moabite covenant is an addition or an *addendum* to the Sinai covenant, since the details of both arrangements are considered valid. But it is the same basic relationship of obligations and

---

35. This could be viewed as an addendum to the covenant with the Levites, which itself is given in the context of the Mosaic covenant. Robertson says, "The covenant with Phineas (Num. 25:12, 13) appears as an adjunct to the Mosaic covenant, developing one specific aspect of the priestly legislation given to Moses" (Robertson, *Christ of the Covenants*, 27).

36. For such uses, Behm calls it "a one-sided disposition or authoritative ordinance which settles things" (*TDNT* 2:126).

promises,[37] only with the consequences of disobedience given in more detail. There is extensive continuity between Sinai and Moab as well as some augmentation in laws and curses.[38] Moses told the people that they were making a covenant not just for themselves, but also *for their descendants* (Deut 29:12–15).[39] First-century Jews would assume that they were included in this covenant. Although the promise to Abraham was unconditional, it was conditional for the Israelites: "If you heed these ordinances . . . the Lord your God will maintain with you the covenant loyalty that he swore to your ancestors" (Deut 7:12).

What were the consequences of disobedience? There is no suggestion that the covenant would simply cease to exist or that God would ignore the people. Rather, the consequences of disobedience were severe curses and exile (Deut 27–28; cf. Lev 26).[40] Leviticus 26:40–45 says that even when the people are exiled, God will have a commitment to them: "When they are in the land of their enemies, I will not spurn them, or abhor them so as to destroy them utterly and break my covenant with them, for I am the Lord their God." Deuteronomy 30:1–5 likewise says that the covenant relationship will always be available—even in exile. If the people repent, God will restore the

---

37. Deuteronomy uses *covenant* both in the sense of promise (4:31) and command (4:13). Hahn, building on the work of McCarthy, argues that the Exodus covenant is a kinship covenant, but the Deuteronomic covenant (made after numerous infractions) is a vassal treaty-type relationship ("Kinship by Covenant," 89, 119). But both covenants give far more emphasis to obligation than to promise.

38. "In substance the terms of the [Moabite] covenant are the same, though they are adapted to aspects of life in the land in a way that reflects needs that will arise in later contexts" (Goldingay, "Covenant," 772). Mann recognizes both continuity and change when he writes, "Since chapters 6–26 represent newly disclosed commandments of Yahweh, and since at the end of the pronouncement of these commandments the people accept them (26:16–19), we can understand Deuteronomy as the *completion* of a covenant-making process stretching back to the original events at Sinai" (*Book of the Torah*, 145).

39. The phrase "with those who are not here today" (v. 15) refers to future generations (see commentaries, such as Christensen, *Deuteronomy* 21:10–34:12, 718).

40. Goldingay says: "Israel's recurrent breaking of the covenant does not have the effect of annulling it but rather of unleashing the sanctions that operate within the covenant's terms" ("Covenant," 769). People suffering penalties might *wish* that the covenant would cease, but the punishments show that they are still under the covenant. The existence of the covenant was not conditional, but the blessings and curses were.

covenant blessings,[41] and the covenant relationship will be revived.

The ratification ceremony for this covenant was to be done between Mount Ebal and Mount Gerizim (Deut 27:12-13). After the people entered Canaan, Joshua gathered them at Shechem and exhorted them to serve the Lord, and they agreed to (Josh 24:1-24). "So Joshua made a covenant with the people" (24:25-26). In the canonical context, it would be understood that this was the Deuteronomic covenant being ratified.[42]

Covenants During the Monarchy

David was given a covenant guaranteeing a dynasty for his family (2 Sam 23:5; 2 Chr 13:5; 21:7; Ps 89:3-4, 28-34).[43] This covenant (also called an oath) could be renewed with subsequent descendants who ruled faithfully (Ps 132:11-12). That is, the covenant with David was guaranteed, but the covenant with subsequent descendants was conditional on their obedience. If a descendant was disobedient, the dynasty

---

41. These blessings and curses disprove Kutsch when he writes, "The OT does not know a reciprocal $b^e rît$ that pairs God and people—a $b^e rît$ in which both God and people accept mutually enforceable responsibilities" (*TLOT* 1:264). He gives his reason: "The individual [or the nation] cannot obligate God to keep his promise by fulfilling these conditions; the promise is guaranteed only by the fact that God stands by his word" (ibid.). But this is a false distinction, for even human treaties depended on people honoring their word. Even though humans cannot *force* God to do anything, the covenant is still presented in a format as if both parties have obligations. McConville writes, "In those places where the covenant idea is conveyed in a form resembling that of the treaty, it has a bilateral character, which ill agrees with Kutsch's view of covenant as 'obligation'" (*NIDOTTE* 1:747).

42. Hahn, "Kinship by Covenant," 123-24.

43. This promise was given in 2 Sam 7:11 without the word *covenant* being used; but a promise from God was easily seen as a covenant. "The promissory nature of the David covenant makes it comparable with the Abraham covenant" (Goldingay, "Covenant," 776).

could be given to a different descendant of David.[44] A postexilic psalm accused God of renouncing this covenant (Ps 89:39, 49).[45]

Centuries later, Josiah was given a "book of the covenant" (probably Deuteronomy) and he "made a covenant before the LORD" (2 Kgs 23:3; 2 Chr 34:31–32), in essence renewing the Mosaic covenant.[46] Jeremiah condemned the people for breaking the covenant God had made with their ancestors (Jer 11). "Cursed be anyone who does not heed the words of this covenant, which I commanded your ancestors when I brought them out of the land of Egypt" (vv. 3–4). They refused to listen, so Jeremiah predicted an irrevocable punishment (v. 11). After the exile, the people entered "a curse and an oath" (equivalent to a covenant) to obey the law of Moses (Neh 10:29).[47]

In summary, some of the covenants stress obligations; others make unconditional promises, but many have a mixture of promises and obligations. Lohfink writes,

> The earlier "deuteronomistic" talk in the Sinai or Horeb covenant is not immediately compatible with the "priestly" talk in the two

---

44. Dumbrell puts it this way: "In general terms the line would not fail. Yet in particular terms, benefits might be withdrawn from individuals" (*Covenant and Creation*, 150). A mixture of unconditional promise to the ancestor and conditional promise to the descendants is also seen in the covenant with Abraham.

Knoppers notes a similar arrangement in a treaty between the king of Hatti and Ulmi-Tešup: If a descendant of Ulmi-Tešup committed an offense, the king could kill the offender, but the offender's land would be given only to another descendant of Ulmi-Tešup ("Ancient Near Eastern," 682; see also Beckman, *Hittite Diplomatic Texts*, 104). Hahn notes that "covenants of grant remain in force even though the human parties may need to be changed" ("Kinship by Covenant," 288, citing Levenson, *Ezekiel 40–48*, 147).

45. McConville takes Ps 89:39 at face value: "The book of Psalms knows that the Davidic covenant came to an end (Ps 89)" (*NIDOTTE* 1:750). But Ps 89 also stresses the faithfulness of God and the perpetuity of the promise; it is best to see v. 39 as an accusation rather than a fact. The Psalmist expects the situation to be temporary and asks, "How long, O LORD?" (v. 46). Tate observes that the psalm presents the contradiction between promise and appearance, but does not resolve the tension (*Psalms 51–100*, 428–30).

46. McKenzie, *Covenant*, 6. Other possible covenant renewals include those of Jehoiada (2 Chr 23:16) and Hezekiah (2 Chr 29:10). They show that "the people had confidence that the commitments that God had previously made to Israel would obligate him to accept their repentance. The common view was that the obligatory covenants were indefinitely renewable" (Freedman and Miano, "People," 10).

47. Freedman and Miano note that Nehemiah begins with language reminiscent of the Mosaic covenant (1:5), and mentions the Abrahamic covenant in 9:7–8 (ibid.).

> interrelated "covenants" of God with Noah and Abraham....
> The word "covenant" has a very different meaning in each case.
> In the one case its meaning is something like a contract which
> can be broken and then is at an end... in the other, its meaning
> is rather a solemn promise made by God.[48]

However, the fact that "covenant" refers to promises on some occasions and obligations on others does *not* indicate that the word has incompatible meanings—rather, we should define the word the way it is used and not try to make it more specific than it really is. It has the more general meaning of relationship involving promises, and although such a relationship can include laws and obligations, the term does not *in itself* mean a legal contract that is terminated when laws are broken—nor does it imply an irrevocable promise. The balance between promise and obligation varies, and it is given by the context, not by the word *covenant*, since a covenant could include both. Elliott summarizes:

> There was a tension or contradiction inherent in the idea of a covenant between God and Israel, the tension between covenant as '*gift*' (emphasizing that the covenant is given by God's grace) and as '*demand*' (emphasizing the requirement of obedience to the covenant by Israel).... This basic inner contradiction was probably not consciously recognized or felt to be problematic. It seems that the extremes—*gift* versus *demand*—existed only hypothetically, while in practice all Jewish theologies embraced both aspects *to an extent*.[49]

I agree with Lohfink when he concludes, "'Covenant' is something very different from a formula which describes definitively something which is quite fixed. It is rather an idea which, depending on its application,

---

48. Lohfink, *Covenant Never Revoked*, 20–21. As Lohfink uses the term, the deuteronomistic covenant stressed obligation; the priestly covenant stressed divine promise. For a review of the history of debate about the covenants, see Nicholson, *God and His People*. Rather than seeing conceptual incompatibility, however, I see differing emphases. The covenant with Abraham included obligations; the covenant at Sinai included some promises. The difference is quantitative, not qualitative.

49. Elliott, *Survivors of Israel*, 246. He notes that a common way of resolving the tension is to apply the promises to a *remnant* of Israel, those who meet the conditions (ibid., 270). Thus the promise is sure to the ancestor, but conditional to individual descendants, much as I argue above.

refers now to this, now to that thing. What this thing is should be derived on each occasion from the context."[50]

This fluidity in covenant concept is important for understanding first-century Jewish views. God's covenant with Israel, rather than being defined by static laws, was a relationship that involved laws, but was primarily a relationship between a living God and a people who moved in history in changing circumstances. Because of this, one covenant led into another, sometimes with blurred boundaries, as the relationship changed in ways appropriate to the circumstances. From one perspective, we can see a series of separate but related covenants (e.g., Deut 5:1–3). From another perspective, it was a single covenant with various stages; it was the relationship between God and Israel.[51]

God made an unconditional promise to Abraham: land and descendants. Later, he offered an ongoing relationship with Abraham's descendants, conditioned on circumcision. Thus God's relationship with Abraham had both unbreakable promises for Abraham and contingent blessings for his descendants. When Israel became a nation, God explained what it would mean for them to be his people. This entailed more requirements, and blessings would accompany obedience, and curses would follow disobedience. As the people of Yahweh, they needed a worship system, so God gave them a calendar, priesthood, and sacrifices as part of the covenant relationship. When the Israelites entered Canaan, additional laws were needed, and were given. Thus the Abrahamic covenant transitioned into a Mosaic covenant with two major manifestations—Sinai and Moab—and various renewals. As the nation developed, the Davidic promises were added, and there continued to be a mix of promises and obligations.

From one perspective, we see a series of distinct agreements. But they could also be seen together, as an amalgamation, since the nation had only one relationship with God, even though different elements within that relationship were based on promises or obligations given at different times. Blessings were promised if the nation as a whole were obedient. However, even if the nation failed miserably, God had

---

50. Lohfink, *Covenant Never Revoked*, 34.

51. Goldingay writes, "The relationship between divine commitment and human obligation is inherently ambiguous, dynamic, volatile, and changeable . . . . The relationship between Yahweh and Israel resembles a personal relationship such as marriage more than a contract, alliance, or treaty" ("Covenant," 771).

promised in Deut 30:1-5 to let them return to the covenant relationship if they wanted to. He demanded loyalty from the people, and promised that he would be loyal to them.

Prophecies of Another Covenant in Isaiah and Ezekiel

Something was wrong with the covenant: the people did not have the heart to obey it (Deut 31:16-29). Deuteronomy predicts apostasy and captivity, repentance and restoration—and after the people turn back to God, God will remedy the deficiency: "God will circumcise your heart and the heart of your descendants . . . . Then you shall again obey the LORD" (30:6). Since descendants are included in this latter promise, it is implied that this covenant offer will be perpetuated indefinitely. This concept of a future covenant based on a changed heart is also found in the later prophets.[52] Lundbom writes that "covenant forms the centerpiece of a larger eschatological hope which includes a new act of salvation, a new Zion, and a new Davidic king."[53]

The Servant Songs in Isaiah say that God will make the servant "as a covenant to the people, a light to the nations" (Isa 42:6; 49:6, 8). This is an unprecedented use of διαθήκη: a person would be a covenant, and there is no indication of whom the covenant is *with*. Perhaps the idea is that the servant would be a *promise* to the people, a visible assurance that the desired salvation would come.[54] Whatever it is, God brings it about.

In Isa 54:9-10, an eschatological restoration is prophesied for Judah, and God says that he will, as he did in the days of Noah, decide never to punish his people in that way again. "The mountains may depart and the hills be removed, but my steadfast love shall not depart from you, and my covenant of peace shall not be removed." What is

---

52. I am assuming that first-century Jews would view all prophecies of an eschatological covenant as predictions of the same covenant for "the age to come."

53. Lundbom, "New Covenant," 1088.

54. Watts suggests that it means that the servant (Cyrus, in his view) "is responsible for government, justice, and order for the peoples under his rule" (*Isaiah 34-66*, 119); he has a similar thought for Isa 49:8 on p. 188. But he gives no evidence to suggest that these governmental functions would be part of the readers' expectations for a covenant. Goldingay suggests that the servant is the nation of Israel, and that the covenant "suggests that Israel can be an embodiment for the world of what it means to be in covenant relationship with Yahweh" ("Covenant," 775). McKenzie suggests that "the servant is the pledge that Yahweh will fulfill his promise" (*Covenant*, 62). McKenzie says the promise is the return from exile (ibid.).

this covenant of perpetual peace? If nations or clans made a covenant of peace, it would probably mean that neither side would attack the other.⁵⁵ The emphasis here is that God will not punish the people;⁵⁶ it also implies that the people will not reject God.

The next chapter says, "I will make with you an everlasting covenant, my steadfast, sure love for David" (Isa 55:3). What is this "everlasting covenant" (διαθήκη αἰώνιον),⁵⁷ and why does it need to be made? The Jews are already in the Mosaic covenant, but nothing is said about renewal, or about *the* covenant; instead, God says that he will make a covenant with them. This implies a new relationship with God—more like the covenant with David, more promissory than conditional.

"He will come to Zion as Redeemer," Isa 59 announces, "to those in Jacob who turn from transgression. And as for me, this is my covenant with them, says the LORD: my spirit that is upon you, and my words that I have put in your mouth, shall not depart out of your mouth, or out of the mouths of your children, or out of the mouths of your children's children, says the Lord, from now on and forever" (vv. 20–21). The Spirit of God would remain with them, and they and future generations would retain the words of God and obey them. A new and effective relationship is being predicted. The covenant will be made possible by God's Spirit—it is promissory, with one condition: it is for those who repent.

Isaiah 61 also predicts a glorious future for the people. "I will faithfully give them their recompense, and I will make an everlasting covenant with them" (v. 8). The content of this covenant is not described, so why is it mentioned? Perhaps the readers feared that their covenant had been forfeited; this verse assures them that they will have one that lasts forever. The future age will not have an ignominious end,

---

55. "For example, the *bᵉrīt* which Abraham and Abimelech made with each other consisted in their mutual pledge to leave each other alone in peace, nothing more" (Nicholson, *God and His People*, 89).

56. The only other biblical uses are Num 25:12–14, the covenant with Phineas, and Ezek 34:25, discussed below. Batto argues that the phrase connotes an end of the hostility from God toward humans—see "Covenant of Peace," 187–211.

57. Other covenants were also given "forever": the covenant with Noah (Gen 9:16), the covenant with Abraham and Isaac (Gen 17:7–19), the Sabbath (Exod 31:16), the showbread (Lev 24:8), sacrificial meat (Num 18:19), the covenant with Phineas (Num 25:13), the covenant between David and Jonathan (1 Sam 20:42), and God's covenant with David (2 Chr 13:5; Ps 89:28). As Barr observes, it is part of the stock vocabulary of covenants ("Some Semantic Notes," 33).

as the previous one had. God promises to initiate a permanent relationship with the people. If readers expected a covenant to be a contract, they would be frustrated by the lack of detail here—but if they viewed covenant as a relationship, they would be encouraged at this promise of a relationship with God that will not be broken any more.

Ezekiel makes similar predictions. "Thus says the LORD God: I will deal with you as you have done, you who have despised the oath, breaking the covenant" (Ezek 16:59). That is, God will give them the punishment appropriate to their faithlessness. But in 16:60 he says, "Yet I will remember [that is, take action on] my covenant with you in the days of your youth, and I will establish with you an everlasting covenant." This does not predict a restoration of the earlier covenant, but it predicts one will be made *because of* the previous covenant.

Deuteronomy 30 and Isaiah 59 predict that repentance will come first, but Ezek 16 has repentance as a *result:* "Then you will remember your ways, and be ashamed when I take your sisters, both your elder and your younger, and give them to you as daughters, but not on account of my covenant with you" (v. 61). The last phrase implies that God will show mercy in a way that the covenant did not require. V. 62 repeats the promise: "I will establish my covenant with you, and you shall know that I am the LORD." Why? "In order that you may remember and be confounded, and never open your mouth again because of your shame, when I forgive you all that you have done" (v. 63). Again, forgiveness and covenant come *before* repentance.

Ezekiel 34 also mentions an eschatological covenant—God promises to gather his people and put David over them. "I, the LORD, will be their God.... I will make with them a covenant of peace and banish wild animals from the land, so that they may live in the wild and sleep in the woods securely" (vv. 24–25). The beasts were part of the Mosaic covenant curses (Deut 32:24), but they will no longer be a threat; peace and prosperity will prevail (Ezek 34:26-29).

Hosea offers a similar promise: "I will make for you a covenant on that day with the wild animals . . . and I will abolish the bow, the sword, and war from the land; and I will make you lie down in safety" (Hos 2:18).[58] It is a relationship characterized by peace and prosperity,

---

58. Literally, this covenant is with the animals, not with the people, but the effect is that God makes a promise toward the people, and the covenant formula is restored to the people (Hos 2:23). I include Hosea at this point, out of chronological and canonical

and the people who had been Lo-ammi (2:23; "not my people," people not in a covenant relationship with God) would become "my people," and Yahweh will be their God (a covenant relationship would be made). Hosea 14:4 promises that God will change the people so they are faithful: "I will heal their disloyalty; I will love them freely, for my anger has turned from them."[59]

A similar pattern is given in Ezek 36. God announces that he will regather his people (v. 24). Forgiveness comes first, then a new heart, followed by obedience: "I will sprinkle clean water upon you, and you shall be clean from all your uncleannesses. . . . A new heart I will give you, and a new spirit I will put within you; and I will remove from your body the heart of stone and give you a heart of flesh. I will put my spirit within you, and make you follow my statutes" (vv. 25–27; cf. Ezek 11:17–20). The prophets had given up hope of the nation ever being obedient, unless God acted to change their hearts. The word *covenant* is not used in this passage, but the same thought is conveyed: God initiates an eschatological renewal of his relationship with his people.

Ezekiel 37 uses the word *covenant*: David will be their shepherd, they will be obedient, and "I will make a covenant of peace with them; it shall be an everlasting covenant with them . . . . I will be their God, and they shall be my people" (vv. 26–27).[60] Although the word "new" is not used, it *is* a new covenant, with new results.

The New Covenant in Jeremiah

Jeremiah 31:31–34 (LXX 38:31–34) is introduced with an eschatological formula: "The days are surely coming, says the LORD, when I will make a new covenant with the house of Israel and the house of Judah. It will not be like the covenant that I made with their ancestors when

---

order, because of its similarity to Ezek 34:25.

59. As Lalleman-de Winkel says, "This comes very close to the promise of a new heart in Ezekiel (36:25–26) and the planting of a new inclination in the hearts of the people to know the LORD (Jer. 31:33–34)" (*Jeremiah in Prophetic Tradition*, 181). She argues that Amos 9:11–15 likewise predicts a relationship restored by divine initiative (ibid., 187).

60. Ezekiel 37:24–27 alludes to the Davidic covenant, the Mosaic covenant, the Abrahamic covenant, and the new covenant (Robertson, *Christ of the Covenants*, 42). But contra Robertson, this does not prove that the covenants are considered one—rather, that elements of each covenant are taken into the new.

I took them by the hand to bring them out of the land of Egypt—a covenant that they broke, though I was their husband, says the LORD" (vv. 31–32). God will make this new covenant because the people broke the old one (v. 32).[61]

Did the covenant cease to exist when it was broken? Lohfink says the Sinai covenant became "nonexistent" when it was broken;[62] Hillers says, "For Jeremiah, the old covenant is a thing of the past. He does not call for a return to it . . . . 'They broke that covenant with me' dismisses the old order laconically but finally."[63] Mendenhall and Herion write, "In the ancient concepts of covenant the ultimate curse for breach of contract was the destruction and scattering of the body politic with which the covenant initially was formed. This had happened in 586 B.C. Thus the old covenant was no more—theoretically, there was no longer any body politic to which the covenant would apply."[64]

However, first-century Jews would not dismiss the covenant so easily. For them, even exile and dispersal could not eliminate the covenant, because the people (although not a nation) were still descendants of Abraham, and Lev 26:44 and Deut 30:1–5 speak of a covenant relationship even after exile.[65] Jeremiah 29:10 also says that God will honor his promises to the people after the exile—hence he still views them as people to whom he has obligations. Freedman writes, "Can covenant bond be broken—and at the same time persist? Can God sever a relationship as a result of covenant violations—and nevertheless maintain it in perpetuity? The Bible seems to answer in the affirmative."[66] When a covenant is "broken," it is not simply terminated—rather, the

---

61. Carroll writes, "According to the deuteronomistic history, that covenant was broken with a regularity which almost beggars the imagination . . . . If ever an institution was created which was a complete failure from the beginning it must be the deuteronomistic covenant!" (*From Chaos to Covenant*, 217).

62. Lohfink, *Covenant*, 48.

63. Hillers, *Covenant*, 167.

64. Mendenhall and Herion, "Covenant," 1192.

65. "According to Old Testament covenant thought, there is no place for a setting-aside of one covenant in favor of another. All the covenants were everlasting, even if broken" (Rayburn, "Old and New Covenants," 163). Heb 8:13 will have a different viewpoint.

66. Freedman, "Divine Commitment," 429.

penalty provisions are invoked.[67] Human actions cannot terminate the covenant that God initiated, but God can choose to revoke the curses if he wishes.[68]

Jeremiah knew that the Josianic reform would not be successful; the people's repentance would not last. Restoration based on national repentance was a vain hope.[69] "All the house of Israel is uncircumcised in heart" (9:26). A more radical change was needed: a covenant that *could not* be broken, a people who would not disobey.[70]

The new covenant will be different in that it will be unbreakable. Jeremiah 31:33 says, "This is the covenant that I will make with the house of Israel after those days, says the LORD: I will put my law within them, and I will write it on their hearts; and I will be their God, and they shall be my people." They will not break the covenant, because the law will be in their minds—which was the (unrealized) ideal of the Mosaic covenant.[71] By God's action, a bilateral covenant is turned into a unilateral obligation. Disobedience will not happen, for God obligates himself to fulfill the responsibilities of *both* parties.

Lohfink argues that the new covenant is the same as the old, because "it is not said that God will give a new torah."[72] It is new only

---

67. "The violation or non-fulfillment of a sworn duty does not terminate a covenant; it simply triggers the curses of the original covenant-ratifying oath" (Hahn, "Kinship by Covenant," 65).

68. "Solange JHWH sein Volk trotz seines Bundesbruches nicht verworfen hat, d. h. solange es das Volk Israel und Juda gibt, *besteht auch der Bund* weiter. Es hat ja die Verpflichtung in feierlichem Gelöbnis als dauernde auf sich genommen" (Schenker, "Der nie aufgehobene Bund," 112).

69. "To encounter a passage in a prophetic book which promises a golden future and a new covenant without repentance, and which envisages a period when there will be no need for such moral change *by* the people because Yahweh will change them automatically, is to enter a world where the prophets have conceded defeat and have withdrawn from the moral struggle to persuade people to change" (Carroll, *From Chaos to Covenant*, 220).

70. "Jeremiah is clearly looking forward to something radically different from past reforms. He witnessed the attempts of Josiah to reestablish a working relationship with the Deity and saw them fail" (Freedman and Miano, "People," 23).

71. Similar predictions are in Deut 30:6–8; Isa 59:21; and Jer 24:7.

72. Lohfink, *Covenant*, 46; similar statements are made by McKenzie, *Covenant*, 59, and Christiansen, *The Covenant*, 57. See my *Sabbath, Circumcision, and Tithing* for a discussion of the theological difficulties of this conclusion, and see below for evidence within Jeremiah that the law *is* different.

in the way that it is given, he says, in that it cannot be broken.[73] But it is not necessary for the text to explicitly say "new torah" in order for the covenant itself to be a new one. The Deuteronomic covenant had different laws than the Sinai covenant; it is even more possible that a covenant that is explicitly called "new" could also have different laws. Lalleman-de Winkel writes, "The new covenant is not just another agreement between God and His people, such as those in Josh. 24 and the other passages.... A substantially new beginning on God's initiative is promised."[74] Goldingay writes, "It will be new because the thing Yahweh intends to do is different; it is new as the Sinai covenant was new over against the Abraham covenant."[75]

Martin-Achard argues for development, saying that the covenant cannot be equated *simpliciter* with the Sinai covenant, but it is the culmination of a series of covenants, from Sinai to Joshua to Josiah:

> La nouvelle alliance n'est donc pas le simple vis-à-vis de la *berit* sinaïtique, avec laquelle elle formerait un diptyque; elle doit être vue de manière génétique et non statique, comme un épisode parmi d'autres des relations de Yahvé avec son peuple....
>
> Jér. 31,31ss. ne nous parle pas d'une simple réparation d'alliance comme on pourrait le penser; le prophète n'envisage pas une pure restauration de la $b^e rit$ des pères. Il faut prendre au sérieux le terme *hadāshāh* qui dépeint l'alliance jérémienne: cet adjectif doit être compris dans un sens fort et ce n'est pas sans raison que la Septante a utilisé à son propos le qualificatif *kainos* plutôt que *neos*.[76]

Jeremiah 31 indicates something new. Yu lists four new elements: "i) the inward inscription of the law; ii) the unmediated knowledge of

---

73. Lohfink, *Covenant*, 47; Martin-Achard makes a similar statement in "Quelques remarques," 156.

74. Lalleman-de Winkel, *Jeremiah*, 200. Pinçon also argues that the covenant is new: "Il ressort que l'expression *«non pas comme l'alliance»* et l'emploi au hiphil du verbe *prr* (c'est-à-dire: séparer, trancher, mettre à part) attestent clairement l'idée d'une rupture par rapport à un temps antérieur" (*Du nouveau dans l'ancien*, 49).

75. Goldingay, "Covenant," 774.

76. Martin-Achard, "Quelques remarques," 148, 154–55. However, he does not argue for a change in law: "Il n'inaugure que sur un point en intériorisant les relations de Yahvé avec Israel ou mieux en combinant audacieusement la notion de *berit* avec le thème deutéronomiste de l'intériorité de la religion yahviste" (ibid.). But if we see the new covenant in a nonstatic way and take "new" seriously, as he says we should, we must be open to the possibility of different laws, just as Deuteronomy is different from Exodus.

God, iii) the forgiveness of sins [without sacrifice]; iv) the promissory characteristic [that God will ensure the results]."⁷⁷ Verse 34 announces several differences: "No longer shall they teach one another, or say to each other, 'Know the Lord,' for they shall all know me, from the least of them to the greatest, says the Lord; for I will forgive their iniquity, and remember their sin no more." A religious hierarchy and written documents will not be needed, because everyone will know God—that is, be loyal to him.⁷⁸

Many interpreters have focused on the internalization of the law in v. 33, but the universality mentioned in v. 34 is an equally important component. As Rayburn notes, some individuals in ancient Israel did have the law in their hearts,⁷⁹ but in the new covenant the nation *as a whole* will be internally motivated to be faithful, and *that* is what makes this covenant notably different.⁸⁰ In ancient Israel, there were some faithful people and some unfaithful ones; in the new covenant there will be only faithful people. The covenant will not be broken, because the nation *in entirety* will keep it, because God, in an act of mercy, will enable all of them to keep it. Hegermann concludes, "The covenant of obligation will be replaced by a covenant of promise."⁸¹ Martin-Achard says, "L'avenir d'Israël repose tout entier sur l'initiative de son Dieu."⁸² Since the covenant will never be broken, there will never be a need for

---

77. Yu, "New Covenant," 17. But Yu errs by saying, "The substance of the law will be the same" (28). Jeremiah makes no such claim.

78. The word *know* is used in ancient treaties to mean "recognize as legitimate sovereign or vassal, and to recognize treaty stipulations as binding" (Hillers, *Covenant*, 121).

79. "It can hardly be maintained that Jeremiah regarded the interiorization of the law to be a heretofore unknown phenomenon" (Rayburn, "Old and New Covenants," 147). Stanley notes that "the uniqueness of the NC lies not in the hope of internalisation, but in how and by whom this would be accomplished—by God . . . . The fundamental improvement of the new over the old is that the Lord himself does under the NC, in some crucial instances, what was left to the people to do under the OC" ("New Covenant Hermeneutic," 85, 88).

80. "The new covenant will involve a heretofore unknown universalism in which the relationship in its true spiritual dimension (cf. Jer. 9:25) is bestowed upon the entire people and not just a portion" (Rayburn, "Old and New Covenants," 159). Note also Martin-Achard: "Il s'agit pour Jérémie d'amener à l'obéissance non quelques individualités religieuses, mais Israël dans sa totalité (cf. y. 34: «tous»)" ("Quelques remarques," 155).

81. Hegermann, *EDNT*, 1:300.

82. Martin-Achard, "Quelques remarques," 149.

another. Robertson says, "It is not only the new covenant; it is the last covenant.... It shall never be superseded by a subsequent covenant."[83]

Is forgiveness part of the *content* of the new covenant, or its precursor? Verse 34 could be understood either way. However, forgiveness is not needed if everyone is keeping the law from the heart. The connection makes more sense in this way: "Because I forgive them, I will make a new covenant that corrects the problem that doomed them before. The Mosaic covenant says they deserve curses, and they show no signs of improvement. They have done nothing to deserve a blessing, but I will give them one. I must waive the penalty, i.e., forgive them, just to get them started again."[84] Potter writes, "The basis of the New Covenant is divine pardon, while the Deuteronomists demand repentance."[85] The nation's disobedience did not annul the covenant—it merely called for the curses to be implemented. It is God who annuls the covenant when he in mercy cancels the penalties—he will no longer remember (or take action on) their sins.[86]

Since much of the Mosaic covenant deals with transgression and atonement, at least that much of the Mosaic covenant would become obsolete when God causes the people to be obedient.[87] Mosaic law also commanded teaching, which will not exist in the new covenant.[88] So *some difference in law is implied*, though the text does not indicate all the differences. The relationship between God and his people will be

---

83. Robertson, *Christ of the Covenants*, 277.

84. "God's forgiveness is not an effect, rather the grounds on which the (new) covenant rests" (Christiansen, *Covenant*, 58). "L'alliance à venir se fonde sur la rémission des fautes.... La *berit* jérémienne est donc en premier lieu un acte de miséricorde de Dieu à l'égard des coupables, elle repose sur le pardon divin" (Martin-Achard, "Quelques remarques," 154).

85. Potter, "New Covenant" 350.

86. Anderson writes, "The presupposition of this prophecy is that the covenant can be revoked by God when, on the human side, it is 'broken.'... Forgiveness... goes contrary to what men have a right, on the basis of the covenant, to expect or claim" ("New Covenant and the Old," 230, 235). The covenant is not automatically terminated when people fail, but it may be set aside at God's discretion.

87. "By saying that sins would be remembered no more, Jeremiah anticipates the end of the sacrificial system" (Robertson, *Christ of the Covenants*, 283).

88. "Even more astonishing is the abrogation of the entire paraphernalia of religious indoctrination.... Instead of the deposit and periodic reading of the covenant text, the knowledge of the divine will is deposited within the conscience of the members of the community" (Mendenhall and Herion, "Covenant," 1193).

restored, not by restoring or perpetuating the Mosaic covenant, but by giving a new one. Although חֲדָשָׁה *could* be translated as "renewed," Jer 31:32 explicitly says that the covenant will *not* be like "the old one," and the LXX translators selected καινός as the appropriate translation.[89] The relationship between God and his people will be changed—it will be based on the new covenant rather than the old, and the *results* will be radically different from the failures of the Mosaic covenant.

Jeremiah 32 also predicts an eschatological covenant:

> I will bring them back to this place, and I will settle them in safety. They shall be my people, and I will be their God. I will give them one heart and one way, that they may fear me for all time, for their own good and the good of their children after them. I will make an everlasting covenant with them, never to draw back from doing good to them; and I will put the fear of me in their hearts, so that they may not turn from me. I will rejoice in doing good to them, and I will plant them in this land in faithfulness, with all my heart and all my soul. (vv. 37–41)

This is another prophecy of restoration, of a divinely changed heart, of humans who are forever faithful, of a covenant without curses. Rayburn says, "Israel's loyalty to God is made possible by God's loyalty to them.... The eschatological covenants... include neither conditions nor curses."[90]

Jeremiah 50:5 again mentions an eschatological covenant as it predicts that both Israel and Judah return to Zion in repentance "and they shall come and join themselves to the LORD by an everlasting covenant that will never be forgotten [that is, they will never forget or break it]." Little is said here about this covenant except that it is everlasting; I

---

89. Gross writes, "Zwar hat der neue Bund vieles mit dem gebrochenen Sinai-Bund gemeinsam—vgl. Tora und Bundesformel—, aber der Text legt sein argumentatives Schwergewicht nicht auf die Kontinuität, sondern auf die Diskontinuität" ("Erneuter oder neuer Bund?" 51).

Lundbom writes, "The new covenant cannot be reduced to a renewed Sinai covenant such as took place on the plains of Moab... at Shechem (Joshua 24), or in Jerusalem at the climax of the Josianic Reform (2 Kings 23). Although this new covenant will have admittedly continuity with the Sinai covenant, it will still be a genuinely new covenant, one that marks a new beginning in the divine-human relationship because 1) it is given without conditions; 2) it will be written in the hearts of the people in a way the Sinai covenant was not (v 33); and 3) it will be grounded in a wholly new act of divine grace" (*Jeremiah 21–36*, 466).

90. Rayburn, "Old and New Covenants," 162, 161.

conclude that it refers to a new covenant because it occurs in the context of national restoration.[91] All these predictions of an eschatological covenant do *not* refer to the Mosaic covenant (except as a contrast in Jer 31:32), but they announce a covenant in which the people will be faithful; few other details of the covenant are mentioned.[92]

Baruch, ostensibly written by Jeremiah's scribe, also mentions a future covenant: "They are a stiff-necked people. But in the land of their exile they will come to themselves and know that I am the Lord their God. I will give them a heart that obeys and ears that hear.... I will bring them again into the land.... I will make an everlasting covenant with them to be their God and they shall be my people" (Bar 2:30–35).[93]

In summary, the prophets predicted an eschatological covenant that would not be broken, a divinely initiated covenant in which all the people would be faithful. Whether we call this a *new* covenant or a covenant *renewal* may depend on our style of categorizing covenants. It is new in the same sense that the Mosaic covenant is different than the Abrahamic. It is different, and yet it is a development of a relationship rather than a complete change. It extends the relationship, but rewrites the *terms* of the relationship in a dramatic way based on changing circumstances.

The new covenant involves a change in the *nature* of the covenant: people will be the people of God in the heart. The unprecedented result—consistent loyalty rather than repeated failure—shows how significant a change this is. The goal—being the people of God—remains the same, and thus there is continuity with the Mosaic and Abrahamic covenants. But the internalization of the people's relationship with God creates a new situation. It merges the promissory and obligatory elements of covenants: the fact that there are laws indicates, *in form*, a conditional covenant that

---

91. Smothers, in Keown et al., *Jeremiah 26–52*, 365. Lohfink argues that the new covenant was fulfilled when the Jews returned from exile. "The new heart, loyal to the torah... was, at that time, available on request to the sinner who repented" (*Covenant*, 52). But this ignores the universality predicted in Jer 31 and the Jews' checkered postexilic history.

92. McKenzie summarizes the predictions: They "describe not so much how the covenant will be different, but how the attitude of the people will change" (*Covenant*, 6).

93. Lehne notes that Baruch does not share Jeremiah's pessimism about human ability to return to God (*New Covenant in Hebrews*, 38). Baruch's next words are a claim of repentance and a plea for mercy (3:1–8).

includes obligations; the fact that God will ensure that the people obey, *in effect*, turns the covenant into a promissory, unconditional covenant.[94] In this new covenant, the obligations are different—but the details are not specified in Scripture. It is a concept awaiting further clarification.

Apocryphal and Pseudepigraphical Literature

Covenant was an important concept throughout Israel's history.[95] This word proclaimed that this people had been given a special relationship with God. The history of the northern tribes was summarized: "They transgressed his covenant" (2 Kgs 18:12; Hos 6:7; 8:1). The ruler of the Jews was the "prince of the covenant" (Dan 11:22). An attack on the Jews was considered an attack "against the holy covenant" (11:28–30). Judith complained that the enemies of the Jews "planned cruel things against your covenant, and against your sacred house, and against Mount Zion" (Jdt 9:13). Here, *covenant* refers to the Jewish religion. Lohfink says that "in the period of the second temple . . . 'covenant' was almost a standard word among the Jewish people for the ancestral religion."[96] They were the covenant people.

One of the oldest writings in the Apocrypha is the Wisdom of Ben Sirach. In a historical hymn, Sirach notes that διαθῆκαι were made with Noah, Abraham, Isaac, Jacob, Moses, Aaron, Phineas, and David (Sir 44:18–23; 45:5, 7, 15, 24, 25; 47:11).[97] Covenant was a major part of the nation's history. Similarly, *T. Mos.* 3:9 asks God to remember the

---

94. Freedman and Miano put it this way: "This covenant type defies classification. It is modeled on the old Sinai covenant and so follows the pattern of conditional covenants, but the chance for termination of the relationship would not exist, nor would the threat of punishment" ("People," 25).

95. Schiffman writes, "These covenants are axiomatic to Second Temple literature and Talmudic texts" ("Covenant in the Qumran Scrolls," 257).

96. Lohfink, *Covenant*, 7; a similar sentence is on p. 22.

97. Mack notes that covenant is one of the seven characteristics that Sirach's heroes have in common (*Wisdom and Hebrew Epic*, 20–21). Vogel notes that "Vermeidet Ben Sira nämlich den Terminus ברית gerade im Zusammenhang mit der Sinai-Gesetzgebung" (*Das Heil des Bundes*, 117).

Διαθήκη is used in its older sense of a secular agreement in Sir 11:20: "Stand by your *agreement* and attend to it." 1 Maccabees 1:11 and 11:9 use it in the sense of a treaty: "Let us go and make a covenant with the Gentiles around us." *L.A.B.* 62:1–3 refers to the covenant between Jonathan and David.

covenant with the patriarchs, "that their seed would never fail from the land which you have given them."[98]

Covenant is an important concept in *Jubilees*. As the patriarchal stories are retold in this work, the covenants are made more prominent—but as Halpern-Amaru notes, they are merged.[99] The covenant with Noah is linked with Mosaic laws in *Jub.* 6:10–18; the Feast of Weeks is said to be an annual renewal of the Noachic covenant (v. 18). The covenant of Noah is also linked with the Abrahamic covenant: On the Feast of Weeks the angels "made a covenant with Abram just as we had made a covenant in that month with Noah. And Abram renewed the feast and the ordinance [i.e., the covenant] for himself forever" (*Jub.* 14:20).[100] Christiansen writes that the author is "operating with *one* covenant, eternally established and valid, with boundaries defined by birth, and envisaging it as a covenant with ethnic Israel."[101] In this merger of covenants, Mosaic laws are retrojected into the patriarchal covenants. The focus is on Israel.[102] Elliott notes that Moses is the "chief character" in *Jubilees*, and yet "a covenant *per se* is never explicitly associated with his name.... This may be due to the fact that Moses' covenant is understood in *Jubilees* as little more than a *renewal* of the ancient laws and covenants."[103]

Circumcision is equated with the covenant in *Jub.* 15 and 20:3. Obedience is stressed in the later chapters (*Jub.* 23:16, 19; 24:11; 30:21; 33:18). VanderKam comments, "For the author of *Jubilees*, the covenant involves not only promises of land and progeny but also laws that are

---

98. Translation by Priest, in Charlesworth, *OTP* 1:928.

99. "The author of *Jubilees* wishes to establish a close, if not singular, relationship between the Noahite, patriarchal, and Israelite covenants" (Halpern-Amaru, *Rewriting the Bible*, 28). Similarly, Christiansen notes, "Jubilees adds that the covenant with Abraham is a *renewal* of the covenant with Noah.... Jubilees envisages the Sinai event ... is a *restoration* of what has already been established with Noah" (*Covenant*, 74–75).

100. Translation by Wintermute, in Charlesworth, *OTP* 2:85.

101. Christiansen, "The Consciousness," 70.

102. Choi argues that the merger of covenants in *Jubilees* serves a particularistic focus on Israel; whereas Sirach shows a more universalistic approach by allowing the Abrahamic covenant to be distinct from the Mosaic. "Sirach ... tended to leave the two covenants as essentially different covenants, one governing the world and the other governing Israel" ("Abraham Our Father," 108).

103. Elliott, *Survivors*, 251.

progressively revealed."[104] Halpern-Amaru says, "*Jubilees* evidences a clear predilection for a covenant defined in terms of adherence to stipulated law."[105] For example, *Jub.* 6:10 says, "Noah and his sons swore that they would not eat any blood which was in any flesh. And he made a covenant before the LORD God forever." In Genesis, the covenant with Noah has only a promise from God and a command; *Jubilees* has added the oath of obedience from the people.

Liber Antiquitatum Biblicarum uses the word *covenant* 52 times, emphasizing the need to obey the law. Enns concludes, "Ps.-Philo never ceases to remind his readers of the obligations God makes on them, but these obligations are nothing less than the special privilege of those who already enjoy covenant status."[106] Levison says, "Covenant and Law are integrally related to one another, so that entrance into the covenant requires adherence to the Law."[107] The covenant at Sinai is called "the Law of his eternal covenant with the sons of Israel"; it contains "his eternal commandments that will not pass away" (11:5).

Despite the stress on obedience, God's faithfulness is also emphasized: The covenant with Abraham "will not be broken, and his seed will be multiplied forever" (*L.A.B.* 4:11).[108] "I will establish my covenant with him and will bless his seed and be lord for him as God forever" (7:4). Although the people will fail, mercy will triumph: "They will forget the covenants that I have established with their fathers; but nevertheless I will not forget them forever" (13:10). According to *L.A.B.*, Deborah told the people, "The Lord will take pity on you today, not because of you but because of his covenant that he established with your fathers and the oath that he has sworn not to abandon you forever" (30:7). Halpern-Amaru observes, "*Pseudo-Philo's* narratives consistently minimize repentance and emphasize how God's mercy sustains the covenantal relationship

---

104. VanderKam, "Covenant," 152; italics added.

105. Halpern-Amaru, *Rewriting*, 43. Christiansen writes, "When I now turn to the covenant consciousness of the Book of Jubilees, . . . covenant blessings and obligations cannot easily be separated" (*Covenant*, 77).

106. Enns, "Expansions of Scripture," 92.

107. Levison, "Torah and Covenant in Pseudo Philo," 122. Part of the evidence that Levison gives is the interchangeability between "law of his covenant" (11:5) and "covenant of this law" (23:2).

108. Translation by Harrington, in Charlesworth, *OTP* 2:304–77. Harrington writes, "At the basis of Pseudo-Philo's views on God and humanity is the biblical notion of covenant" (ibid., 301).

in spite of Israel's behavior . . . . The reconstructed narratives explicitly confirm that the covenantal promises made by God will not be undone even as a consequence of Israel's infidelities."[109] Nevertheless, obedience was enjoined, for although the covenant itself was sure, an individual's participation in the blessings was not.

L.A.B. presents the covenant as unconditional, but some other writers imply that it is not. Azariah prayed that God would not annul his covenant (Pr. Azar. 1:11). Just before a battle, the Maccabeans appealed to God on the basis of the covenant, asking him to "remember his covenant with our ancestors and crush this army before us today" (1 Macc 4:10; 2 Macc 1:2). The covenant did not obligate God, but could provide the basis for a request.

The Psalms of Solomon also refer to the covenant, and Falk writes, "Although covenant is rarely explicitly mentioned, God's covenant with Israel is unmistakably an underlying presupposition of this community's self-perception . . . . The community represented by *Psalms of Solomon* interpreted the woes of Israel in light of the covenantal warnings" (cf. Neh 9:32).[110] That is, the Jews' lack of power was assumed to be a consequence of their unfaithfulness. In contrast, the *Testament of Moses* makes the astonishing claim that "never did (our) fathers nor their ancestors tempt God by transgressing his commandments" (*T. Mos.* 9:5).[111] The surviving text ends with an assurance that God will preserve his nation,

---

109. Halpern-Amaru, *Rewriting*, 91. Levison acknowledges this when he writes, "God gives the law to people who participate fully in human sinfulness and thus will continue to require God's patient exercise of mercy" ("Torah and Covenant," 125). Murphy writes, "What is note-worthy, however, is the relatively small space devoted to repentance or to the people's calling on God's help. More often than not the people are completely passive, even when appeal for help is present in the biblical text. Israel's deliverance usually does not depend on its own action in any way" ("Eternal Covenant in Pseudo-Philo," 43).

110. Falk, "Psalms and Prayers," 50; he cites *Pss. Sol.* 9:8–11; 10:4; 17:15; cf. 11:7; 17:4–5, 23. Yu concludes, "The author [of *Pss. Sol.*] is convinced that the covenant promises extend to all Israel except for those whose sins are so willful that they consequently exclude themselves" ("New Covenant," 76). For example, Ps. Sol. says, "the Lord will remember his servants in mercy, for the testimony of it (is) in the Law of the eternal covenant" (10:4). Although this might imply that the covenant is an unconditional promise of mercy, 10:3 clarifies that "the mercy of the Lord is upon those who truly love him" (Wright, in Charlesworth, *OTP*, 2:661).

111. Translation by Priest, in Charlesworth, *OTP* 1:931.

somehow because of the covenant (12:12–13).¹¹² No matter what happens, no matter how deserved or undeserved it is, "covenant" is assumed to be the basis for the preservation of the Jewish people.

In the time of Antiochus Epiphanes, Jews were forbidden to keep their distinctive laws. Their identity as a people was at stake, so it is understandable that an emphasis on law-keeping permeates the books of 1 Maccabees. But this emphasis on law is tightly associated with the covenant, since the covenant gave the people both identity and laws. The renegades "removed the marks of circumcision, and abandoned the holy covenant" (1:15). "Anyone found possessing the book of the covenant, or anyone who adhered to the law, was condemned" (1:57). Eating forbidden food would "profane the holy covenant" (1:63). Mattathias said that he would "continue to live by the covenant of our ancestors. Far be it from us to desert the law and the ordinances" (2:20-21). He said, "Let everyone who is zealous for the law and supports the covenant come out with me!" (2:27). He encouraged his sons, "Show zeal for the law, and give your lives for the covenant of our ancestors" (2:50). Covenant was tightly associated with law, and with national, ethnic, and religious identity.¹¹³

Sirach often uses διαθήκη to indicate a law: "All living beings become old like a garment, for the decree¹¹⁴ from of old is, 'You must die!'" (Sir 14:17). Decrees and covenant are parallel ideas: "He established with them [human beings] an eternal covenant, and revealed to them his decrees" (17:12; cf. 45:5) and "Remember the commandments . . . remember the covenant of the Most High" (28:7). In Sir 24:23, "the book of the covenant" is equated with "the law that Moses commanded us." A good person "will glory in the law of the Lord's covenant" (39:8). Other close associations: "Do not be ashamed of the law of the Most High and his covenant" (42:2) and Abraham "kept the law of the Most High, and entered into a covenant with him" (44:20).

---

112. Since the remaining text is lost, it is not possible to say what covenant is meant, nor how it is connected with the continuation of the Jewish people.

113. However, *covenant* was not the only means of expressing the special relationship Israel had with God. Josephus and Philo make little use of the term, though they have the concept. See Spilsbury, "Josephus," 249–52, and Hay, "Philo," 369–70. Grässer writes, "Im hellenistischen Bereich (Philo, Josephus, 3/4 Makk etc.) Diatheke fast ganz fehlt" (*Der Alte Bund im Neuen*, 129).

114. The Hebrew has "decree" where the Greek has "covenant" in several verses in Sirach; see Appendix D.

Rayburn gives a good summary:

> In the Apocrypha, Pseudepigrapha, and Rabbinic Literature covenant . . . occurs by far the most frequently in the earlier literature (Sirach, 1 Maccabees, and Jubilees). In later works the term appears at least several times in Assumption of Moses and 4 Ezra. However, a large number of the occurrences in this literature are either non-theological, part of some stylized phrase, or occur in a résumé of Old Testament history. Virtually all of the remaining instances clearly equate the covenant with the law or individual laws. The remaining few occurrences refer to the theological covenant(s) with a contemporary application. Though the number of times covenant is identified with law in this literature is striking, the uses of the term in the Apocrypha and Pseudepigrapha do not appear to differ significantly from its uses in the Old Testament.[115]

Although law dominates the concept of covenant in these writings, *L.A.B.* shows that Jews also viewed the covenant as a promise. 2 Esdras 3:15 acknowledges that God chose Abraham and "made an everlasting covenant with him, and promised him that you would never forsake his descendants."[116] De Roo shows that some writers believed that God was *obligated* to bless them because of the good deeds of the patriarchs: "God graciously allowed the good deeds of some to be salvific for others due to their membership in the same covenant."[117] After the Romans

---

115. Rayburn, "Old and New Covenants," 166–67. However, as *L.A.B.* shows, early documents were not the only ones to use "covenant" frequently. Harrington dates *L.A.B.* "about the time of Jesus" ("Pseudo-Philo," 299).

116. 2 Esdras (also called 4 Ezra) was probably written after A.D. 70 (Nickelsburg, *Jewish Literature*, 270), but it reflects attitudes that existed earlier. Rabbinic writings are too difficult to date to be of much use here. At any rate, covenant does not have a prominent role in rabbinic writings (Lohfink, *Covenant*, 6). "Sectarian Jewish usage of the idea [e.g., the DSS and the NT] might have led to a Rabbinic avoidance of it" (Lehne, *New Covenant*, 57). Rayburn notes that covenant "appears with striking infrequency in this literature . . . refers . . . almost invariably to some specific commandment, usually circumcision" ("The Contrast," 168). "For the most part . . . the בְּרִית is specifically equated with circumcision on the basis of Gn. 17:10" (Behm, *TDNT* 2:129). "The rabbinic need to coin a new word in its place to refer to the Exodus 'pact' between God and Israel (Talmudic *dĕyāytîqî*, loan word from Gk *diathēkē*) is evidence that the functional significance of 'covenant' had been largely replaced by other concerns" (Mendenhall and Herion, "Covenant," 1197).

117. E.g., *T. Ash.* 7:7. De Roo, "God's Covenant with the Forefathers," 202. Choi notes that Bar 2:19 is unusual in disavowing the merits of the ancestors ("Abraham," 113). Assumptions of divine blessing seem to be based on the Abrahamic covenant

destroyed Jerusalem and the temple, some Jews felt betrayed, because they felt that the covenant had obligated God to give them mercy. Bauckham writes, "These arguments imply that God has broken his covenant with Israel in that he has not exercised mercy to his people in order to fulfill his covenant promises to them."[118] The writer "felt the destruction of Jerusalem to be in inexplicable contradiction" with the covenant with Abraham.[119] Nevertheless, "God will [eventually] be faithful to his covenant with Abraham."[120] Even if the Jews were unfaithful, God would give them mercy, they thought, because they believed that the covenant was a promise that God would not break.

Philo stressed the gracious nature of the covenant, says Schwemer:

> Fassen wir zusammen: Philo geht von der Grundbedeutung von διαθήκη als „Testament" und „Schenkung" aus und versteht die διαθήκη als „Sinnbild" der unverdienten Gabe der Gnade Gottes. Wie der Tragiker Ezechiel betont er den Geschenkcharakter des „Bundes". Zugleich hebt er die Festigkeit und Unumstößlichkeit dieser Gabe hervor, die er mit dem Logos, dem Gesetz und der Weisheit identifizieren kann.[121]

In addition to divine favor for the nation, Israel's covenant with God was also understood to include *a promise of individual salvation*. The youngest of the seven martyrs said that his brothers "after enduring a brief suffering have drunk of everflowing life, under God's covenant" (2 Macc 7:36). In 1 *En.* 60:6, the word *covenant* is used to refer to the reward of the righteous: The day of judgment "will become a day of covenant [i.e., a reward] for the elect and inquisition for the sinners."[122] Although the word *covenant* usually referred to obligations, it was assumed that the covenant also involved rewards for the faithful.

---

even when that is not made explicit—although the Mosaic covenant included national blessings, it would be difficult to construe that covenant formulation as providing unconditional promises.

118. Bauckham, "Apocalypses," 163.

119. Ibid., 167.

120. Ibid.

121. Schwemer, "Zum Verhältnis von Diatheke und Nomos," 101. Grabbe argues that Philo stressed the gracious nature of διαθήκη because that Greek word normally meant a testamentary disposition ("Covenant in Philo and Josephus," 257). He concludes, "The covenant concept was not very important to some significant writers in Second Temple Judaism" (ibid., 264).

122. Translation by Isaacs, in Charlesworth, *OTP* 1:40.

What about the new covenant, the eschatological covenant? Jewish hopes for the future were based more on past covenants (probably the Abrahamic covenant) than on the covenant predicted in the Major Prophets. Jewish literature makes few references to the eschatological covenant.[123] (As I show below, even the eschatologically minded Qumran community looked more to the past than to the future in their concept of the covenant.) As noted above, Bar 2:30–35 refers to a future covenant; *Jubilees* provides the only other reference from this period. Although the word *covenant* is not used, the intent is clear: "I shall cut off the foreskin of their heart and the foreskin of the heart of their descendants. And I shall create for them a holy spirit, and I shall purify them so that they will not turn away from following me from that day and forever.... And they will do my commandments. And I shall be a father to them, and they will be sons to me" (*Jub.* 1:23–25).[124]

The Dead Sea Scrolls

The writers of the Dead Sea Scrolls viewed themselves as an eschatological community. Not all the writings use *covenant* in the same way, but there are major consistencies. Hillers writes, "For a rough measure of the importance of the covenant idea in the sectarian writings from Qumran, we may note that they use the word 'covenant' (*berit*) over five times as often as do the New Testament writers."[125]

Sanders summarizes the two primary ways in which the DSS use the term *covenant:* 1) "God had made with the community a *new* covenant" and 2) "The other formulation, which is the more frequent, is that God made a covenant with Moses (or the patriarchs) but that it contained hidden things understood only in the community."[126] These

---

123. Perhaps this is a sign of optimism—the people believed that the Mosaic obligations could be kept, rather than believing that their only hope was something new in the future. Although many Jews had eschatological hopes and messianic expectations, these did not seem to be associated with a new covenant or even with a covenant renewal.

124. Translation by Wintermute, in Charlesworth, *OTP* 2:54. Christiansen argues that this does not predict a new covenant, but a restoration of the old one (*Covenant*, 87). However, she argues that *all* of God's covenants are essentially the same, and her stress on unity obscures the differences that do exist.

125. Hillers, *Covenant*, 171. The MT uses the term about three times as often (per 1000 words) as the NT does.

126. Sanders, *Paul and Palestinian Judaism*, 240.

two formulations "appear to amount to the same thing."[127] That is, the community's "new" covenant is simply a new interpretation of the Mosaic covenant, and they believed that a person could be faithful to the Mosaic covenant only if faithful to the new understanding.[128] When people joined the community, they swore "the covenant oath which Moses established with Israel, the covenant to rev[ert to] the law of Moses with the whole heart" (CD XV, 8-9).[129] Returning to the Law of Moses meant obeying it "in compliance with all that has been revealed concerning it to the sons of Zadok, the priests who keep the covenant and interpret his will and to the multitude of the men of their covenant" (1QS V, 8-9).[130] Although the sectarians acknowledged the role of grace in beginning the covenant, they stressed the role of obedience in remaining in the covenant.

Kutsch notes several references to God's self-obligation: "God 'remembers' his b^{e}rît (1Q34 3:2, 5; 6Q15 3:5; CD 1:4; 6:2; 4QDibHam 5:9), 'keeps' his b^{e}rît (e.g., 1QM 18:7). The 'promise' to the fathers (1QM 13:7; 14:8; CD 8:18 = 19:31), to David (4QDibHam 4:6), and to the priests (1QM 17:3) should also be mentioned."[131] The promise

---

127. Ibid. He describes their belief: "The sectarian covenant is the only true covenant" (242).

128. "Its newness consists in an improved understanding" (Elliott, *Survivors*, 256). The *Rule of the Community* points out the role of new revelation: "With those who remained steadfast in God's precepts, with those who were left from among them, God established his covenant with Israel forever, revealing to them hidden matters in which all Israel had gone astray: his holy sabbaths and his glorious feasts, his just stipulations and his truthful paths" (CD III, 12-15; translation from García Martínez, *Dead Sea Scrolls*, 35). In effect, the covenant with Israel was transferred to "those who were left"—the sectarians.

It is not clear whether the covenant in view is that of Abraham or that of Moses; it is possible that the DSS community viewed them as the same covenant, as seen in *Jubilees* (see p. 127), a document that may reflect the tradition in which the sectarians originated. Sinai is mentioned specifically in 1Q22 I, 8; II, 8; other texts may refer to the Sinai covenant. Schiffman notes, "The 'laws of the covenant' . . . also refer simply to the laws of the Torah, although it is assumed that these laws existed already in the time of the Patriarchs. . . . For Qumran texts, the Sinai covenant is the central referent of the term *berit*" ("Covenant in the Qumran Scrolls," 266, 269).

129. García Martínez, *Dead Sea Scrolls*, 39.

130. Ibid., 8.

131. Kutsch, *TLOT* 1:265. The covenant with Abraham, Isaac, and Jacob is mentioned in CD III, 2-4; the covenant with Jacob at Bethel is mentioned in 11Q19 XXIX, 6-9.

and covenant with Noah is mentioned in 4Q370, line 7; the promise to Abraham is mentioned in *Genesis Apocryphon* XXI, 8–14, though the word *covenant* is not used.[132]

Kutsch notes some passages that mention the obligations of the sectarians:

> The *bᵉrît* "to act according to all that he (God) has commanded, and not to turn aside from him" (1QS 1:16f.) and "to separate oneself from all evildoers" (5:10, etc.) appears as an "obligation." It is meant when one enters into the *bᵉrît* (*bô*' 1QS 2:12, 18, etc.; *'br* 1:18, 20, etc.). The *bryt hdšh* (CD 6:19; 8:21; 19:33), which, according to CD 20:12 has been placed in effect (*qym* pi.) "in the land of Damascus (= Qumran?)" and into which one enters there, is also understood as an "obligation."[133]

The covenant was given by God, and it required a response of obedience—it "is conditional on keeping the law . . . . Covenant is almost synonymous with statutes, and covenant validity [is] tied to obedience."[134] When people entered the covenant (that is, entered the community), they accepted the obligations. Hillers says, "Covenant is understood as an oath of loyalty to an established set of precepts, as interpreted by a clearly defined authority, the Zadokite priests."[135] Murphy-O'Connor writes, "While lip service was paid to the fundamental concept of election, in practice all attention was concentrated on observance of the commandments."[136] Schiffman writes, "The covenant of Abraham is primarily tied up with the commitment of the Patriarchs to follow God's teachings."[137] Bockmuehl writes,

---

132. Schiffman, "Covenant in the Qumran Scrolls," 258–60; see García Martínez, *Dead Sea Scrolls*, 224, 235. Schiffman argues that CD I, 4–5 and VI, 2 refer to the covenant with the forefathers, but the translation in García Martínez is "covenant of the very first" (ibid., 33, 36). Vermes has "Covenant of the forefathers" (*The Complete Dead Sea Scrolls*, 129, 133).

133. Kutsch, *TLOT* 1:265. Unfortunately, Kutsch includes these human obligations in the section labeled "God's self-obligation."

134. Christiansen, *Covenant*, 109–10. Freedman and Miano write, "They felt human obligation was the leading principle behind covenant maintenance" ("People," 21).

135. Hillers, *Covenant*, 178.

136. Murphy-O'Connor, "New Covenant," 202. Although the Qumran community focused on law-keeping, a stress on covenant does not *necessarily* lead to that focus; it could also be used to emphasize God's promises.

137. Schiffman, "Old and New Covenants," 263.

> One central theme for this as for other key sectarian documents (notably CD, 1QH, 1QM) is that of the *covenant*, sometimes explicitly the "covenant of God." However, unlike the biblical use of the term to denote a normative divine relationship with the whole nation, the divine "covenant" has here become the defining characteristic of the sectarian community or *yahad* in particular, *over against* the nation (and of course the nations) at large. In this sense the covenant, while still divinely established, is no longer sufficiently defined as God's pact of grace with Abraham and his descendants or with all Israel at Sinai, but has become more particularly the sect's own exclusive alliance devoted to Torah observance.... Even the *Damascus Document's* notion of a "new" covenant... merely fulfils and validates, but does not displace, the old.[138]

Collins describes three uses of ברית in the Damascus Document: "the covenant of the Patriarchs, the covenant of Sinai, and the [new] covenant of Damascus."[139] God gave his covenant to the patriarchs because he loved them, but "the eternal covenant imposed on the human partner... a dual obligation. He must love... God and he must keep the commandments of God."[140] The emphasis throughout the DSS is on the obligations of the covenant. The DSS say little about the blessings,[141] and they alter the biblical concept of covenant in three major ways: 1) The sectarians (rather than Israel) are the covenant people,[142] 2) Eschatological reward has replaced national prosperity,[143] and 3) Community life has replaced temple worship.

---

138. Bockmuehl, "1QS and Salvation," 389, 391. "What is indeed 'new' is the revelation to the community of hitherto unknown religious mysteries" (392).

139. Collins, "Berith-Notion of the Cairo Damascus Document," 556.

140. Ibid., 558.

141. "Although covenant stands for both law and blessings in principle, in reality covenantal blessings are never accentuated" (Christiansen, "Consciousness of Belonging to God's Covenant," 78).

142. Sanders points out that the DSS community "generally refrained from simply calling themselves 'Israel'" (*Paul*, 247). Instead, they were people called *out* of Israel.

143. The sectarians viewed themselves as an eschatological people, but they still looked for a future day of judgment. A covenant with God was assumed to involve blessings, but since they were not evident in this life, they would presumably be given on the day of judgment. For those who obey, "God's covenant is a guarantee for them that they shall live a thousand generations.... Those who remained steadfast in it will acquire eternal life" (CD VII, 5; III, 20; 1QS IV, 8 promises "eternal enjoyment with endless life") (García Martínez, *Dead Sea Scrolls*, 37, 35, 7; one manuscript of CD

The DSS use the phrase "new covenant" five times (CD VI, 19; VIII, 21; XIX, 33; XX, 12 and 1QpHab II, 3). Did the community see themselves as the fulfillment of Jer 31:31? They *did* view themselves as the eschatological fulfillment of various other prophecies, but they made little use of Jeremiah.[144] In proclaiming themselves the eschatological fulfillment of biblical prophecies, they normally cited the text and created a detailed pesher, but this is not done for Jer 31. Further, they would find it difficult to reconcile their own emphasis on study and teaching with Jeremiah's prediction that teachers would not be needed.

The phrase "new covenant" is found primarily (four times) within the larger phrase "new covenant in the land of Damascus."[145] Although the phrase "new covenant" by itself could refer to Jer 31, it is less likely that the larger phrase does, and it appears to be a technical term in the history of the sect, perhaps when the community rules were revised.[146] People who had refused to accept the Teacher of Righteousness were unfaithful to the new covenant (1QpHab II, 3). The community's "new" covenant is believed to be in complete agreement with the Mosaic covenant (after the Teacher reinterpreted the laws). Collins says, "The new

---

VII, 5 cites Deut 7:9 for support—ibid., 45). Christiansen notes that "nowhere in CD is the possession of the land said to be a present or future blessing of the covenant" ("Consciousness," 77).

144. "Allusions to *Jer.* in CD are rather sparse, and . . . none among them is a literal citation" (Collins, "Berith-Notion," 572). "Only six manuscripts of the biblical book [Jeremiah] were discovered (Isaiah accounts for twenty-one) and there is no Pesher" (Abegg, "Covenant of the Qumran Sectarians," 84). Jer 31:27-40 is not in any of the extant scrolls (Abegg et al., *Dead Sea Scrolls Bible*, 400-401).

145. Collins concludes that this is also the covenant meant by "covenant of God," "his covenant," "the covenant," and the "covenant of repentance" ("Berith-Notion," 562). Most uses of ברית therefore refer to the community's own covenant rather than biblical covenants.

146. Christiansen suggests that "'new covenant' may be a polemical phrase, coined by one group in opposition to another" ("Consciousness," 83-84). Bockmuehl writes that the new covenant "concerns not the Qumran community's *present* self-understanding, but denotes the prior (and arguably pre-sectarian) group constituted 'in the land of Damascus'" ("1QS," 391). Lichtenberger writes, "Vielmehr ist 'die Gemeinde des neuen Bundes im Lande Damaskus' die Vorgängergemeinde, die entweder, nach J. Murphy-O'Connor, mit dem Beginn der essenischen Bewegung in Babylon oder mit der in der seleukidischen Verfolgung treu gebliebenen 'Gemeinde der Frommen' identifiziert werden kann . . . . Zunächst fällt auf, dass der 'neue Bund' eine Grösse der Vergangenheit ist. Vom Eintreten in den 'neuen Bund' wird stets im Tempus der Vergangenheit berichtet" ("Alter Bund und Neuer Bund," 404).

covenant in the land of Damascus is the Sinai covenant renewed."[147] Jaubert says, "La comparison des texts prouve suffisamment qu'il n'existe qu'une seule et unique alliance." Entering the new covenant of the DSS is the same thing as promising to keep the laws of Moses in the way that community leaders said they should be kept.[148]

Collins gives four significant differences between the Jer 31 covenant and the "new" covenant of the DSS: 1) one is with all Israel, the other with a remnant; 2) one is in the heart, but CD never mentions laws written in the heart; 3) one is by divine initiative, the other by humans;[149] 4) one includes only blessings, but CD includes threats.[150] Collins examines all other uses of חדש in the DSS and concludes, "the notion expressed by the חדש root is essentially eschatological, and that the new covenant is always linked to the community which appears to be living in (realized) eschatological times."[151] But he also notes that "CD does not give any evidence of a direct allusion to the Jeremian text."[152]

Lehne writes, "Both C. Wolff . . . and R. F. Collins . . . deny a relationship between the NC [new covenant] in CD and Jer 31:31–34 on the grounds that 1) The Qumranites usually reveal their biblical sources and 2) the specific content of Jeremiah's prophecy is absent at Qumran or even partially contradicted by the insistence on instruction of Torah."[153] Yu argues that the Qumran community did see its covenant as a fulfillment of Jer 31:31, but that their emphasis on teachers would have made it "difficult to interpret this passage by the pesher method."[154]

---

147. Collins, "Berith-Notion," 566. Evans reaches the same conclusion in "Covenant in the Qumran Literature," 59, 79.

148. Sanders, *Paul*, 241. Similarly, Kim writes, "In content, then, the Qumranian new covenant was the re-establishment of the old Sinaitic covenant by its sharing of the same Law of Moses" ("Eschatological Examination," 9).

149. Christiansen writes that in the DSS, the new covenant "was neither given nor established by God, but was rather based on what humans had entered into the past" ("Consciousness," 79). See also Freedman and Miano, "People," 22.

150. Collins, "Berith-Notion," 574–75.

151. Ibid., 580.

152. Ibid. Collins tries to cover both options by suggesting that the concept may have originated with Jer 31, but that the "ultimate biblical foundation" of this idea "had long since been practically forgotten" (ibid.).

153. Lehne, *New Covenant in Hebrews*, 135 n. 48, citing Wolff, *Jeremia im Frühjudentum*, 125, 130, and Collins, "Berith-Notion," 572–75.

154. Yu, "New Covenant," 104, 124.

In contrast to Yu, I conclude that this difficulty means it is *unlikely* that the community members thought of themselves in terms of Jer 31. They viewed themselves as the fulfillment of some eschatological prophecies, but this does not mean that they had the same approach to all such prophecies, particularly for the ones they did not quote. They still expected a future eschaton, which means that they did not view themselves as the fulfillment of *all* eschatological predictions. Their new covenant cannot be equated with Jer 31 (or any other biblical prophecy). In fact, since their primary use of the phrase "new covenant" is found in the non-Jeremian phrase "new covenant in the land of Damascus," it is far more likely that the solitary use of "new covenant" refers to this Damascus covenant rather than the Jeremian text. Their concept of covenant is focused on their own rules, and rewards that are not mentioned in the biblical covenants.

Christiansen points out that in the Rule of the Community, the covenant is de-historicized. Unlike CD, there is no mention of a covenant with any patriarchs, no mention of remembering a covenant, and no mention of Israel being formed by a covenant. The ancestral covenants are not mentioned because the community did not see Israel as a whole as being faithful to the covenant. Covenant is an important term for the identity and obligations of the group, and it is the *community's* covenant that distinguishes them from other Jews who also claim to keep the covenant of Moses.[155] Christiansen concludes that for the DSS community, "'Covenant of God' stands for a *timeless principle*, rather than a historical foundation . . . . The most important covenant aspect is that of *obedience* . . . . Election is reinterpreted so that being chosen means being obliged to live according to the law and being devoted to the study of Torah."[156] Lundbom points out another difference: "The *Manual* reads much like Deuteronomy. The main difference between the two is that in the *Manual* the older corporate sense is gone; the blessings and curses, for example, fall now upon individuals."[157]

---

155. Christiansen, "Consciousness," 85.

156. Christiansen, *Covenant*, 147, 158. 1Q14, the pesher on Micah, indicates that people can freely choose to join "the elect" to be saved on the Day of Judgment. The word *elect* there simply means the community, without any indication of divine predetermination. Covenant is identified with law, "understood primarily in its obligatory aspect" (Christiansen, "Consciousness," 87–88).

157. Lundbom, "Covenant," 1090. Christiansen notes that "the emphasis has *shifted*

Due to the emphasis on community rules, the DSS covenant is a covenant of sectarians *with one another* as much as it is a covenant with God; the term evoked the community, with its distinctive rules, as much as it did a relationship with God. Kutsch notes that the term "$b^e r\hat{\imath}t$ can also describe a group of people: as in 1QS 5:11, 18 '(the evildoers) will not be reckoned to his (God's) $b^e r\hat{\imath}t$' (cf. CD 19:35: '[the apostates] will not be reckoned to the assembly of the people'); as in 1QM 14:4, where 'his $b^e r\hat{\imath}t$' parallels 'people of his redemption' and in 17:7, where 'Israel's $b^e r\hat{\imath}t$' parallels 'lot/portion (= people) of God.'"[158] These uses equating covenant with the people are the end result of viewing covenant primarily in terms of community rules. It was a covenant entered by choice, not by ancestry and circumcision. They had a narrow view of covenant, a rule-based view in which only a small remnant of Israel pleases God.

Summary

Jews in the Second Temple period viewed the covenants in various ways—some with an emphasis on promise; others emphasizing obligation. But they all viewed the word *covenant* favorably; it did not suggest an onerous burden. It suggested obligations, but also the honor of being God's chosen people and the implication of eternal rewards. Jews were aware of different covenants with Noah, Abraham, and Moses,[159] but when viewing their own relationship with God, they generally amalgamated the promises given to Abraham with the obligations given through Moses.

Sectarians tended to stress the necessity of individuals choosing to obey the terms of the covenant. They stressed conditions—and that if people really wanted to, they could meet the conditions. Sectarians

---

from concrete blessings of place and collective existence, to an individualized reward . . . an eschatological hope" ("Consciousness," 88). Whereas CD suggested that Israel would eventually be faithful, in 1QS only the remnant will be rewarded; thus the covenant with Israel is downplayed and the covenant with the community is stressed (ibid., 97).

158. Kutsch, *TLOT*, 1:265.

159. There are few references to the Davidic covenant. Since the Jews had been many centuries without a Davidic king, the Davidic covenant may have been a puzzle or an embarrassment (cf. Ps 89). Messianic expectations of a Davidic king could have been based on prophecies of national restoration rather than the covenant texts. Vogel writes, "Redet Ben Sira weder in 45,15 noch in 47,1l von einer „ewigen" Dauer der Davidverheissung" (*Das Heil des Bundes*, 119).

viewed the covenant as a contract, and when they amalgamated the covenants, they forced them all into the Mosaic mold, assuming that the requirements God gave through Moses must have been required for Abraham and Noah, too. When they included a promise of eternal life within the covenant, they did so on the basis of a scripture.

Writers who wanted to include most Jews within the covenant did the opposite: They stressed the nation. When they amalgamated the covenants, the Abrahamic promises dominated, even though the laws of Moses were also taught. If people really wanted to, they could disqualify themselves, but God would still be faithful to the nation as a whole. They viewed the covenant more flexibly,[160] and when they included a promise of eternal life, no exegetical justification was necessary; it was simply believed that God would reward his people. Since the concept of covenant was flexible, there was no need to make Noah and Abraham keep Mosaic laws.[161]

Sectarians believed that all the covenants had the same obligations, so they had no room in their theology for a new covenant. They believed that they were complying with the covenantal obligations, and felt no need for God to alter their hearts. The nonsectarian majority also felt no need for a new covenant, since God's promises to the nation could already be counted on. Consequently, few first-century Jews were looking for a new covenant, or expecting any major changes. They rarely referred to the eschatological or new covenant. For the most part, the concept of a *new* covenant was dormant.

---

160. In other words, *covenant* was a term capable of carrying new meaning. Outside the DSS community, it was an umbrella term rather than a technical term with narrow meaning. If the Jews understood something as part of their relationship with God (whether obligation or promise), they understood it as part of the covenant. The covenant was a living relationship that allowed development.

161. This eventually made a place for Gentiles, who could comply with the "terms" of the Noahic covenant without complying with all the laws of Moses—though there is no evidence from Second Temple Jewish literature that anyone had developed this idea this far. Even in rabbinic writings, people who met the terms of the Abrahamic covenant—circumcision—were expected to keep the Mosaic covenant as well; the two covenants were functionally considered as one.

5

"Covenant" in the New Testament

IN THE FIRST CENTURY, A NEW SECT AROSE WITHIN JUDAISM, TEACHING that the Messiah had come and had, contrary to all expectations, inaugurated a new covenant by dying on a cross. We will examine the writings of this sect to see what concept of covenant they had. One initial observation is that the concept is not as important in the NT as in the Hebrew Bible—although בְּרִית occurs 284 times in the HB, διαθήκη occurs only 33 times in the NT.[1] We will begin with references to previous covenants, then survey references to a new covenant.

Ancestral Covenants in the Gospels and Acts

Luke 1 reports the earliest use of διαθήκη in the NT—before Jesus was born.[2] The angel Gabriel may have alluded to the Davidic covenant when he told Mary that her child would be given "the throne of his ancestor David" (v. 32). Mary alluded to the Abrahamic covenant when she said that God "has helped his servant Israel, in remembrance of his mercy, according to the promise he made to our ancestors, to Abraham and to his descendants forever" (v. 55). The covenant "to be their God" was assumed to include a promise of mercy even though Genesis does not explicitly say that. Similarly, the priest Zechariah said that God had given the Jews a savior in the house of David, as predicted in the prophets, to save the Jews from their enemies. "Thus he has shown the mercy

---

1. Porter notes that the *concept* of covenant can also be conveyed by other words ("Concept of Covenant in Paul," 269–85), but the word frequencies do reflect a different emphasis.

2. Although Luke was probably a Gentile, he reports traditions from Jewish believers. I am not concerned with the historicity of these accounts—I am exploring what this literature reports in order to see what the people believed about covenants.

promised to our ancestors, and has remembered [i.e., taken action on] his holy covenant, the oath that he swore to our ancestor Abraham" (vv. 69–72). The passage alludes to several covenants: God promised to give the land of Canaan to the descendants of Abraham (Gen 17:8); he promised military success within the Mosaic covenant (Deut 28:7), and in the Prophets he promised to raise the house of David (Jer 33:15; Ezek 34:23, etc.). All these promises are amalgamated into the same package, as if all are based on the Abrahamic covenant.[3] The implication is that God had obligated himself to show mercy to the Jewish people, and this is part of what it means for Yahweh to be God to his people. The promises given to Abraham, Israel, and David were all invoked, with little need for discriminating between them.

Matthew 1:1 mentions Abraham and David as the most noteworthy ancestors of Jesus, hinting that he is the inheritor of the promises or covenants given to them. Matthew 3:9 (par. Luke 3:8) says that John the Baptist told Jews that they could not count on escaping "the wrath to come" simply because they had Abraham as their ancestor. This alludes to the Abrahamic covenant, and when John says, "God is able from these stones to raise up children to Abraham," it implies that only children of Abraham will be saved. Salvation on the day of judgment was understood to be part of the covenantal benefits.

Jesus implied that privileges were due to the children of Abraham when he argued that a healed woman was "a daughter of Abraham" and a tax collector was "a son of Abraham" (Luke 13:16; 19:9).[4] He spoke favorably of sacrificial laws (Matt 8:4; Luke 5:14) and of Moses (Mark 7:10; 12:26; 16:29; John 3:14; 5:46). Although he did not use the word *covenant* when referring to the patriarchs, the Gospels portray him as believing that the people had a special relationship with God that entailed privileges and obligations. The Jews were the people of God, which meant that a covenant existed.

---

3. Nolland writes, "The covenant with Abraham and the patriarchs is in mind, but no clear distinction from the later Mosaic covenant is intended" (*Luke 1—9:20*, 87). "According to the Gospels, Jesus came to fulfill the covenant" (Goldingay, "Covenant," 775).

4. Jesus could have been using an *ad hominen* argument, using an idea that was merely sufficient for his critics. However, other passages also support his preferential treatment for Jews (e.g., Matt 10:6; 15:24, 26; John 4:22). Space does not permit a discussion of the historicity of these sayings, but it seems unlikely that the early church would have invented sayings that gave the Jews special status or favor.

Matthew says that people called Jesus "the Son of David" (Matt 9:27; 12:23; 15:22; 20:30; 21:9; 22:42); this may allude to the Davidic covenant. The people allude to the eschatological promise when Jesus entered Jerusalem: "Blessed is the coming kingdom of our ancestor David!" (Mark 11:10). The people expected the restored kingdom to be ruled by a descendant of David; this may be due to the Davidic covenant or simply to statements in the Major Prophets. Luke tells us that the disciples expected the messiah "to redeem Israel" (Luke 24:21), "to restore the kingdom to Israel" (Acts 1:6); these nationalistic expectations are probably rooted in their belief in a covenant with God.

In general, the Gospels *allude* to the ancestral covenants in a fair number of places, but do not use the word "covenant" for them,[5] perhaps because the word suggested a need to keep laws that were unique to Israel. Jesus' teachings come under the rubric of the reign of God,[6] a less nationalistic term that could be given new meaning.

According to Luke, Peter referred to the Abrahamic covenant while preaching after Jesus' death and resurrection: "You are the descendants of the prophets and of the covenant that God gave to your ancestors, saying to Abraham, 'And in your descendants all the families of the earth shall be blessed'" (Acts 3:25, quoting Gen 22:18). Genesis 22 does not use the word *covenant*, but says that God swore this as an unconditional promise. Peter considers this oath as part of God's covenant with Abraham.[7] Acts 26:6 calls resurrection a "promise made by God to our ancestors," but does not cite any text or say which ancestors. The πατέροι are generally Abraham, Isaac, and Jacob, rather than Moses. Peter says that God raised Jesus "to give repentance *to Israel*" (Acts 5:31); even when he speaks to the Gentile Cornelius, Peter says that God has given the message "to the people of Israel" (10:36). The blessings of salvation were seen as a national privilege, probably based on the covenant with God.

---

5. Because of the allusions, I cannot agree with Grässer when he says, "Dass für die Ausprägung der theologischen Entwürfe der Synoptiker die Bundestheologie keine Rolle spielt, kann man nicht als zufällig bezeichnen" (*Der Alte Bund im Neuen*, 11).

6. "The underlying thought has been taken over [in the Synoptics] in the sayings about the kingdom of God" (Guhrt, *NIDNTT* 1:369).

7. Grammatically, it is possible that Peter considered Gen 22:16–18 to be a covenant in its own right (making three Abrahamic covenants, as Hahn advocates in "Kinship by Covenant," 185–86), but there is no Jewish precedent for seeing even two Abrahamic covenants.

The only covenant mentioned in Luke's summary of Stephen's speech is Abraham's "covenant of circumcision" (Acts 7:8).[8] Luke also reports an allusion by Paul to the Davidic promises: "God has brought to Israel a Savior" from the descendants of David "as he promised" (Acts 13:23). He applies a scripture to the risen Jesus: "I will give you the holy promises made to David" (Acts 13:34, possibly paraphrasing Isa 55:3). These promises given to David of a Savior among his descendants *may* allude to the Davidic covenant. Luke refers to the laws of Moses several times (Acts 6:14; 15:5; 21:21), but does not call them a covenant; the word *covenant* is used in Acts only for the nation's relationship to God based on their descent from Abraham.

Paul's References to Ancestral Covenants

Paul refers to previous covenants in both positive and negative ways. Perhaps the earliest mention (the date does not affect my study) is Gal 3, where Paul argues that the law of Moses cannot annul the covenant with Abraham or annul those promises, because the law came 430 years later (v. 17). Just as a human διαθήκη[9] cannot be changed (v. 15), the promises given "to Abraham and to his offspring"[10] (v. 16) cannot be taken away—and his offspring include those who "belong to Christ,

---

8. Luke argues against the law of Moses (e.g., in Acts 15) and apparently did not find it helpful to call it a covenant. Although Luke reports that circumcision is not required for Gentiles, his willingness to call circumcision a covenant may indicate that he believes it is still required for Jews, even those who believe in Jesus.

9. Scholars debate whether διαθήκη here means a covenant or a testament. What Paul says is true of a covenant—an oath could not be altered—and true of a will, as long as we understand Paul to mean that *no one else* can modify the will. It is difficult to ascertain what the Gentile readers would have understood from this first use of διαθήκη in the epistle. "Will" was the normal meaning in secular Greek, but Paul has already alluded to the Abrahamic covenant, and the readers were apparently familiar with that meaning of διαθήκη. But Paul is alluding to a human custom, and in the first century, the only human διαθήκαι were wills, and Paul is discussing descendants and inheritance. Longenecker writes, "Paul's use of διαθήκη in 3:15 is not exactly in accord with the legal situation of the day.... It may be that Paul felt no compulsion to speak in precise legal parlance" (*Galatians*, 130). Whether Paul means will or covenant is of minor significance for my study, since my primary interest is to know what first-century Jews thought about *divine* covenants. Either way, Paul's point here is that a διαθήκη cannot be annulled—a point that conflicts with what he writes about the Mosaic covenant, as I discuss below.

10. This reference to the offspring of Abraham is probably an allusion to the Abrahamic covenant.

heirs according to the promise" (v. 7, 29). The law of Moses was a temporary measure, appointed only until "the offspring would come to whom the promises had been made . . . until faith would be revealed . . . until Christ came" (vv. 19, 23–24).[11]

Paul does not call the law of Moses a covenant here (although he calls it that in the next chapter), for that would make the contrast in Gal 3 unnecessarily confusing. However, Paul's argument has a potential problem, for he implies that a ratified covenant could not be revoked—but the Mosaic covenant *was* ratified. Why then could it be revoked? Paul's strongest answer is that obligations cannot nullify a previous promise (v. 17).[12] Dunn observes, "The key term in the passage is actually 'promise' (eight times in 3.14–29 [as opposed to only twice for διαθήκη]). That is the term which provides the cutting edge of Paul's exposition in Gal 3. That is the term which carries the contrast with νόμος."[13] This suggests that "covenant" is not a term that Paul prefers—it was a term he had to argue *against*, as much as a term he could use in his favor.[14] Dunn

---

11. As Grässer notes, Paul is contradicting Jewish tradition, which considered the law eternal (*Der Alte Bund*, 63). Surprisingly, Paul does not give any exegesis to support his view; the enigmatic v. 20 is where we might expect for some rationale to be given; the γάρ suggests that v. 20 explains why mediation is relevant to the law's termination at the coming of the seed (v. 19), but the logic is obscure.

12. That response, if taken to an extreme, would mean that the law never had any validity at all. Paul does not take that approach. Rather, he says that the law had validity only until the seed had come (v. 19). Why did its validity terminate then? It apparently had something to do with the fact that the law was given through a mediator (v. 19d), and the mediator is not like God (v. 20). Paul *could* have argued that the law dealt with transgressions and was rendered moot by the forgiveness that came through Christ, but he did not, and it is not clear why he brought in the fact that the law had a mediator. In the final analysis, Paul argues that a διαθήκη made through a mediator had a temporary validity, and he does not explain why it is so.

13. Dunn, "Did Paul Have a Covenant Theology?" 291. Paul is aware that a covenant could include obligations (Gal 4:24), but he stresses the promissory nature of the Abrahamic covenant (3:17).

14. Das suggests that "'Covenant' would have been a key term for the apostle's opponents in their discussion of Abraham . . . . The Abrahamic texts clearly fit the opponents' case much better, with circumcision acting as the sign of the Abrahamic covenant" (*Paul, the Law, and the Covenant*, 76). Lundbom says, "The Mosaic covenant serves Paul only for the purpose of making a contrast with the Abrahamic covenant" (*Jeremiah*, 475–76).

says, "His usage seems to be more reactive than expressive of his own cutting edge reflection."[15]

Paul's reference to the Mosaic covenant in the next chapter is even more negative. Paul uses an allegory about Sarah and Hagar: "These women are two covenants. One woman, in fact, is Hagar, from Mount Sinai, bearing children for slavery. Now Hagar is Mount Sinai in Arabia and corresponds to the present Jerusalem, for she is in slavery with her children" (4:24–25). A covenant associated with Sinai and Jerusalem—the Mosaic covenant—is said to involve slavery—the obligations given in the law of Moses. Paul does not even name the better covenant (again suggesting that "covenant" is not the term he prefers), but implies that the readers would be aware of it under the name "covenant" (perhaps from the Lord's Supper), and aware that they should be in it. He implies that this covenant is based on or identified with the promises given to Abraham.

Paul has done something atypical for Jews of his time period: He has separated the covenants. Whereas previous writers amalgamated the Abrahamic and Mosaic covenants, treating one covenant as an outgrowth or development of the other, Paul has pitted one against the other. Although he has not categorized the covenants in the way scholars do today, his terminology stresses the promissory nature of the Abrahamic relationship and the obligatory nature of the Mosaic covenant. He has seen a fundamental difference in the nature of these two covenants.

Writing about AD 55 or 56, in 2 Cor 3, Paul calls the law of Moses "the old covenant" (v. 14). He is negative about this covenant, associating the stone tablets with condemnation and death. Although this covenant came with glory, its glory has been eclipsed by "a new covenant" (vv. 6–10). Paul argues that, just as the glory of Moses' face is now set aside (vv. 7, 13),[16] the old covenant "has lost its glory" and has been "set aside" by the more glorious new covenant (vv. 10–11). He says that the new covenant is permanent, implying that the old covenant was temporary (v. 11). The primary purpose of the passage is not an exposition of the covenants—it is to defend Paul's ministry. Dunn writes, "It was

---

15. Dunn, "Did Paul," 287.

16. Grässer points out, against v. 13, that the glory on Moses' face was permanent in Exod 34 and in most Jewish tradition (*Der Alte Bund*, 86). I will say more below about the contrast that Paul draws between the old and new covenants.

a way of countering a glorification of Moses' ministry which sought to denigrate his own."[17] It is likely that here, too, Paul's opponents initiated the use of διαθήκη as well as the comparison with Moses.

Not long after 2 Corinthians was written, Paul writes in Romans that promises were given to Abraham and his descendants, and others share in the promise of salvation by being counted among his descendants (4:13, 16). He clarifies that descent from Abraham is by faith, not through the flesh (9:7–8), just as circumcision is a matter of the heart rather than the flesh (2:28–29).[18] This redefinition of the terms of inclusion shifts the focus to individual response, rather than being part of an ethnic group, as also happened for the DSS sectarians.

Paul is redefining who the people of God are, but one thing remains constant: The relationship must be rooted in the promises given to Abraham rather than the law given to Moses. Paul further reasons that since the promise was given to Abraham when he was uncircumcised, the promise is extended to uncircumcised people who have faith, for faith is the means by which they descend from Abraham (Rom 4:1–12). Here again, Paul prefers the word "promise" to characterize the Abrahamic covenant.

Paul writes that the Jews have "the adoption, the glory, the covenants [plural],[19] the giving of the law, the worship, and the promises" (Rom 9:4). He does not specify which covenants he is talking about, but he associates them with being the people of God (Gen 17), the Mosaic law, and "promises" (which could be associated with Abraham, Moses, David, and/or the eschatological prophecies). This is a more positive reference, but Paul does not give enough detail here for us to draw further conclusions about his view of the covenants.

His analogy of grafting in Rom 11 implies a privileged relationship for *Israel*—Gentiles receive salvation by being grafted into Israel; unbelieving Jews are rejected by being removed from Israel. The constant is that salvation is for *Israel* (which is now defined by faith in Christ)—and

---

17. Dunn, "Did Paul," 299.

18. Similarly, the Jerusalem council concluded that believers did not have to be circumcised or to obey the law of Moses in order to be saved (Acts 15). Col 2:11 says that believers are *spiritually* circumcised in Christ. The true definition of circumcision, Paul says in Phil 3:3, is boasting in Christ, not in the flesh—that is, relating to Abraham through faith in Christ rather than in physical descent and physical circumcision.

19. Although some MSS have the singular, the best ones have the plural.

for Paul, "Israel" is defined by descent from Abraham, not by the Mosaic covenant. "I myself am an Israelite, a descendant of Abraham" (11:1). Even though most Jews rejected Jesus, God loves them because of the patriarchs (11:28). Yet in Paul's view, most of them are disenfranchised (Rom 9:2–3; 10:1). As noted earlier, he defines Israel as those who are descended from Abraham in terms of faith, not by physical descent and circumcision. He uses the old name *Israel*, but by it he means a reconstituted people, with only a partial overlap with the old people. Israelites may have the covenants, but most of them are disenfranchised from the blessings of those covenants.

A positive but nonspecific mention of plural covenants is also seen in Eph 2: The Gentiles, before they believed in Christ, were "aliens from the commonwealth of Israel, and strangers to the covenants of promise, having no hope and without God in the world" (v. 12). The covenants here are associated with hope and being part of "the household of God" (v. 19). The Gentiles have been brought near because Christ "has abolished the law with its commandments and ordinances," that is, the law that divided Jew from Gentile (vv. 14–16).[20] Thus there is a positive mention of covenants with a negative mention of law; the covenants are associated with promises and contrasted with law. A privileged role for Israel is implied, but it is altered by the inclusion of Gentiles—again, "Israel" is being defined in a new way.[21]

The New Covenant in the Lord's Supper

The NT also uses the word "covenant" for a *new* relationship between God and humans. I will examine these passages to see what they reveal about the concept of covenant. That background will then be used to explore the role of covenant in the argument of Hebrews.

---

20. Precisely what is meant by "law" here is debated, but it includes Mosaic commandments that applied to Jews but not Gentiles. Several NT passages argue that a broad category of law is obsolete: the law of Moses (Acts 15), the old covenant (2 Cor 3; Heb 8), and all the laws added by Moses (Gal 3).

21. Grässer writes, "Eine merkwürdige Spannung durchzieht den ganzen Abschnitt Eph 2,11–18. Einerseits bleibt der Vorzug Israels als das von Gott berufene Volk anerkannt, und die „Bündnisse der Verheissung" sind *das* signum der Erwählung (v 12). Andererseits wird der Vorzug Israels in einer erheblichen Weise relativiert" (*Der Alte Bund*, 32).

The Synoptic Gospels and Paul report that Jesus used the word διαθήκη at the Last Supper.[22] The Markan/Matthean version is, "This is my blood of the covenant, which is poured out for many" (Mark 14:24; Matt 26:28 adds "for the forgiveness of sins"). The Lukan/Pauline version is, "This cup that is poured out for you is the new covenant in my blood" (Luke 22:20; 1 Cor 11:25 omits "that is poured out for you").

"Blood of the covenant" is an echo of Exod 24:8;[23] Mark and Matthew thereby suggest that Jesus' blood (i.e., his death) brought a new relationship between God and his people—suggesting that the people of God are defined in some way by the death of Jesus. The Matthean version specifies what God promises: forgiveness. Although the phrase about blood evokes the Sinaitic covenant, which stressed obligations, there are no obligations mentioned with Jesus' cup-word. Hillers points out a major shift:

> In Moses' use of the words "blood of the covenant," the blood helps bring the curse into effect; the people are identified with the victim, whose fate will be theirs if they sin. The eucharistic words . . . the emphasis is not on bringing them under a curse but rather of a sacrifice made on their behalf. Thus, though there is a verbal echo of the Sinai covenant, the real conceptual link is to the new covenant of forgiveness of which Jeremiah spoke.[24]

Since forgiveness is secured by the death of Jesus, without any mention of obligations, this covenant implies a promise, and it does not have the nationalistic associations that are often found in Second Temple literature uses of *covenant*.

The Lukan/Pauline version also connects the covenant with blood, but in a different way. Instead of alluding to Exodus, it probably alludes to the Jer 31 prophecy of a covenant that will be based on forgiveness.[25]

---

22. Although there is considerable debate about what words are most likely original to Jesus, I will bypass that debate, since my concern is how the *literature* uses the concept, as an indicator of how διαθήκη was understood by people who believed in Jesus as the Messiah.

23. The phrase is also found in Zech 9:11, but readers would be more likely to think of Exodus.

24. Hillers, *Covenant*, 187. Readers could connect the cup-word with an earlier saying, "The Son of Man came . . . to give his life a ransom for many" (Mark 10:45; Matt 20:28). It might also evoke Isa 42:6.

25. Grässer argues that, other than the words "new covenant," there is no reason to connect this to Jer 31 (*Der Alte Bund*, 119–20). Jer 31 says nothing about blood; the Lukan cup-word says nothing about laws, hearts, teaching, knowing or forgiveness. But

But what would it mean to say that a covenant was *in* a person's (shed) blood? It suggests that the death enabled the covenant, but says little about whether the covenant entailed obligations, promises, or both. Nor does this fit into the way the word *covenant* was usually used; by itself, the saying does not indicate whether the covenant is with God, or merely a covenant among sectarians.

How were readers expected to understand this term, when the Gospels do not prepare the readers for it? It would be difficult to interpret διαθήκη in either of its traditional meanings—in the sense of a national relationship with God, or the secular Greek sense of a person's last will indicating inheritance rights. Apparently the readers were already familiar with the cup-word through liturgical use. Paul had received it as part of the earliest tradition (1 Cor 11:23).

The NT reveals a people who 1) believed they had forgiveness with God because of what Jesus had done, 2) in the Eucharist, regularly used the word *covenant* for the resulting relationship with God, and 3) connected this covenant with Jesus' death. Writers could assume that readers already knew through liturgical use that Jesus brought them a forgiveness-enabled relationship with God. Even if the word *new* was not part of the original saying, it would be easy for Jesus' followers to call it a "new covenant" (the word was implied, for this was clearly different from previous covenants[26]), and especially with the word "new,"

Grässer seems to be asking for more evidence than is reasonable. The mention of "new covenant" in Heb 8 clearly alludes to Jer 31, but there is nothing in the *context* of Heb 8 (other the quote itself) about laws, teaching, knowing, heart, or other Jer 31 themes. The NT picks up the phrase from Jer 31 but invests it with new meaning rather than building on details in Jer 31.

At this point it might seem that I am inconsistent—saying that the eucharistic "new covenant" alludes to Jer 31, but the DSS use of the exact same words does not. In neither case is there any reference to other themes from Jer 31, but Heb 8 shows that such references should not be required. The primary differences are: 1) The phrase "new covenant" in the DSS refers to something in the community's history. 2) Although the Lukan/Pauline eucharistic words are not overtly linked to forgiveness, the Mark/Matthean version of the words is linked to forgiveness, a theme found in Jer 31. 3) The Gospels and Paul have literary affinities to Hebrews, which quotes Jer 31, whereas the DSS corpus never quotes Jeremiah.

26. "The covenant established by Jesus' blood must be a new covenant, different from the Sinaitic covenant, because whereas the Sinaitic covenant was established by the blood of animal sacrifice, the covenant at the Last Supper was established by the blood of Jesus" (Yu, "New Covenant," 177).

it would be easy for readers to connect this covenant of forgiveness with Jer 31.[27]

What would it mean to have a covenant with God? Based on LXX usage, it would imply a relationship in which loyalty is expected—and when that relationship is with God, rewards are expected as part of God's loyalty to his people. The eucharistic covenant was the new relationship with God that came with the forgiveness that was given to believers through Jesus' death. The eucharistic words announced that people who drank the wine were God's people, and the eucharistic context implied that God accepted them not because of their ancestry or their works, but because of Jesus' death. The eucharistic context did not tell them what they were expected to *do* in the covenant; it referred only to what Jesus had done for them.

The New Covenant in Paul

Paul alluded to the new covenant when he told the Galatians there were two covenants (Gal 4:24). One covenant he associated with Sinai, bondage, and first-century Jerusalem; he associated the other covenant with promise, freedom, and "Jerusalem above" (Gal 4:26). He wanted the readers to be in the covenant of freedom, but he did not name it or develop it.[28] This suggests that his objective was more in dissuading the readers away from the Sinaitic law, rather than trying to get them to see their faith under the term *covenant.*

Paul was not interested in explaining the gospel under the category of *covenant*—perhaps the term was too associated with Jewish nationalism and Mosaic laws and conditions, all of which he argued against.[29] He was willing to use the word *covenant*, but he preferred other words,

---

27. "Jesus adds that the pouring out of his blood brings about 'the forgiveness of sins.' He thus takes up Jeremiah's talk of a new covenant" (Goldingay, "Covenant," 775).

28. Paul calls the Abrahamic promise a covenant, and he connects the covenant of freedom with the child of promise, so he may intend readers to see themselves under the Abrahamic covenant of promise. However, he probably taught them the same Lord's Supper tradition he gave in Corinth, so it is likely that the readers already associated their faith with the term "new covenant." But he does not exploit the word "new."

29. Wright says, "Since in NT times 'covenant' had come to mean almost exclusively obedience to the Jewish law, one can observe that NT writers were not comfortable with the term" ("Theological Study of the Bible," 986).

such as promise, justification,[30] faith, or being in Christ.[31] In Gal 4:23, Paul associated the Christ-covenant with Sarah and "the child . . . born through the promise," and we can probably connect this with his earlier statement, "If you belong to Christ, then you are Abraham's offspring, heirs according to the promise" (3:29). In other words, the Christ-covenant *is* the Sarah covenant, the Abrahamic covenant.[32] The new covenant does not *replace* the Mosaic covenant—it terminates it, and God's covenant reverts back to the Abrahamic promises, with Christ being the means by which people participate in them. Grässer observes the irony that "dieses ‚völlig Neue' für Paulus eigentlich *älter* ist als die Sinaidiatheke."[33]

Paul reveals more of his thoughts when he contrasts the old covenant with the new in 2 Cor 3. Paul's main purpose is to defend his style of ministry, not to explicate the covenants, but he reveals numerous aspects of old and new:

Verse	The old covenant	The new covenant
4	written on tablets of stone	written on the heart
6	the letter that kills	the Spirit that gives life
7	a ministry that brought death	a ministry that brings life
7	engraved in letters on stone	a ministry of the Spirit
7	came with glory	is even more glorious

30. Righteousness and justification can have covenantal connotations—Porter points out that Paul uses the δικαιο word group "in the context of the covenant relation" ("Concept," 282)—but even so, Paul rarely uses the word *covenant*. One result of this is that the social connotations of *covenant* are lost, and salvation becomes more individualized. Since new boundaries are defining a new "group," it may have been counterproductive to use the old term, which was associated with the old definition of the group.

31. "It is the common belonging to Christ, *not* belonging to the covenant, to which Paul relates ecclesiastical identity" (Christiansen, *Covenant*, 214).

32. Lohfink says, "According to the thought patterns of this text Christians belong not to a 'new covenant' but to the 'Abrahamic covenant' which both precedes and overarches the law of Sinai" (*Covenant*, 30). But the new covenant includes details about Jesus that the Abrahamic covenant did not. Freedman and Miano write, "Paul sees the Abrahamic covenant as the foundation upon which the obligatory covenants are built and upon which the new covenant is built (Gal. 3.15–18)" ("People," 23).

33. Grässer, *Der Alte Bund*, 75. Paul does not use the word "new" in Gal 3–4; the irony comes only when we couple the term "new" from 2 Cor 3 with his argument in Gal 3.

Verse	The old covenant	The new covenant
9	the ministry that condemns	ministry bringing righteousness
10	has no glory in comparison	the surpassing glory
11	came with glory	has much greater glory
11	is now set aside	a permanent ministry

Paul is writing to people who already knew about a new covenant (1 Cor 11:25), but here, he appears to be arguing against people who had a high respect for the Sinaitic covenant. This passage shows that Paul perceived *covenant* to be a broad category that could include obligatory relationships as well as promissory ones, but Paul again makes a sharp contrast in the nature of these covenants. The Sinai covenant, with its conditions, could bring only condemnation for failure, and Paul said it is terminated.[34] The new covenant brought salvation, and it was obviously *different* from the old. Goldingay writes, "Apostles such as Paul saw themselves as 'ministers of a new covenant,' whose novelty lies in its being 'not of letter but of spirit' (2 Cor 3:6). This antithesis corresponds to but restates the one in Jer 31:31–34."[35]

Even though 2 Cor 3 is Paul's longest passage on the new covenant, he says nothing about how a person enters this covenant, what makes it possible, or what it entails. His purpose here is not to explain what the new covenant is, but to reject the old, to respond to opponents who said that the old was glorious.[36] Just as in Galatians, he is *willing* to call the Christ-faith a covenant, but he apparently does not think that the word *covenant* is the best way to describe the people's relationship

---

34. Lohfink argues that it not the old covenant, but the veil that covers it, that comes to an end. "The 'new covenant' is nothing else than the unveiled, no longer covered 'old covenant' which radiates God's splendor already contained in it" (*Covenant*, 39). But this ignores the many contrasts that Paul draws in 2 Cor 3; Paul is clearly describing the old covenant itself, not a misinterpretation, as inferior. Thielman points out that "Paul's use of the neuter participle shows that he means that the entire Mosaic ministry—the Mosaic covenant, its sentence of condemnation and the death that it dealt to those who disobeyed it—is passing away" (*Paul and the Law*, 113).

35. Goldingay, "Covenant," 775.

36. "It is quite possible that Paul's use of covenant terminology reflects a situation in which the covenant or questions of 'old' and 'new' were forced on him by opponents' use of one or both terms" (Christiansen, *Covenant*, 252–53).

with God.³⁷ He does not find the first-century concept of covenant to be congenial to his purpose. After arguing that the new covenant has even more glory than the old, he abandons the term; he probably uses the word here only because his opponents used it. "Covenant" was the word traditionally used by Jews to express the idea that they had a relationship with God that others did not have, and it is not surprising that Paul has to argue against the term, since he wants to include people on a different basis.

In Romans, Paul mentions salvation as a covenant only obliquely. He acknowledged that covenants were important for the Jews (9:4). The plural word may acknowledge a difference between the Abrahamic and the Mosaic covenant, or it may refer to a covenant from the past and the promise of one in the future. Paul notes the prediction of future salvation and a covenant for the people in Rom 11:26-27: "All Israel will be saved; as it is written, 'Out of Zion will come the Deliverer; he will banish ungodliness from Jacob.' 'And this is my covenant with them, when I take away their sins'" (quoting Isa 59:20-21a).³⁸ Here, Paul associates the eschatological covenant with forgiveness—more of a gift of salvation than a set of obligations. Again, Paul did not describe the covenant in any detail, even though an easy transition to it was offered by Isa 59:21b-c, with its mention of the Spirit and the internalization of God's words. The term *covenant* could refer to Jewish particularism and obligations, or it could be used for a promise of salvation and life. Probably because of potentially negative connotations, Paul preferred other terms, such as *promise*, that more clearly expressed his view.³⁹

---

37. Murphy-O'Connor writes, "His repeated use of *diakonia* (four times in 3:7-9) rather betrays a deliberate intention to avoid *diathēkē*. . . . The concept of a new covenant was fundamentally alien to Paul's theology, and . . . his use of it was a grudging concession to external pressure. . . . [He] was prepared to accept the idea of covenant and *a fortiori* that of new covenant, provided that it was completely divorced from law" ("New Covenant," 195, 204).

38. The first part of the quote is from Isa 59:20-21a; the last part is often attributed to Isa 27:9 or Jer 31:34, but may be Paul's own summary of the prophecies of the eschatological covenant.

39. "In the Pauline corpus as a whole διαθήκη does not play a significant role" (Lehne, *New Covenant*, 166). "Covenant in its narrow sense, that is in its association with law, is no longer an obvious term for the present community's relationship with God. . . . Paul never uses the term 'covenant' as a designation for the Christian community. . . . Paul found covenant as a term inadequate, if and when it is overloaded with ethno-centric values" (Christiansen, *Covenant*, 249, 270-71).

Summary

The NT uses the word *covenant* in several ways—often as a description of the past, for Israel's relationship with God. Luke notes that God made various promises to the Jewish people under the term *covenant*, and he presents Jesus as the fulfillment of those promises. But the Gospels do not use the word διαθήκη until the Last Supper, where the word has almost none of the earlier associations. It designates a relationship with God and is associated with forgiveness, but is given few other details.

Early in the first century, there was an undifferentiated, amalgamated view of the ancestral covenants. Abrahamic promises were mixed with Mosaic laws; national blessings were mixed with rewards for individuals. But some[40] who believed in the resurrection of Jesus *separated* the laws and covenant of Moses from the promises given to Abraham. The covenant with Abraham was considered permanent, and circumcision, its accompanying sign, was reinterpreted instead of being dismissed. The Mosaic covenant, in contrast, was considered obsolete, and its laws could be dismissed without any specific reinterpretation required, because it had come to an end, and another covenant had been made. Even so, covenant is not a prominent conceptual category, perhaps because it implied either a descent from Abraham (which had to be redefined), or the laws of Moses (which had to be set aside, at least for Gentiles).

Paul also uses the word *covenant* as a descriptor for the past (the promises given to Abraham and the laws given to Moses), and for Judaism of his own day. He acknowledges that faith in Jesus as Messiah is associated with a new covenant, but he develops that concept only in contrast to previous covenants; he does not develop it as a concept on its own. I will say more about Paul's use of the term in the conclusion of this chapter, when I contrast Paul and Hebrews.

Ancestral Covenants in Hebrews

Hebrews has more than half of the NT uses of the word διαθήκη (17 out of 33). The epistle draws a contrast between two covenants—the Mosaic

---

40. Acts 21:20 reports that some believed in the continuing validity of the laws of Moses *for Jews* who believed in Jesus, but Paul did not believe the laws were required, even for Jews (Gal 2:14; 1 Cor 9:20–21). Since there were different views of law, it is likely that there were different views of covenant, too.

covenant and the new covenant. To avoid confusing the contrast, it does not use the word *covenant* for Abraham—probably due to rhetorical strategy.[41] However, it alludes to the Abrahamic covenant in 6:13-15. Hebrews 6:13 refers to "a promise to Abraham" and quotes from Gen 22:17, and Heb 6:15 says that Abraham obtained the promise. Isaac is not the promise, since he was already alive in Gen 22, so the "promise" apparently refers to covenantal promises.[42]

The "first covenant" that Hebrews considers is the Mosaic, and Hebrews has several references to it.[43] The author argues that the Israelites received the law under the Levitical priesthood (7:11) and that Christ has become a priest (6:20; 7:17), necessitating a change in the law (7:12). The flow of the argument in 7:17-22 shows that the concepts "law" and "covenant" are equivalent:

> There is, on the one hand, the abrogation of an earlier commandment because it was weak and ineffectual (for the law made nothing perfect); there is, on the other hand, the introduction of a better hope, through which we approach God.... Accordingly Jesus has also become the guarantee of a better covenant.... Consequently he is able for all time to save those who approach God through him.

When Christ is called the mediator of a "better" covenant (7:22; 8:6), the word "better" implies that there was a previous hope and a previous covenant, and a negative judgment is implied for it. It was ineffective, so Jesus brought a better arrangement. The law/covenant was received in conjunction with the Levitical priesthood and was valid only while that priesthood was valid. Since Jesus is a different type of priest, his appointment implies the termination of the previous priesthood, and therefore the termination of the law that restricted the priesthood to the family of Aaron, which in turn implies an end to the validity of

---

41. Eisenbaum notes that none of the role models of Heb 11 is explicitly associated with a covenant, unlike the list in Sirach ("Heroes and History," 392).

42. As noted earlier in reference to Acts 3, Gen 22 was considered to be part of the Abrahamic covenant.

43. The first occurrence of διαθήκη is in Heb 7:22, referring to the new covenant, but the *concept* of covenant is addressed earlier in the chapter with the word νόμος, referring to the Mosaic covenant. See pages 55-59 for the rhetorical strategy involved in the author's use of "law" in Heb 7.

the covenant that included that law—it all stands or falls together, according to the author.

God appointed Jesus a priest, the author repeats, and then concludes, "accordingly Jesus has also become the guarantee of a better covenant" (7:22). Not just individual commandments have been abrogated, but the law as a whole (the covenant) has been replaced. The Mosaic covenant was viewed as a package of laws. Although Hebrews focuses on worship regulations, the word *covenant* indicates that the author believed other regulations to be obsolete, too.[44]

Heb 8:7 says that the Mosaic covenant was not faultless, and its weakness (the inability of the people to keep it)[45] necessitated the promise of a "second" covenant, which supersedes the Mosaic covenant. Thus the Mosaic covenant is viewed negatively, as something that makes demands that cannot be kept, although the word *covenant* itself can just as easily be used for a better covenant.

Hebrews 8:9, quoting Jer 31:32, states that the new covenant will not be like the Mosaic covenant, because the people were not faithful to it. The implication is that no one could *ever* be faithful to it, so a different covenant was needed. As Grässer notes, Jer 31 is cited not as a word of promise (as it was in Jeremiah), but in Hebrews as a word of criticism.[46] The covenant is viewed as a package of obligations, and in this case, they could not be kept.

---

44. Some regulations are different; others remain the same (e.g., Heb 13:4b). Although individual laws might remain the same, the new covenant brings a different *package* of instructions.

45. The fault was in the people (8:8), but Hebrews does not comment on why God would give people a covenant that he knew they could not keep. "The covenant fails practically by not providing for the weakness of the people" (Stanley, "New Covenant," 92). Frey notes that the author was not interested in the fault of the people here; his concern was to blame the system under which they sinned: "Die im Prophetenwort angesprochenen Teilhaber der ersten covenant interessieren den Autor hier nicht weiter, der Tadel an ‚ihnen' begründet in seiner Argumentation lediglich den Tadel an der für sie gültigen Ordnung" ("Die alte und die neue διαθήκη," 279). The author's concern is the need for a new covenant, not a new people; he does not even stress the need for a new heart, even though Jer 31 mentions it. Hegermann concludes, "The first covenant is powerless, not because the people of God have broken it (8:7–13), but because it is weak in itself" (*EDNT* 1:301).

46. Grässer, *Der Alte Bund*, 108. Lehne says, "In Heb. Jeremiah's oracle is made to function as an indictment of the Sinai covenant" (*New Covenant*, 48).

The most negative comment about the covenant is (perhaps as a matter of rhetorical strategy and tact) in a sentence that does not use the word *covenant*. Heb 8:13 uses substantives to say, "In speaking of a new [covenant], he has made the first one obsolete" (8:13).[47] Just as the Mosaic laws of priesthood were declared to be "weak and ineffectual" (7:18), the entire covenant is declared passé. But covenant as a concept does *not* disappear, for Christ has brought a new covenant.

Chapter 9 includes a brief description of the worship regulations of the first covenant. Verse 4 refers to "the ark of the covenant" and "the stone tablets of the covenant," but this description does not imply a judgment. The ark may be associated with mercy or the presence of God; the tablets are associated with legal obligations. Verse 18 notes that the "first covenant" was inaugurated with blood; Moses is quoted as saying, "This is the blood of the covenant that God has ordained for you" (v. 20; quoting Exod 24:8). This description likewise does not imply a judgment, either negative or positive (the new covenant was also inaugurated with blood).

A slightly negative mention occurs in Heb 9:15: Christ's death redeems people "from the transgressions under the first covenant." This verse, while implying the validity of the Mosaic laws, also implies that the covenant could not alleviate the situation it placed the people in. The sacrifices of the Mosaic covenant could not forgive sin.[48]

---

47. Kim makes a similar observation: "By not explicitly mentioning the Sinai covenant, the author demonstrates a bit of caution as he voices such a radical statement" (*Polemic*, 137). The harshest polemic in Hebrews is against the sacrificial system; comments about "the law" are almost as strong, but criticism associated with the word *covenant* is more muted. For example, Heb 7:11–12 states that there must be "a change in the law"; 7:18–19 says that there is an "abrogation of an earlier commandment because it was weak and ineffectual (for the law made nothing perfect)." This passage is not about a specific law, but the entire law (or covenant) of Moses. As Grässer says, there is hardly any difference in meaning between νόμος and διαθήκη in these verses (*Der Alte Bund*, 99). However, the author preserves a more positive role for διαθήκη. Grässer also notes that "die eigentlich gewichtigen theologischen Diatheke-Vorkommen ihren Ort ausschliesslich in der Schriftexegese haben" (ibid.).

48. Rayburn points out that "the cult is criticized and maligned in Hebrews primarily for failing to achieve something it was not designed to achieve: the perfection of the conscience in and of itself. It is clear that Hebrews knows that the cult was not intended intrinsically to take away sin" ("Contrast," 460). But if the Hebrew Bible did not give this as a purpose of the cult, where did the idea come from? It was probably from the readers, or at least the readers' idea was close enough to it for it to be a useful foil for the author. There would be little point in arguing that Christ was better than

The meaning of διαθήκη in Heb 9:16–17 is debated. The majority view is that the author is using it in the sense of "will," its common meaning in non-Jewish Greek writings.[49] The author is talking about death and inheritance, and although the logic is not tight, the point is illustrated by an analogy: Just as a will becomes effective on a person's death, so also a covenant becomes inaugurated with a death. Just as the Mosaic covenant was ratified with blood, so also the new covenant was put into effect through the death of Jesus. However, Hahn, building on the work of Westcott and Hughes, points out some problems with the traditional view:[50]

1) In other Greek literature, ἰσχύω and βέβαιος (9:17) refer to validity, not execution, and a will is valid when signed; it does not become valid only on the death of the testator.

2) Inheritance before death was sometimes permitted, contra 9:17b.

3) Φέρεσθαι in 9:16b is a peculiar way to say that a person has died.

4) Ἐπὶ νεκροῖς (plural, 9:17) is a peculiar way to refer to death.

5) Hebrews uses διαθήκη to mean covenant, and the term is important to the argument; a play on words would weaken the logic. The argument assumes a consistent meaning of διαθήκη from 9:15 to 9:22; there is no verbal indication that the logic is irregular (unlike in 7:9, for example).

6) Nowhere else in Hebrews does the believer's inheritance come through testamentary means, since God is the testator and cannot die.[51]

---

something completely ineffective, unless that "something" was already regarded highly. The author not only has to argue *for* Christ, but also *against* the old cult.

49. Ellingworth begins by arguing, "There is *prima facie* no reason to press the various occurrences of διαθήκη in vv. 15–20 into a single meaning" (*Hebrews*, 462). But *au contraire*, the logical connectors in 9:16, 18 are *prima facie* evidence that the author is working with a consistent meaning. Westcott writes, "The connexion of vv. 15–18 is most close: v. 16 ὅπου γάρ . . . : v. 18 ὅθεν οὐδέ . . . . This connexion makes it most difficult to suppose that the key-word (διαθήκη) is used in different senses in the course of the verses" (*Hebrews*, 300, ellipses in original).

50. Hughes, "Hebrews IX 15," 66–91; Hahn, "A Broken Covenant," 416–36; Hahn, "Covenant, Cult, and the Curse-of-Death," 65–88.

51. Hahn, "A Broken Covenant," 422.

7) A mediator is not involved in the vast majority of testaments.
8) Hebrews always builds its case on Jewish scriptures, not secular law. "The problematic passage occurs in the middle of Heb 9, the chapter with the densest concentration of cultic language and imagery."[52]

Hughes, following Westcott, suggests that the meaning "covenant" works if vv. 16–17 refer to the animal sacrifices that were done during covenant ratification to represent the death of covenant-breakers. But Hahn points out two difficulties with this:

1) Contra v. 17, not all covenants required animal sacrifices—some involved only an oath. Hebrews is not making a general statement about all covenants.
2) Vv. 16–17 more naturally refer to the *actual* death of the people who make the covenant, not merely to a death symbolized in a ritual.[53]

Hahn suggests that these verses refer to a *broken* covenant—and v. 15b sets that context by referring to transgressions of the first covenant. "The purpose of vv. 16–17 is to explain *why a death* [i.e., of Jesus] *was necessary*."[54] I will summarize Hahn's view with an expansive paraphrase of vv. 15–18:

> Jesus is the mediator of a new covenant so that people can receive the promises, because a death has occurred to redeem them from the penalty that they deserved under the first covenant. Since[55] the transgressions occurred in the context of a covenant, the transgressors must die, for this covenant can be considered valid only if death is carried out on transgressors, since the covenant specified that death is the penalty for transgression. The covenant is not in force if it is not being enforced and transgressors are allowed to live. That is why the first covenant was inaugurated with blood—to symbolize the death of the

---

52. Hahn, "Covenant, Cult," 69.
53. Ibid., 430–31.
54. Ibid., 431, italics in original.
55. This takes ὅπου with the meaning "since" rather than "where." "Under different circumstances, . . . transgressions might have been inconsequential or given rise to some lesser punishment, but 'since there is a covenant' . . . entailing a curse of death for unfaithfulness—'the death of the covenant maker must be borne'" (ibid., 432).

covenant-breaker. But now, since the penalty has been carried out in Christ, who represented the people, the old covenant has no further claim, and he can make a new covenant.[56] In brief, people can receive the promises because a death has occurred to redeem them from the legal claims of the Mosaic covenant.

Hahn's proposal coheres well with my earlier conclusion that a covenant does not cease to exist when it is broken; rather, the penalties are invoked.[57] The covenant could not simply be *declared* obsolete— v. 15 indicates that the transgressions incurred legal consequences that had to be fulfilled. The purpose of the passage in Heb 9 is to defend the necessity of and the efficacy of the death of Jesus in terminating the old covenant and inaugurating the new—he had to die because the previous covenant required death for transgressions. This suggests that the covenant was viewed as a contract with detailed stipulations and consequences. However, the author does not view the new covenant in exactly the same way. Rather, he distinguishes between the nature of the Mosaic covenant and the new covenant, much as Paul did.

Hebrews 12:18–21 refers to the inauguration of the Sinaitic covenant, and characterizes Sinai as a place of fear and death. But the problem is not covenant *per se*, but the laws and punishments associated with Sinai. The new covenant has penalties, too, but in chapter 12 the author chooses to emphasize the blessings.

The New Covenant in Hebrews

Although Hebrews argues against the old covenant, it also uses the word *covenant* in a more positive way than Paul does. Hebrews 7:21–22 tells us that Jesus brought a better covenant, or a better hope. In what way is his covenant better? The author does not directly say; the argument of Heb 7 implies that the major benefit is that it allows people to approach God; this is something the readers presumably want.[58]

---

56. "Christ's death is simultaneously the legal execution of the curses of the old covenant and the liturgical ritual of sacrifice which establishes the new" (Hahn, "Covenant, Curse," 88).

57. See chapter 4, pages 94 and 103.

58. A covenant means that God offers a special relationship. But why should the people want it? In Hebrews, eternal life is an implicit benefit; the *stated* benefit is permission to be with God.

The author again says that the covenant is better in 8:6: "Jesus has now obtained a more excellent ministry, and to that degree he is the mediator of a better covenant, which has been enacted through better promises." The author implies that the previous covenant had some promises, but he does not say what they are, nor even how the new covenant is better. Instead, he is content to argue that the previous covenant was not faultless and that a new one was predicted (8:7). At this stage of the argument, it is apparently more important to remind the readers about the *prediction* of a new covenant, than to explain what the new covenant actually is. He quotes Jer 31:31–34 and proclaims the end of the old covenant (8:13). But he does not exegete Jer 31 or explain the new covenant.[59] He says nothing about the covenant formula or the blessing of knowing God, although these points could have encouraged his readers. Instead, he launches into a description of the old covenant (9:1–10).

After saying that Christ purifies the conscience and enables true worship (9:14), the author gives a purpose of the new covenant: "For this reason he is the mediator of a new covenant, *so that* those who are called may receive the promised eternal inheritance, because a death has occurred that redeems them from the transgressions under the first covenant" (9:15). The purpose of the new covenant is salvation, and this salvation is possible because Jesus' death redeemed people from the penalty of transgressions. The first covenant condemned because the people could not keep its laws; the new covenant redeems by the death of Christ and thereby enables people to receive the eternal inheritance. Because people transgressed the laws of the first covenant, it could not give anyone the promise.[60] But because Christ purifies the conscience (v. 14), forgiving sins, he brings a new covenant, and this new covenant enables people to approach God and inherit the promise. The burden of keeping the covenant has been shifted from the people, to the accomplished work of Christ. People can receive the inheritance because his death was efficacious.

---

59. Schunack notes, "Die Aussagen über die beiden *diathêkai* eigenartig unbestimmt bleiben. Die neue, bessere *diathêkê* ist nirgends *als solche* ein theologischer Begriff zur Charakterisierung des eschatologischen Heilsgeschehens" (*Der Hebräerbrief*, 100).

60. The author takes "the promised eternal inheritance" for granted as an assumption that his readers share; he does not attempt to connect it with either Moses or Abraham.

The first covenant had obligations that the people failed to fulfill; the new covenant has a gift of forgiveness. The author does not say whether the new covenant can be transgressed, but the strongly worded warning sections of Hebrews imply that it is possible for people to fail to receive the benefits of the new covenant.[61]

Hebrews presents *covenant* as a term for the readers' relationship with God—it is a word that can be used for the law-based Sinai covenant, or it can equally be used for the forgiveness-based new covenant. The author exhorts the readers away from a relationship based on laws, transgressions, guilt, human priests, and repetitious rituals; he exhorts them to have a relationship rooted in something Christ has done for them once for all. Because of what Christ has done, the laws are repealed, the transgressions are taken care of, the guilt is cleared, and the priests and rituals are obsolete. What the old covenant offered but could not deliver, the new covenant gives—and it gives more, since it supposedly has better promises.[62] It enables people to approach God by forgiving their sins and cleansing their consciences.

The next mention of covenant comes in chapter 10, where part of the Jer 31 passage is quoted again. In Heb 8, the author focused on the beginning of the quote, the mention of a "new" covenant. In chapter 10, he focuses on the end of the quote: forgiveness.[63] This may be one of

---

61. Rejecting the mediator, or actions that implied a rejection, apparently result in punishment, not blessing. The "penalties" of the new covenant do not seem to be in the new covenant itself; they are the results of not entering the covenant, or of exiting it.

62. The new covenant enables people to receive "the [previously] promised inheritance," but the author does not say whether any *additional* promises come with the new covenant.

63. He repeats the clause about laws being put in the heart, but he does nothing with the concept. Indeed, he has already argued that old covenant laws are set aside (7:18). As Lehne observes, Hebrews talks of a better covenant, better sacrifices, and better blood, "but nowhere do we hear of a 'new' or 'better' law" (*New Covenant*, 27). This is not because the law is exactly the same, but probably because the author does not want to discuss the role of law in the new covenant. Whereas the DSS version of the "new covenant" was an intensified version of the old, in Hebrews the new is quite different, with many elements typologically reinterpreted.

Hillers writes, "The Essenes had a covenant, but it was not new; the Christians had something new, but it was not a covenant [by that he means it was not like the Sinaitic]. That is to say, to call what Jesus brought a covenant is like calling conversion circumcision, or like saying that one keeps the Passover with unleavened bread of sincerity and truth. For Christians, the coming of the substance made shadows out of a rich array of Old Testament events, persons, and ideas, among them covenant" (*Covenant*, 188).

the "better promises."[64] Since sins are forgiven, sacrifices are no longer needed (10:18). The old covenant required many sacrifices; the new involved only one, and it has been accomplished once for all time.

After a lengthy contrast of old and new covenants in Heb 7–10, the author exhorts the readers to be confident that Christ has qualified them to approach God (10:18–23). This was apparently something the readers wanted from the covenant, and he argues that it cannot be obtained from the Mosaic covenant, but is guaranteed through the new.

Hebrews mentions covenant three more times, and these reveal a little more about the new covenant, although covenant is not the focus of subsequent passages. The author refers to "the blood of the covenant by which they were sanctified" (10:29).[65] He implies that the Mosaic covenant failed to sanctify the people, but the new covenant does it effectively, and it does it by the blood of Jesus. The covenant is a relationship between God and humans, and the intended result is that people can approach God.

Hebrews 12:24 mentions that Jesus is "the mediator of a new covenant"; this is again in the context of approaching God—and contrasted to the Sinaitic covenant. Sinai is characterized as a place of fear and death; the new covenant is characterized as a place of community, joy, and glory. The new covenant is again connected with blood: "and to the sprinkling of blood that speaks a better word than the blood of Abel" (12:24b). Son writes, "Abel's blood could not atone for Cain's sin but functions only as a reminder of his sin (Gen. 4:10-16), whereas Christ's blood cleanses the sins of worshippers and thus announces forgiveness and acceptance."[66]

However, it is not necessary to discard the concept of covenant when we remember that it could be dominated by promises, as the Abrahamic covenant was. Christiansen, who stresses continuity between old and new, nevertheless admits that in Hebrews "a grandiose reinterpretation has taken place" (*Covenant*, 228). The reinterpretation is so extensive that it is simpler to see it as a *new* covenant. As she says for Paul, "when God's covenant is thus reinterpreted, it becomes a different covenant" (ibid., 239).

64. Although forgiveness and freedom from a guilty conscience can be a blessing in itself, it might also be understood as simply removing the barrier that prevented access to greater promises.

65. Ellingworth notes, "Grammatically, the subject [of "sanctified"] could be the covenant; if so, this would not greatly affect the meaning, since the blood and the covenant are inseparable" (*Hebrews*, 541).

66. Son, *Zion Symbolism*, 101.

Hebrews' closing doxology refers to "the blood of the eternal covenant" (13:20). The author believes that the blood of Jesus is an important part (indeed, the part that makes it possible) of the new relationship that believers have with God through Jesus. Here again *covenant* is used as a positive term that summarizes the people's relationship with God; it was apparently a term that the readers valued.

The readers were apparently attracted to the old covenant, and the author takes the points in which the old covenant seemed attractive (such as having a priesthood and elaborate rituals), and responds that faith in Christ has all of these, only better. Traditional Jews said that they had a covenant with God, and the author responds by saying, 1) that covenant was ineffective, 2) God said he would replace it, 3) it is now obsolete, 4) believers have a better covenant through Christ, 5) it gives confidence instead of fear, 6) it gives forgiveness and sanctification instead of condemnation, and 7) it gives eternal life instead of death. If someone wants to approach God, he argues, Christ is the only means there is.

Obligations and condemnation were part of one covenant; forgiveness and privilege are part of the other. The word *covenant* could include either type of relationship, and the author characterizes the Sinai covenant negatively, as a relationship of fear, and the Christ covenant positively, as a relationship of privilege and boldness.

Conclusion

Hebrews is the only NT writing to use the covenant concept in an extended way, but even here the use seems to be primarily comparative, not developed in its own right. Nevertheless, the positive uses of the term in chapters 12 and 13 show that the writer is more comfortable with the term than Paul is.[67] The new covenant brings forgiveness and thereby allows access to God through a cult radically redefined and restructured by Christ. For Paul, writing to a largely Gentile audience, covenant was a concept for the past, or for comparing present with the

---

67. "In Hebrews the stress is on the new as foreshadowed in the old. The new covenant is better than the Sinai covenant, but it does not contradict it; it fulfills it and reveals its deepest meaning. In Paul, on the other hand, the two are contrasted so sharply that there is no apparent continuity left between the Sinai covenant and the new covenant in Christ, and the apostle has to reach back to the covenant with Abraham as an anticipation for his gospel, and has to elaborate the view that the Sinai covenant is only an episode, an interruption in the history of faith" (Hillers, *Covenant*, 182–83).

past. For Hebrews, designed for an audience attracted to the laws of Moses, covenant was still a useful concept even after the author explained that the Mosaic covenant had been replaced with a new and better covenant. The *community* connotations of covenant may have also been congenial to the author's desire that the readers remain in community (10:25).

Hebrews argues that the second covenant (the Christ covenant) has replaced[68] the first (the Mosaic covenant)—unlike Paul, who argued that a later covenant could *not* negate an earlier one (Gal 3:17). Why this difference? In both cases, the annulled covenant was a conditional covenant (dominated by laws). Since humans are imperfect, a conditional covenant can never be an effective means of salvation. Both Paul and Hebrews argue that the Sinaitic covenant was *designed* to be temporary, but they reach that conclusion by different means. Paul argues on principle: that the laws could not annul the Abrahamic promises; whereas Hebrews argues based on details: the old predicted its own demise, it has been legally terminated because of its ineffectiveness, legally fulfilled through the death of Jesus, and a new covenant begun. The two authors also differ on the reason for the permanence of the new covenant. For Paul, the new covenant is permanent because it is based on unconditional promises; in Hebrews, the new covenant is permanent because of its details: the sacrifice of Christ is effective and there can never be a better one.

A covenant based on promises is based only on God, and is therefore permanent. So Paul applies the Abrahamic promises to his Gentile

---

68. This is a supersession of a covenant and of worship rituals, not of peoples. The Abrahamic promises are retained, so the supersession is not complete. The word *supersession* means different things to different people and should not be used without stating *what* has been superseded. Some aspects of Second-Temple Judaism (e.g., animal sacrifices) have been superseded within Judaism itself, so using the word *supersession* without qualification paints with a rather indistinct brush (see Lincoln, *Hebrews*, 118, for a good discussion).

Johnson says "the proper sense" of supersessionism is "the replacement of Israel by Gentiles as God's people" (*Hebrews*, 33). But that definition involves a category mistake, for neither the OT nor the NT defines the people of God simply by ethnicity. "As we examine various polemical passages in Hebrews we need to ask what specifically is being superseded? Is the text arguing for the replacement of the Jewish people, or simply Jewish practices and institutions?" (Kim, *Polemic*, 7). "The author is not arguing for the abandonment by God of the Jewish people, but rather for the abandonment [by the readers] of the shadowy means by which God's people draw near to him" (ibid., 201). He was a Jew writing to Jews about the right way to follow the living God.

mission, implying that the new covenant of Christ is a development of the Abrahamic covenant. Hebrews does not call the Abrahamic promise a covenant,[69] but dismisses the Mosaic covenant by emphasizing Jeremiah's promise of a new covenant, particularly the forgiveness on which it is based, a forgiveness that eliminates the need for the rituals that dominated Mosaic covenant worship. Hebrews uses typology (e.g., blood) to point out similarities between the Mosaic covenant and the new, but does not attempt an exposition of what the new covenant entails. Although the readers liked the term *covenant*, other terms could convey the new focus (forgiveness) more clearly.

---

69. Although the author and the readers were no doubt *aware* that the Abrahamic promises were given as a covenant, it was apparently not an issue in their concern for approaching God. The "promise" taken for granted in 9:15 may be an allusion to the Abrahamic covenant, as it is in 6:13–15.

# 6

Conclusion

Role of the Covenant Motif in the Exhortations in Hebrews

ALTHOUGH HEBREWS HAS LONG EXPOSITORY SECTIONS, THEY SUPPORT a hortatory purpose. After each section of doctrinal explanation, the author writes, "Therefore, let us [do this, or do that; see table]." These exhortations, rather than being homiletic "applications" tacked on to the end of the expositions to give them a veneer of contemporary significance, are actually the primary purpose of the epistle, and the author has selected which texts to exposit based on his prior goal of exhorting the readers to be loyal to Christ and the community of believers. The epistle ends with exhortations, not with "I hope you understand these scriptures better now." The epistle was occasioned by an urgent situation, and the author writes in the hope that the epistle will effect a change in the readers' minds and lives.

Exhortations in Hebrews 1–12	
(negative exhortations are boldfaced)	
2:1	We must pay greater attention to what we have heard, **so we do not drift away from it.**
2:3	(implied) **We should not neglect so great a salvation.**
3:1	Consider that Jesus . . . was faithful to God.
3:6	(implied) We should hold firm the confidence . . . that belongs to hope.
3:8	**Do not harden your hearts as in the rebellion.**

153

Exhortations in Hebrews 1–12	
3:12	Take care that none of you may have an evil, unbelieving heart that turns away from God.
3:13	Exhort one another every day.
3:14	(implied) We should hold our first confidence firm to the end.
4:1	Let us take care **that none of you should fail to reach God's rest.**
4:11	Let us make every effort to enter his rest, **so that no one may fall through disobedience.**
4:14	Let us hold fast to our confession.
4:16	Let us approach the throne of grace with boldness.
5:9	(implied) Obey Jesus if you want salvation.
6:1	Let us go on toward perfection.
6:11	We want each one of you to show the same diligence (serving the saints) . . . to the very end, **so that you may not become sluggish.**
7:25	(implied) Approach God through Jesus if you want to be saved.
8:1	(implied) We should make use of the high priest we have.
9:28	(implied) Eagerly wait for Christ if you want him to save you.
10:22	Since we have a high priest, let us approach God in full assurance of faith.
10:23	Let us hold fast to the confession of our hope **without wavering.**
10:24	Let us consider how to provoke one another to love and good deeds, **not neglecting to meet together.**
10:35	**Do not abandon your confidence** (i.e., continue your previous behavior).
10:39	(implied) **Do not shrink back,** but have faith and thereby be saved.
11:6	(implied) We must have faith.
12:1	Let us lay aside every weight and sin; let us run with perseverance, looking to Jesus as the model. Consider (imitate) him **so that you may not grow weary.**
12:7	Endure trials for the sake of discipline; God is treating you as his children.
12:12	Lift your drooping hands and strengthen your weak knees.
12:15	**See to it that no one fails to obtain the grace of God.**
12:25	**See to it that you do not refuse the one who is speaking.**
12:28	Let us give thanks.

I summarize the book's exhortations in this way: *continue looking to Jesus as the means by which you approach God.* But this theme, starting with the very first exhortation (2:1), is paired with consistent warnings to avoid failure: Do not neglect, do not harden, do not fail, do not become sluggish, do not refuse—in other words, do not abandon your faith in Jesus. The readers *had* faith in Jesus, but there was a danger that they would not keep it. Something was vying for their allegiance, and the only alternative ever addressed in Hebrews is the old covenant. The author is not exhorting faith in Christ as an abstract notion—he is advocating faith in the context of a specific situation in the congregation, and he addresses that situation in part by comparing Christ with various aspects of the old covenant.

How does the covenant motif support the author's purpose?

In chapter 1 I showed that the readers were Jewish—at least culturally, and probably in ethnicity, too. In chapter 2 I showed that they were experiencing a crisis of faith, a crisis due to external pressures and a desire to worship God. In chapter 3 I showed that they had a prior allegiance to Jesus as the Christ, but were in danger of looking to the old covenant rather than to Jesus for forgiveness and salvation. The opponents were not simply using threats in order to enforce compliance—they were using the Jewish Scriptures to argue that the readers should seek atonement through the Levitical priesthood and rituals. In this situation, it was necessary for the author to base his argument on the Scriptures, using the Scriptures to show that certain aspects of the Scriptures were obsolete. Rather than showing that individual verses are obsolete, he argues that the entire Levitical package of laws is obsolete—and the biblical name for this package is a *covenant*.[1] He argues for allegiance to the Christ community not by denigrating the old covenant *community,* but by arguing against the efficacy of the old covenant rituals; this switch from rituals to community shows that he is thinking in terms a package that combines ritual and community together—in other words, one religious *system* as

---

1. Johnson summarizes some of this quite well: "The portrayal of Christ as a high priest . . . involves the apprehension of Judaism as a religious system. A network of interconnected premises runs through Hebrews' argument, especially in chapters 7–10. Among them are the convictions that God and God's people are bound by covenant (7:22; 8:6–13), that every covenant is explicated by laws (7:11–14), that among these laws are requirements concerning sacrifice (8:3–4) . . . . In Hebrews the cult of Israel serves as a sort of synecdoche for the covenant with God" (*Hebrews*, 25).

opposed to another. The label he uses for the religious systems, both old and new, is *covenant*.

In chapter 4, I argued that a biblical covenant is a relationship that could include varying mixtures of promise and obligation. An unconditional promise to an ancestor could be coupled with conditions placed upon individual descendants, who would then incorporate both aspects into the covenanted relationship. The covenant, as a relationship between living entities, could develop with various additions as new situations arose. Despite the flexibility permitted in a covenant, the Hebrew prophets predicted a *new* covenant rather than a restoration or modification of the old. This newness is made explicit in Jer 31:31, but is implicit in the other predictions of an eschatological covenant. Rather than saying that the people already had a secure covenant, the prophets said that an everlasting covenant *would be made,* involving a dramatic change in the faithfulness of the people. However, they did not give details for this new relationship, and the concept was for the most part dormant in the Second Temple period.

Jews in the Second Temple period often focused either on the promises given to Abraham or on the obligations given through Moses, but they usually spoke of covenant in the singular—the people had one relationship with God. However, the NT writers began to make a distinction, as I showed in chapter 5. By separating Abrahamic promises from Mosaic laws, and connecting salvation with the Abrahamic promises, they taught that salvation was available without any need to keep the laws of Moses—thus making salvation more accessible to Gentiles. As shown in their traditions of the Last Supper, they said that this expanded opportunity for salvation was a new covenant. However, since the word *covenant* was often associated with Jewish nationalism and Mosaic laws, other terminology (salvation, justification, grace, etc.) more effectively conveyed the nature of the new relationship; the word *covenant* was used primarily when advocates of the old covenant had introduced it into the debate. Paul was willing to use the word *covenant* for the new relationship with God when he was contrasting it with the old system, but once he had dismissed the old covenant, he abandoned the term and did not explain the new relationship under the rubric *covenant.*

There was an ambiguity in the term *covenant*—it could connote a gracious promise of salvation, or contract-like obligations of law, and whereas Jews had traditionally amalgamated these disparate aspects,

NT authors separated them. Hebrews treats the old covenant as a contract by stressing the penalties of the laws of Moses and the rituals that were prescribed by the law for transgressions. Hebrews has less to say about the new covenant, but stresses the promise of forgiveness found in Jer 31. The prophecy of a new covenant in Jer 31 gave the author a crucial, almost indispensable, step in the argument—rather than arguing law by law, he was able to argue more comprehensively, considering the entire package of laws together.

For example, suppose that the opponents claimed that sins can be atoned only through the rituals of Yom Kippur, which is a plausible argument for first-century Jews to make.[2] This would make Jesus soteriologically insignificant and require believers to be connected to a synagogue, which would be sociologically limiting. How could the author refute such a claim? He could observe, as he did, that Jesus has been raised to God's right hand, which implies that he was righteous. He could claim that Jesus had performed an efficacious sacrifice, which he does, but the opponents could easily respond that Scripture still requires the Levitical rituals.

The author could observe that Jesus has been appointed a priest according to the order of Melchizedek, thus invalidating the Levitical priesthood. The author makes this argument, and assumes that the readers will accept the logic. However, it is only a partial answer, because it does not address nonpriestly rituals, and Diaspora synagogues could function quite well without priestly rituals. For example, the law says that everyone must go without food and water on Yom Kippur, and opponents could still say—with biblical support—that atonement came only through observance of the day, which in their area would be done by fasting, and probably meeting together for readings from Lev 16. Besides, rituals can be observed even *after* their meaning has been fulfilled,[3] and the law of Moses still prescribes certain behavior on Yom Kippur. Such an argument is plausible, and the author could address it only by demonstrating that those laws are obsolete.

---

2. We should expect the author to address the strongest arguments of the opponents, but we should not expect him to repeat those arguments in their most forceful form.

3. For example, the week of unleavened bread was a ritual commemorating the haste with which the Israelites left Egypt, and the temporary shelters of Succoth were also rituals commemorating the past.

Covenant provides the crucial link between the priesthood and the rituals that involved the laity; covenant provides the umbrella term by which all the laws could be undercut simultaneously. Since Jeremiah predicted a new covenant, he implied the termination of the Mosaic covenant. The author thereby gains biblical evidence that the Mosaic covenant as a whole was ineffective and temporary; he does not have to show that each particular law is ineffective and has been terminated. At the end of his longest doctrinal section, he brings the covenant concept to bear on what is apparently the key point in the controversy: because a new covenant has been made, sin offerings are no longer necessary (Heb 10:18). Starting in 10:19, he draws hortatory conclusions from this point.

Covenant is a key element in the doctrinal argument—but what is its role in the subsequent exhortations? Here again, covenant provides a crucial link between the doctrinal argument and the behavior that the author wants to see in the readers. That is because he wants to do more than dissuade the readers from old covenant rituals; he wants to do more than persuade them to trust in the sacrifice of Christ for their atonement. What more does he want? He wants allegiance to the community of believers. The exhortations sometimes make the communal dimension explicit: "Take care that *none* of you . . . Exhort one another . . . so that *no one* may fall . . . We want you to serve the saints . . . Provoke one another to good deeds, not neglecting to meet together." This responsibility for mutual assistance is never addressed in the doctrinal arguments. Although the author does not make the connection explicit, the covenant motif helps bridge the gap between doctrine and exhortation in three ways:

1) "Covenant" implies a *group* of teachings, and just as the author did not have to refute every single law within the old covenant, he does not have to prove every single behavioral component of the new covenant. The readers are already familiar with the competing faiths as *systems*, as collections of beliefs and practices, and when the author refutes one system as ineffective, he is implicitly urging the readers to embrace the other system *in entirety*, including its behavioral expectations. Just as the old covenant was assumed by Diasporan Jews to include synagogue

attendance, the author assumes that the new covenant includes regular meetings and mutual exhortations among its adherents.

2) "Covenant" implies *the people of God*, a community. Jews in the Second Temple period, whether sectarian or not, assumed that "covenant" included a people who had relationships with one another. The author does not state this explicitly, but it seems to be the step by which he assumes that the new soteriological situation offered in Jesus also necessitated new sociological responsibilities for believers—duties so incumbent that the author implies that people who fail to meet together are persisting in grievous sin (Heb 10:25–27).

3) The frequent exhortations to avoid failure show that the author thought of the new covenant, like the old, more as a *contract* than an irrevocable relationship.[4] He says there is a punishment worse than death for people who once accepted the covenant but then refuse to follow through with its terms.[5] The author apparently expects the readers to view the covenant as a contract as well, and this helps explain the way that he reasons in the warning passages. If we refuse to comply with the obligations, he seems to say, the deal is off and we are worse off than when we started, so let us persevere because the reward is worth it. The contract has both carrot and stick.

In my introduction and in Appendix A, I note that the argument in Hebrews is cogent without any mention of covenant. This is true for the Christology (Jesus as high priest exalted to heaven) and for soteriology (he offered a sacrifice effective for salvation), but it falls short when it comes to the exhortations. In particular, it fails to explain why the existence of a Savior necessitates meeting together (10:19–25). The covenant is the comprehensive concept the author needs to bridge the gap between the readers' doctrinal questions and their behavioral patterns.

---

4. I do not agree with the author in this; I wish that he had said more about the way that God changes the heart so that people are faithful.

5. The duty to be loyal to a benefactor may also be explained in sociological terms, as part of an implied contract between patron and beneficiary (deSilva, *Perseverance*, 238–39, 355). Although the author would think that these social expectations supported his argument, the biblical concept of covenant is the style of argumentation he chose to use, because Scripture was viewed as the highest authority.

In chapter 2 I asked, What is wrong with being lethargic? What were the readers not doing, or what were they in danger of not doing, that prompted the author to write lengthy doctrinal expositions and strongly worded warnings? The most explicit danger is that they were in danger of forsaking the meetings. The meetings are not a means of salvation, but they are, in the author's view, an essential corollary of faith in Christ—part of the package, part of the covenant. Just as the author argued that if one law in the old covenant is obsolete, then the whole package is obsolete, he also seems to think that if this one part of the new covenant is neglected, the rest will surely follow. So, to forestall an attraction to the old covenant, the author found it necessary to argue that the old covenant is obsolete, superseded by another. This done, he assumes that the readers will then embrace the only alternative: allegiance to Christ, and along with that, allegiance to the community of people who believed in Christ. "Covenant" is the term that links doctrine and exhortation in the argument of Hebrews.

Appendix A

The Text of Hebrews with All References to Covenant Removed

THE ARGUMENT OF HEBREWS IS COHERENT AND COGENT WITHOUT ANY mention of covenant. With minor modifications, the argument can be restricted to the priesthood, as shown below with the NRSV text. A few sections and phrases can be deleted, as shown with strikeout, or modified, as shown in boldface.

7:1 This "King Melchizedek of Salem, priest of the Most High God, met Abraham as he was returning from defeating the kings and blessed him"; 2 and to him Abraham apportioned "one-tenth of everything." His name, in the first place, means "king of righteousness"; next he is also king of Salem, that is, "king of peace." 3 Without father, without mother, without genealogy, having neither beginning of days nor end of life, but resembling the Son of God, he remains a priest forever.

4 See how great he is! Even Abraham the patriarch gave him a tenth of the spoils. 5 And those descendants of Levi who receive the priestly office have a commandment in the law to collect tithes from the people, that is, from their kindred, though these also are descended from Abraham. 6 But this man, who does not belong to their ancestry, collected tithes from Abraham and blessed him who had received the promises. 7 It is beyond dispute that the inferior is blessed by the superior. 8 In the one case, tithes are received by those who are mortal; in the other, by one of whom it is testified that he lives. 9 One might even say that Levi himself, who receives tithes, paid tithes through Abraham, 10 for he was still in the loins of his ancestor when Melchizedek met him.

Now if perfection had been attainable through the levitical priesthood, ~~for the people received the law under this priesthood~~ what further need would there have been to speak of another priest arising according to the order of Melchizedek, rather than one according to the order of Aaron? 12 For when there is a change in the priesthood, there is necessarily a change in the law as well. 13 Now the one of whom these things are spoken belonged to another tribe, from which no one has ever served at the altar. 14 For it is evident that our Lord was descended from Judah, and in connection with that tribe Moses said nothing about priests.

15 It is even more obvious when another priest arises, resembling Melchizedek, 16 one who has become a priest, not through a legal requirement concerning physical descent, but through the power of an indestructible life. 17 For it is attested of him,

"You are a priest forever, according to the order of Melchizedek."

18 There is, on the one hand, the abrogation of an earlier commandment ~~because it was weak and ineffectual 19 (for the law made nothing perfect)~~; there is, on the other hand, the introduction of a better hope, through which we approach God.

20 This was confirmed with an oath; for others who became priests took their office without an oath, 21 but this one became a priest with an oath, because of the one who said to him, "The Lord has sworn and will not change his mind, 'You are a priest forever'" 22—accordingly Jesus has also become ~~the guarantee of a better covenant.~~ **a better high priest.**[1]

23 Furthermore, the former priests were many in number, because they were prevented by death from continuing in office; 24 but he holds his priesthood permanently, because he continues forever. 25 Consequently he is able for all time to save those who approach God through him, since he always lives to make intercession for them.

26 For it was fitting that we should have such a high priest, holy, blameless, undefiled, separated from sinners, and exalted above the heavens. 27 Unlike the other high priests, he has no need to offer sacrifices day after day, first for his own sins, and then for those of the people; this he did once for all when he of-

---

1. This conclusion works well in the context.

fered himself. 28 For the law appoints as high priests those who are subject to weakness, but the word of the oath, which came later than the law, appoints a Son who has been made perfect forever.

8:1 Now the main point in what we are saying is this: we have such a high priest, one who is seated at the right hand of the throne of the Majesty in the heavens, 2 a minister in the sanctuary and the true tent that the Lord, and not any mortal, has set up. 3 For every high priest is appointed to offer gifts and sacrifices; hence it is necessary for this priest also to have something to offer. 4 Now if he were on earth, he would not be a priest at all, since there are priests who offer gifts according to the law. 5 They offer worship in a sanctuary that is a sketch and shadow of the heavenly one; for Moses, when he was about to erect the tent, was warned, "See that you make everything according to the pattern that was shown you on the mountain." 6 But Jesus has now obtained a more excellent ministry, ~~and to that degree he is the mediator of a better covenant, which has been enacted through better promises. 7 For if that first covenant had been faultless,~~ ~~there would have been no need to look for a second one.~~

~~8 God finds fault with them when he says: "The days are surely coming, says the Lord, when I will establish a new covenant with the house of Israel and with the house of Judah; 9 not like the covenant that I made with their ancestors, on the day when I took them by the hand to lead them out of the land of Egypt; for they did not continue in my covenant, and so I had no concern for them, says the Lord. 10 This is the covenant that I will make with the house of Israel after those days, says the Lord: I will put my laws in their minds, and write them on their hearts, and I will be their God, and they shall be my people. 11 And they shall not teach one another or say to each other, 'Know the Lord,' for they shall all know me, from the least of them to the greatest. 12 For I will be merciful toward their iniquities, and I will remember their sins no more."~~

~~13 In speaking of "a new covenant," he has made the first one obsolete. And what is obsolete and growing old will soon disappear.~~

9:1 Now even the first ~~covenant~~ **priesthood** had regulations for worship and an earthly sanctuary. 2 For a tent was constructed, the first one, in which were the lampstand, the table, and the bread of the Presence; this is called the Holy Place. 3 Behind the second curtain was a tent called the Holy of Holies. 4 In it stood the golden altar of incense and the ark ~~of the covenant~~ overlaid on all sides with gold, in which there were a golden urn holding the manna, and Aaron's rod that budded, and the tablets ~~of the covenant~~; 5 above it were the cherubim of glory overshadowing the mercy seat. Of these things we cannot speak now in detail.

6 Such preparations having been made, the priests go continually into the first tent to carry out their ritual duties; 7 but only the high priest goes into the second, and he but once a year, and not without taking the blood that he offers for himself and for the sins committed unintentionally by the people. 8 By this the Holy Spirit indicates that the way into the sanctuary has not yet been disclosed as long as the first tent is still standing. 9 This is a symbol of the present time, during which gifts and sacrifices are offered that cannot perfect the conscience of the worshiper, 10 but deal only with food and drink and various baptisms, regulations for the body imposed until the time comes to set things right.

11 But when Christ came as a high priest of the good things that have come, then through the greater and perfect tent (not made with hands, that is, not of this creation), 12 he entered once for all into the Holy Place, not with the blood of goats and calves, but with his own blood, thus obtaining eternal redemption. 13 For if the blood of goats and bulls, with the sprinkling of the ashes of a heifer, sanctifies those who have been defiled so that their flesh is purified, 14 how much more will the blood of Christ, who through the eternal Spirit offered himself without blemish to God, purify our conscience from dead works to worship the living God!

15 For this reason he is **a better priest, for he offered a better sacrifice.** ~~the mediator of a new covenant, so that those who are called may receive the promised eternal inheritance, because a death has occurred that redeems them from the transgressions under the first covenant. 16 Where a will is involved, the death of the one who made it must be established. 17 For a will takes effect only at death, since it is not in force as long as the one who made it is alive. 18 Hence not even the first covenant was inaugurated~~

~~without blood. 19 For when every commandment had been told to all the people by Moses in accordance with the law, he took the blood of calves and goats, with water and scarlet wool and hyssop, and sprinkled both the scroll itself and all the people, 20 saying, "This is the blood of the covenant that God has ordained for you." 21 And in the same way he sprinkled with the blood both the tent and all the vessels used in worship. 22 Indeed,~~ under the law almost everything is purified with blood, and without the shedding of blood there is no forgiveness of sins.

23 Thus it was necessary for the sketches of the heavenly things to be purified with these rites, but the heavenly things themselves need better sacrifices than these. 24 For Christ did not enter a sanctuary made by human hands, a mere copy of the true one, but he entered into heaven itself, now to appear in the presence of God on our behalf. 25 Nor was it to offer himself again and again, as the high priest enters the Holy Place year after year with blood that is not his own; 26 for then he would have had to suffer again and again since the foundation of the world. But as it is, he has appeared once for all at the end of the age to remove sin by the sacrifice of himself. 27 And just as it is appointed for mortals to die once, and after that the judgment, 28 so Christ, having been offered once to bear the sins of many, will appear a second time, not to deal with sin, but to save those who are eagerly waiting for him.

10:1 Since the ~~law~~ **priesthood** has only a shadow of the good things to come and not the true form of these realities, it can never, by the same sacrifices that are continually offered year after year, make perfect those who approach. 2 Otherwise, would they not have ceased being offered, since the worshipers, cleansed once for all, would no longer have any consciousness of sin? 3 But in these sacrifices there is a reminder of sin year after year. 4 For it is impossible for the blood of bulls and goats to take away sins. 5 Consequently, when Christ came into the world, he said, "Sacrifices and offerings you have not desired, but a body you have prepared for me; 6 in burnt offerings and sin offerings you have taken no pleasure. 7 Then I said, 'See, God, I have come to do your will, O God' (in the scroll of the book it is written of me)."

8 When he said above, "You have neither desired nor taken pleasure in sacrifices and of-

ferings and burnt offerings and sin offerings" ~~(these are offered according to the law)~~, 9 then he added, "See, I have come to do your will." He abolishes the first in order to establish the second. 10 And it is by God's will that we have been sanctified through the offering of the body of Jesus Christ once for all.

11 And every priest stands day after day at his service, offering again and again the same sacrifices that can never take away sins. 12 But when Christ had offered for all time a single sacrifice for sins, "he sat down at the right hand of God," 13 and since then has been waiting "until his enemies would be made a footstool for his feet." 14 For by a single offering he has perfected for all time those who are sanctified. ~~15 And the Holy Spirit also testifies to us, for after saying, 16 "This is the covenant that I will make with them after those days, says the Lord: I will put my laws in their hearts, and I will write them on their minds," 17 he also adds, "I will remember their sins and their lawless deeds no more." 18 Where there is forgiveness of these, there is no longer any offering for sin.~~

19 Therefore, my friends, since we have confidence to enter the sanctuary by the blood of Jesus, 20 by the new and living way that he opened for us through the curtain (that is, through his flesh), 21 and since we have a great priest over the house of God, 22 let us approach with a true heart in full assurance of faith, with our hearts sprinkled clean from an evil conscience and our bodies washed with pure water. 23 Let us hold fast to the confession of our hope without wavering, for he who has promised is faithful. 24 And let us consider how to provoke one another to love and good deeds, 25 not neglecting to meet together, as is the habit of some, but encouraging one another, and all the more as you see the Day approaching.

26 For if we willfully persist in sin after having received the knowledge of the truth, there no longer remains a sacrifice for sins, 27 but a fearful prospect of judgment, and a fury of fire that will consume the adversaries. 28 Anyone who has violated the law of Moses dies without mercy "on the testimony of two or three witnesses." 29 How much worse punishment do you think will be deserved by those who have spurned the Son of God, profaned the blood of the covenant by which they were sanctified, and outraged the Spirit of grace? 30 For we know the one who

said, "Vengeance is mine, I will repay." And again, "The Lord will judge his people." 31 It is a fearful thing to fall into the hands of the living God.

32 But recall those earlier days when, after you had been enlightened, you endured a hard struggle with sufferings, 33 sometimes being publicly exposed to abuse and persecution, and sometimes being partners with those so treated. 34 For you had compassion for those who were in prison, and you cheerfully accepted the plundering of your possessions, knowing that you yourselves possessed something better and more lasting. 35 Do not, therefore, abandon that confidence of yours; it brings a great reward. 36 For you need endurance, so that when you have done the will of God, you may receive what was promised.

37 For yet "in a very little while, the one who is coming will come and will not delay; 38 but my righteous one will live by faith. My soul takes no pleasure in anyone who shrinks back."

39 But we are not among those who shrink back and so are lost, but among those who have faith and so are saved . . . .

(no changes in chapter 11)

12:1 Therefore, since we are surrounded by so great a cloud of witnesses, let us also lay aside every weight and the sin that clings so closely, and let us run with perseverance the race that is set before us, 2 looking to Jesus the pioneer and perfecter of our faith, who for the sake of the joy that was set before him endured the cross, disregarding its shame, and has taken his seat at the right hand of the throne of God.

3 Consider him who endured such hostility against himself from sinners, so that you may not grow weary or lose heart. 4 In your struggle against sin you have not yet resisted to the point of shedding your blood. 5 And you have forgotten the exhortation that addresses you as children—"My child, do not regard lightly the discipline of the Lord, or lose heart when you are punished by him; 6 for the Lord disciplines those whom he loves, and chastises every child whom he accepts."

7 Endure trials for the sake of discipline. God is treating you as children; for what child is there whom a parent does not discipline? 8 If you do not have that discipline in which all children share, then you are illegitimate and not his children. 9 Moreover, we had human parents to discipline us, and we respected them. Should we not

be even more willing to be subject to the Father of spirits and live? 10 For they disciplined us for a short time as seemed best to them, but he disciplines us for our good, in order that we may share his holiness. 11 Now, discipline always seems painful rather than pleasant at the time, but later it yields the peaceful fruit of righteousness to those who have been trained by it.

12 Therefore lift your drooping hands and strengthen your weak knees, 13 and make straight paths for your feet, so that what is lame may not be put out of joint, but rather be healed.

14 Pursue peace with everyone, and the holiness without which no one will see the Lord. 15 See to it that no one fails to obtain the grace of God; that no root of bitterness springs up and causes trouble, and through it many become defiled. 16 See to it that no one becomes like Esau, an immoral and godless person, who sold his birthright for a single meal. 17 You know that later, when he wanted to inherit the blessing, he was rejected, for he found no chance to repent, even though he sought the blessing with tears.

18 You have not come to **an imperfect priesthood and ineffective sacrifices that must be continually offered, and to a curtain that prevents your approach to God** ~~something that can be touched, a blazing fire, and darkness, and gloom, and a tempest, 19 and the sound of a trumpet, and a voice whose words made the hearers beg that not another word be spoken to them. 20 (For they could not endure the order that was given, "If even an animal touches the mountain, it shall be stoned to death." 21 Indeed, so terrifying was the sight that Moses said, "I tremble with fear.")~~ 22 But you have come to Mount Zion and to the city of the living God, the heavenly Jerusalem, and to innumerable angels in festal gathering, 23 and to the assembly of the firstborn who are enrolled in heaven, and to God the judge of all, and to the spirits of the righteous made perfect, 24 and to Jesus, ~~the mediator of a new covenant,~~ and to the sprinkled blood that speaks a better word than the blood of Abel.

25 See that you do not refuse the one who is speaking; for if they did not escape when they refused the one who warned them on earth, how much less will we escape if we reject the one who warns from heaven! 26 ~~At that time his voice shook the earth; but~~ now he has promised, "Yet

once more I will shake not only the earth but also the heaven." 27 This phrase, "Yet once more," indicates the removal of what is shaken—that is, created things—so that what cannot be shaken may remain. 28 Therefore, since we are receiving a kingdom that cannot be shaken, let us give thanks, by which we offer to God an acceptable worship with reverence and awe ; ~~29 for indeed our God is a consuming fire.~~

13:1 Let mutual love continue. 2 Do not neglect to show hospitality to strangers, for by doing that some have entertained angels without knowing it. 3 Remember those who are in prison, as though you were in prison with them; those who are being tortured, as though you yourselves were being tortured. 4 Let marriage be held in honor by all, and let the marriage bed be kept undefiled; for God will judge fornicators and adulterers. 5 Keep your lives free from the love of money, and be content with what you have; for he has said, "I will never leave you or forsake you." 6 So we can say with confidence, "The Lord is my helper; I will not be afraid. What can anyone do to me?"

7 Remember your leaders, those who spoke the word of God to you; consider the outcome of their way of life, and imitate their faith. 8 Jesus Christ is the same yesterday and today and forever. 9 Do not be carried away by all kinds of strange teachings; for it is well for the heart to be strengthened by grace, not by regulations about food, which have not benefited those who observe them. 10 We have an altar from which those who officiate in the tent have no right to eat. 11 For the bodies of those animals whose blood is brought into the sanctuary by the high priest as a sacrifice for sin are burned outside the camp. 12 Therefore Jesus also suffered outside the city gate in order to sanctify the people by his own blood. 13 Let us then go to him outside the camp and bear the abuse he endured. 14 For here we have no lasting city, but we are looking for the city that is to come. 15 Through him, then, let us continually offer a sacrifice of praise to God, that is, the fruit of lips that confess his name. 16 Do not neglect to do good and to share what you have, for such sacrifices are pleasing to God.

17 Obey your leaders and submit to them, for they are keeping watch over your souls and will give an account. Let them do this with joy and not with sighing—for that would be harmful to you.

18 Pray for us; we are sure that we have a clear conscience, desiring to act honorably in all things. 19 I urge you all the more to do this, so that I may be restored to you very soon.

20 Now may the God of peace, who brought back from the dead our Lord Jesus, the great shepherd of the sheep, ~~by the blood of the eternal covenant,~~ 21 make you complete in everything good so that you may do his will, working among us that which is pleasing in his sight, through Jesus Christ, to whom be the glory forever and ever. Amen.

Appendix B

The Rhetorical Genre of Hebrews

Aristotle described three types of rhetoric: judicial, deliberative, and epideictic. In general, these ask the audience to (respectively) decide about what someone did in the past, decide what the audience should do in the future, and praise a person or reinforce a value that the audience currently holds (*Rhet.* 1.3).[1] The genre often influences the style. Watson writes: "Epideictic usually employs amplification to stir emotion rather than arguments to effect proof. Deliberative chiefly relies upon ethos and examples and comparison of examples; whereas judicial is characterized by the use of enthymeme."[2]

How has Hebrews been evaluated in these categories? Watson reports that "Von Soden (1899: 11) proposed that Hebrews was judicial rhetoric," but this opinion has been abandoned.[3] Some modern commentators classify Hebrews as epideictic, and some as deliberative. This often reflects their view on the situation and purpose of Hebrews: If the audience is seen as simply lethargic, then Hebrews is epideictic, designed to strengthen their faith and keep them where they are. If the audience is drifting away and the readers need to change their behavior, then Hebrews is classified as deliberative. Pfitzner states that "Hebrews conforms more closely to epideictic oratory."[4] Seid "classifies Hebrews as a written speech of encomium (epideictic rhetoric) belonging to the genre

---

1. A concise summary is in Kennedy, *New Testament Interpretation*, 19–20.

2. Watson, *Invention, Arrangement, and Style*, 19. Kennedy gives this definition: "Epideictic is perhaps best regarded as including any discourse, oral or written, that does not aim at a specific action or decision but seeks to enhance knowledge, understanding, or belief" (*New Testament*, 45).

3. Watson, "Rhetorical Criticism," 182. Lane writes, "No one today would follow von Soden in identifying Hebrews with forensic rhetoric" (*Hebrews 1–8*, lxxvii).

4. Pfitzner, *Hebrews*, 21.

of *synkrisis*."[5] Aune and Witherington also call Hebrews epideictic.[6] On the other hand, "Nissilä . . . classifies Hebrews as a speech conforming to the conventions of ancient deliberative rhetoric . . . . Übelacker . . . also argues that Hebrews is deliberative rhetoric."[7] Garuti, Lindars, Lincoln, and Maxey also categorize Hebrews as deliberative.[8]

Several commentators choose both epideictic and deliberative. "Attridge argues that Hebrews is mainly an epideictic oration with some deliberative elements . . . . The purpose of Hebrews is to keep the audience faithful to the Jesus tradition and values and commitments."[9] "DeSilva . . . classifies the letter as deliberative rhetoric which relies upon epideictic rhetoric. Which species of rhetoric dominates depends in part upon the hearer."[10] Koester writes, "For listeners who remain committed to God and Christ, Hebrews is epideictic, since it maintains

5. Watson, "Rhetorical Criticism," 195.

6. Aune, *Literary Environment*, 212, and Witherington, *Letters and Homilies*, 44. In *Westminster Dictionary*, 212, Aune summarizes the views of Übelacker and Koester without giving a conclusion about rhetorical genre.

7. Watson, "Rhetorical Criticism," 182-83.

8. Garuti, *Alle origini dell'omiletica Cristiana*, 200; Lindars, "Rhetorical Structure," 383; Lincoln, *Hebrews*, 16; and Maxey, "Rhetoric of Response," 125. Garuti writes, "From the rhetorical point of view, Hebrews belongs to the deliberative kind: the audience is not invited to judge a person or to receive an encomium of a hero or a virtue. Much less it must judge the ability of the orator, which was often the case in epideictic speeches. The audience must instead decide about their behavior . . . the opportunity to join or continue in the new salvific economy" (*Alle origini*, 200, my translation).

Maxey writes, "Hebrews as a whole is deliberative rhetoric. Deliberatively, Hebrews is paraenetic discourse (παράκλησις) . . . . That Hebrews is paraenesis is established by the following: (1) the extensive use of exhortation/advice, both positive and negative (e.g. 2:1-4; 3-4); (2) the extensive use of historical examples and chreiai; (3) the call to imitate/not to imitate known examples (12:15-16; 13:7); (4) the presence of synkrisis or comparison (e.g. chs. 7-10); (5) the call to remember/not to forget particular information or the presence of familiar information (e.g. 10:32-24; 11:32-38; 12:4-6, 16-17), the presence of a virtue/vice list (ch. 13)" ("Rhetoric of Response," 125). He also argues that 10:32-12:13 is a deliberative "speech" embedded within Hebrews (ibid., 126-27, 455).

9. Watson, "Rhetorical Criticism," 183.

10. Ibid., 186. Stowers observes, "It is difficult to fit the literature of the hortatory tradition completely into either epideictic or deliberative, i.e., advising, rhetoric. When advice calls for a specific course of action it is deliberative; when it only seeks to increase adherence to a value or to cultivate a character trait it is epideictic" (*Letter Writing in Greco-Roman Antiquity*, 107). Since an audience could include some people who held the value and others who did not, the same exhortation could be epideictic to one and deliberative to the other.

the values they already hold. For those tending to drift away from the faith, Hebrews is deliberative, since it seeks to dissuade them from apostasy and move them toward a clearer faith commitment."[11] Thurén says, "Rhetorically the text can be divided into *epideictic* and *deliberative* passages."[12] Olbricht says: "Hebrews best conforms to the epideictic genre in its superstructure even though the body of the argument may be conceived as deliberative."[13]

A mixture of genres is not unusual. Aristotle advised people to praise (which is characteristic of epideictic) what they advocate (deliberative), and to advocate the praiseworthy.[14] *Rhetorica ad Herennium* notes that epideictic "is only seldom employed by itself independently," but epideictic praise is often used in sections of judicial and deliberative speeches.[15] Fairweather notes that "Chrysostom was familiar with the theory of what was known as 'figured' rhetoric, in which a positive delight was taken in the notion that discourse could simultaneously fulfil several functions."[16] Watson writes, "Quintilian makes it clear that the threefold division is arbitrary and there are numerous gradations of each of the three styles (12.10.66–68) . . . . All three species of rhetoric rely on the others, each often temporarily using the other."[17] Kennedy

---

11. Koester, *Hebrews*, 82.

12. Thurén, "New Testament Writings," 590. Isaacs writes, "Parts of its paraenetic sections could be classified as deliberative, since they are aimed at leading the readers to take some paths of action and to avoid others. In other respects, it conforms more closely to epideictic speech . . . in its exposition it largely seeks to reinforce already established Christian convictions" (*Hebrews and James*, 16).

13. Olbricht, "Hebrews as Amplification," 378. Buck says that Thurén has a similar approach: He "applies the elements of deliberative rhetoric to the body of the letter . . . while viewing the framework as epideictic" (Buck, "Rhetorical Arrangement," 80, n. 94).

14. "Praise and counsels have a common aspect; for what you might suggest in counseling becomes encomium by a change in the phrase. . . . Accordingly, if you desire to praise, look what you would suggest; if you desire to suggest, look what you would praise" (Aristotle, *Rhet.* 1.9.35–36; trans. J. H. Freese; online at http://www.perseus.tufts.edu/cgi-bin/ptext?doc=Perseus%3Atext%3A1999.01.0060&layout=&loc=1.9; accessed 2 Jan. 2008). Similarly, Quintilian writes that epideictic "has some similarities to deliberative oratory, because its subjects of praise are often the same as the subjects of advice in that type of speech" (*Inst.* 3.7.28 [Russell, LCL, 2:117]).

15. *Rhet. Her.* 3.8.15 (Caplan, LCL).

16. Fairweather, "Epistle to the Galatians," 6.

17. Watson, *Invention*, 10, 24 n. 225, citing *Rhet. ad Alex.* 5.1427b.31ff and Quint., *Inst.* 3.4.11, 16.

notes that "any one speech may involve deliberative, judicial, and epideictic elements."[18] Some orators would use one genre to accomplish the purpose of a different genre.[19] Lincoln writes that in Hebrews, the expository sections are epideictic, the hortatory sections are deliberative, and "the epideictic material is in fact in service of the deliberative."[20] Black writes,

> The distinction between judicial, deliberative, and epideictic discourse is not hard and fast. Quintilian (*Inst.* 3.4.16) admits that the lines between the different species of rhetoric are sometimes blurred: like judicial rhetoric, deliberative discourse often inquires about the past (ibid., 3.8.6), and both species are frequently colored by epideictic concerns (ibid., 3.7.28; 3.8.15). In both theory and practice, the identification of the species of rhetoric affords a relative, not an absolute, indication of the primary intentions of a speech.[21]

Several facts combine to suggest that categorizing Hebrews into a rhetorical genre is an exercise of dubious value:

- The three-part scheme was not designed to govern letters, didactic messages or religious discourse.
- The scheme was designed to guide the creation of messages by beginning orators, not to analyze the results.
- Genres were flexible, often mixed, and could be used outside of their primary purpose by skilled speakers.[22]
- The rhetoric of Hebrews may be influenced by Jewish synagogue speeches and may not fit into Greek styles of oratory. A homily of scripture exposition and exhortation, the most likely genre of Hebrews, simply does not fit into Aristotle's three categories.

---

18. Kennedy, *New Testament*, 45.
19. Ibid., 44.
20. Lincoln, *Hebrews*, 16.
21. Black, "Hellenistic Jewish and Early Christian Sermon," 5, n. 17.
22. "Greek rhetorical practice was, and always had been, more flexible than is suggested by the rigid divisions drawn by most ancient theorists, for the sake of pedagogic clarity, between the principal types of oration" (Fairweather, "Epistle to the Galatians," 23).

- The evident lack of agreement among scholars about the genre of Hebrews also suggests that it cannot be definitively categorized.[23]

Lane concludes, "Hebrews cannot be forced into the mold of a classical speech."[24] Guthrie says it well: "Hebrews is not easily categorized according to any one speech form of ancient Greek rhetoric.... While the speech forms in the classical handbooks were crafted in the judicial and political spheres, the book of Hebrews has the characteristics of the hellenistic synagogue homily. This form, while containing a wide range of rhetorical features described in the Greek handbooks, cannot be forced into the mold of a classical speech. Rather, the author's means of argument follow the rhetorical and exegetical skills of the rabbis."[25] And what Olbricht says about another epistle applies as well to Hebrews: "Must we force 1 Thessalonians into one of the categories, regardless? In the spirit of Aristotle, I think not; rather, we should add a genre."[26]

Part of the difficulty is that some scholars see the defining characteristic of deliberative to be "urging a change in behavior," and other scholars see the defining characteristic as "making a decision about a future action." To illustrate the difference, let us suppose a city assembly is meeting to decide whether to go to war—one speaker may advocate war (deliberative by everyone's definition) but another may argue for not going to war (deliberative by some definitions, epideictic by others since it advocates maintaining existing behavior). I believe that both speeches should be categorized as deliberative, for both have a similar purpose: to urge people to make a decision about future action.[27]

---

23. "The debate as to whether *Hebrews* represents deliberative or epideictic rhetoric shows, this author cannot so easily be pigeon-holed" (Gordon, *Hebrews*, 22). What Porter says about Philippians is true for Hebrews as well: "The wide diversity among those who treat the entire letter throws into serious question any claim that ancient rhetorical analysis can arrive at an objective estimation of structure.... This should make any interpreter cautious about claims made for rhetorical analysis" ("Paul of Tarsus," 61).

24. Lane, *Hebrews 1–8*, lxxix.

25. Guthrie, *Structure*, 32. Koester reports that Garuti also argues against classifying Hebrews ("Hebrews, Rhetoric," 104).

26. Olbricht, "Aristotelian Rhetorical Analysis," 225–26.

27. Lincoln writes, "Deliberative rhetoric is concerned with persuasion and dissuasion, urging the audience to take *or not to take* a particular course of action in the future" (*Hebrews*, 15, italics added).

Some scholars judge Hebrews to be epideictic because it urges the readers to remain faithful[28]; others judge it to be deliberative for the exact same reason. When two scholars can agree about the basic purpose of Hebrews and yet disagree about the rhetorical category, it seems that categorization serves no purpose.

Further, Kennedy admits, "In general, identification of genre is not a crucial factor in understanding how rhetoric actually works in units of the New Testament."[29] Sumney observes, "Since invention was versatile, identifying the rhetorical species is not as useful for helping us understand the flow of an argument as is identifying the stasis."[30] The purpose of a written work must be ascertained before a genre can be assigned; hence the genre is more of a label at the end of a process, rather than a help toward anything else.[31] As Classen says, "A term alone does not really assist one in understanding the letter's intention or any of its details."[32] Malina agrees: "To mark off a pattern still does not yield information about the meaning of the pattern."[33] Watson concludes, "Making Hebrews conform to the typical elements of arrangement now seems forced.... There is a move beyond simplistic labeling of a New Testament letter as one of the three rhetorical species. It is recognized that these letters are mixed letters, that is, they use all three species of rhetoric."[34] In summary, Hebrews should be analyzed on its own terms, not forced into a mold it may not fit, nor given a label that might artificially limit what the reader expects the text to say.

---

28. For example, Witherington: "This discourse is not about urging a change in direction or a new policy.... This act of persuasion is surely epideictic in character, appealing to the values and virtues that the audience has already embraced in the past" (*Letters and Homilies*, 44). But even someone who advocated a *change* in behavior would generally appeal to values and virtues the audience already held.

29. Kennedy, *New Testament*, 33.

30. Sumney, "Argument of Colossians," 339.

31. The structures suggested for each genre were suggestions, not formulas that must be followed. Hence ascertaining a genre is at best a vague hint about structure. Buck argues that since the author showed some freedom in the way he quoted the OT, he could be similarly creative with any use of Greco-Roman rhetorical patterns (Buck, "Rhetorical Arrangement," 95, n. 135).

32. Classen, *Rhetorical Criticism*, 23.

33. Malina, "Rhetorical Criticism," 97.

34. Watson, "Rhetorical Criticism," 187, 201.

Appendix C
Date of the Epistle

THE EPISTLE INCLUDES A FEW CLUES ABOUT THE DATE—BUT THEY ARE only clues, and commentators draw very different conclusions about it. An important clue is in 2:3: The gospel message "was attested to us by those who heard" the Lord. The church was taught by people who were contemporary with Jesus. Thus the letter could be as early as 10 years after Jesus died, or perhaps 60 years afterwards. Hebrews 12:4 suggests that no one in the community had been killed for the faith, which would not be true for Jerusalem after AD 50, or Rome after AD 64, but a later date would be possible if the epistle was written to another city. "There are various indications in Hebrews that some time had elapsed since the readers first became Christians," Ellingworth writes.[1] Most notably, they had grown lax, even though they had enough time to become teachers. This might have taken several decades, but it might have happened more quickly. None of the details "absolutely requires a time span of more than a few years."[2]

Hebrews 10:32 refers to a time of persecution some years before the epistle was written; this could refer to the edict of Claudius if the epistle was written to Rome,[3] but uncertainties about the location of the recipients weakens this argument. Heb 13:7 suggests that the original leaders (plural) have died, presumably of natural causes; which could happen as early as AD 60, or as late as 90.[4] The epistle mentions Timothy, and assuming that this is Paul's co-worker, we are again left with a range of dates from 60 to 90.[5] Ellingworth notes, "One firm piece of external evidence is that Hebrews was known to Clement of Rome,

1. Ellingworth, *Hebrews*, 30.
2. Ibid.
3. Koester, *Hebrews*, 52.
4. Ibid., 50.
5. Ibid.

whose authentic epistle is traditionally dated c. 96," but this does not narrow the range at all.[6]

The present-tense verbs used throughout the epistle for the Levitical sacrifices are *not* good evidence that sacrifices were still being performed.[7] For one, the author is not describing worship at the temple, but at the tabernacle, which had not existed for 1,000 years, so the present-tense verbs are anachronistic.[8] Also, Josephus uses present-tense verbs for temple rituals even after the temple had been destroyed.

However, there are other hints in Hebrews that *suggest* that sacrifices were still being offered. Ellingworth writes that if the author knew about the destruction of the temple, "it is difficult to believe that he would have stated that the old covenant was merely ἐγγὺς ἀφανισμοῦ (8:13), or that he would not have referred to the fall of Jerusalem."[9] Another piece of evidence is in Heb 10:2: "Otherwise, would [sacrifices] not have ceased being offered . . . ?"—an odd argument to make

---

6. Ellingworth, *Hebrews*, 29. However, he notes some uncertainties about the date of 1 Clement: "Recent studies . . . have raised serious doubts about whether there was a special persecution of Christians under Domitian, an event to which the phrase 'our recent series of unexpected misfortunes and set-backs' (*1 Clem.* 1.1) was assumed to refer" (ibid., 29–30, citing Welbourn, "On the Date of 1 Clement," 35–54).

7. Porter points out that Greek tenses do not always indicate time, and the present tense is often gnomic ("Date of the Composition," 299).

8. Koester suggests that the author might have referred to the tabernacle "because the Mosaic statutes concerning the Tabernacle constituted the divinely revealed basis for the sanctuary" (*Hebrews*, 52–53); he suggests that the author might have assumed that the destruction of the temple was permanent, since "it was not immediately clear that it would not be rebuilt" (ibid., 53). DeSilva writes, "I would disagree with those who claim that the author would not allude to the temple's destruction out of sensitivity for his (Jewish) hearers. He is so unsparing in his critique of the inefficacy of the levitical cultus and his affirmation of the obsolescence of Torah that it is hard to see how he could have made his sermon any more offensive by adding the destruction of the 'copy' and 'shadow' to his generally unappreciative assessment of the OT cult!" (*Perseverance*, 20–21). Nevertheless, it could be argued that the author did not use the destruction of the temple as a supporting point because he did not want his argument to be negated if the Jews ever reinstituted the sacrificial system.

9. Ellingworth, *Hebrews*, 32. Koester notes that "many recent scholars find that a pre-70 date best accounts for the references to persecution (10:32–34) and the absence of any reference to the destruction of the temple. Others prefer a date in the 80s or 90s, understanding the text to be dealing with the fatigue of second-generation Christians or a sense of loss over the destruction of Jerusalem" (*Hebrews*, 54). In general, scholars who prefer a diagnosis of fatigue prefer a later date, whereas those who see an attraction to the old covenant cultus prefer an earlier date.

if in fact they had ceased.¹⁰ The author also alludes to a functioning priesthood when he says that believers "have an altar from which those who officiate in the tent have no right to eat" (13:10). Although he puts the argument in terms of the long-gone tabernacle, he appears to be referring to priests who officiate in the temple, and it would be pointless to argue that non-existent persons could not partake of the new covenant altar.

The situation of the readers (as implied by arguments in the epistle) also provides evidence that the temple rituals were still being performed when the epistle was written. The only form of Judaism ever addressed in the epistle is a religion in which sacrifices are central—which implies that *a post-Temple Judaism, in which sacrifices have been de-emphasized and reinterpreted, is not yet an option for the readers.* There is no hint that any sort of rituals could be effective in the absence of actual sacrifices. Walker argues, "It is hard to see how a post-70 Judaism would have presented Hebrews' audience with such an alluring and hard-to-resist temptation."[11]

The urgency reflected in the epistle implies that the readers had recently experienced renewed pressures to abandon the Christ community and to look to the old covenant sacrifices for atonement, and a *sudden* increase in pressure is sociologically to be expected in the mid 60s, but less likely after 70. As nationalistic tensions rose in Judea in the 60s, there would be pressure not only in Palestine but also in the Diaspora for Jewish solidarity.[12] Jews who did not support Jewish traditions might be viewed as traitors. This would explain why the readers were facing a renewed threat of persecution after a time of relative toleration.[13]

This does not prove a pre-70 date for the epistle, but it seems to me that the arguments in the epistle would be more appropriate *before*

---

10. "The question expects that listeners will agree with the author, instead of pointing out that sacrifices have in fact ceased" (Koester, *Hebrews*, 53).

11. Walker, "Jerusalem in Hebrews 13:9–14," 60.

12. "The Jews were putting pressure on Christian Jews to show their loyalty and solidarity with the nation and their support for the holy city and temple by participating in festive meals" (Young, "Bearing His Reproach," 251).

13. This might also explain why the author has focused his argument on the tabernacle: In the 60s, any denigration of the temple would be viewed as treason (ibid.); the mere mention of the temple might risk setting off emotions that would distract people from the real subject of the epistle. This would be true to a lesser extent after AD 70 as well.

the destruction of the temple than after. But for my purposes, this is an inconsequential conclusion, since the date does not affect the meaning of the epistle, nor the role of the covenant motif. Rather, the meaning of the epistle is analyzed first, and then that becomes the basis for ascertaining the date. Since I am not basing any conclusions on the date of the epistle, I have kept this discussion in an appendix, and I have not attempted a more comprehensive discussion, nor a detailed response to all the arguments used in favor of a later date.

Appendix D

Translation Irregularities of בְּרִית and Διαθήκη

Of the 284 occurrences of בְּרִית in the MT, about 96 percent are rendered as διαθήκη in the LXX.[1] Table 1 shows the exceptions. Table 2 shows verses in which διαθήκη appears in the LXX without having any counterpart in the MT. Table 3 lists verses in which διαθήκη corresponds to a different Hebrew word. Table 4 shows verses in the Apocrypha, which is not in the MT, although in some cases a Hebrew text is extant.

Table 1

Verses in Which בְּרִית Is Not Translated as Διαθήκη

	NRSV translation of MT; the word corresponding to בְּרִית is in italics	NETS Translation of LXX[a]
Gen 14:13	Then one who had escaped came and told Abram the Hebrew, who was living by the oaks of Mamre the Amorite, brother of Eshcol and of Aner; these were *allies* of Abram.	And one of those who had been rescued, when he arrived, told Abram the emigrant. Now he, Amoris, used to live near the oak of Mambre, the brother of Eschol and brother of Aunan, who were confederates [συν–ωμόται] of Abram.

---

1. Based on a comparison of two concordances: Kohlenberger and Swanson, *Hebrew-English Concordance to the Old Testament*, and Hatch and Redpath, *Concordance to the Septuagint*.

Deut 9:15	So I turned and went down from the mountain, while the mountain was ablaze; the two tablets of the *covenant* were in my two hands.	And after I had turned, I went down from the mountain, and the mountain was burning with fire; and the two tablets [A text has μαρτυρίων—of the testimonies; Rahlfs and NETS omit the phrase] were in my two hands.
Judg 8:33	As soon as Gideon died, the Israelites relapsed and prostituted themselves with the Baals, making Baal-*berith* their god.	And it came about even as Gedeon died that the sons of Israel turned around and prostituted themselves after the Baalim, and they made a *covenant* [διαθήκη] for themselves with Baal[b] that he should be for a god to them.
Judg 9:4	They gave him seventy pieces of silver out of the temple of Baal-*berith* with which Abimelech hired worthless and reckless fellows, who followed him.	And they gave him seventy pieces of silver out of the house of Baal-Berith,[c] and Abimelech hired himself vain and cowardly fellows, and they walked after him.
Judg 9:46	When all the lords of the Tower of Shechem heard of it, they entered the stronghold of the temple of El-*berith*.	And all the men of the towers of Sychem heard of it, and gathered to the assembly-place at Baithel-Berith.[d]
2 Kings 17:15/4 Kgdms 17:15	They despised his statutes, and his *covenant* that he made with their ancestors, and the warnings that he gave them. They went after false idols and became false; they followed the nations that were around them, concerning whom the LORD had commanded them that they should not do as they did.	[The LXX does not have text corresponding to the MT *covenant*] And his testimonies that he testified to them they did not keep but went after the worthless things and were rendered worthless and after the nations that were around them of whom he had commanded them not to do in accordance with these.

2 Chr 16:3	Let there be an *alliance* between me and you, like that between my father and your father; I am sending to you silver and gold; go, break your *alliance* with King Baasha of Israel, so that he may withdraw from me.	Make a covenant [διαθήκη] between me and you and between my father and between your father. See, I have sent you gold and silver. Come, and shake off from me Baasa, king of Israel [no mention of covenant in this part], and let him withdraw from me.
2 Chr 23:1	But in the seventh year Jehoiada took courage, and entered into a *compact* with the commanders of the hundreds, Azariah son of Jeroham, Ishmael son of Jehohanan, Azariah son of Obed, Maaseiah son of Adaiah, and Elishaphat son of Zichri.	And in the seventh year Iodae gained strength and took the officers of hundreds, Azarias son of Ioram and Ismael son of Ioanan and Azarias son of Obed and Maasaias son of Adaias and Elisaphas son of Zacharias, with him into a house.[e]
Jer 11:8	Yet they did not obey or incline their ear, but everyone walked in the stubbornness of an evil will. So I brought upon them all the words of this *covenant,* which I commanded them to do, but they did not.	V. 7 and most of v. 8 are not in the LXX. Only the final words of v. 8 are represented: And they did not.

184   APPENDIX D

Jer 33:20 (2)	Thus says the LORD: If any of you could break my *covenant* with the day and my *covenant* with the night, so that day and night would not come at their appointed time,	
Jer 33:21	only then could my *covenant* with my servant David be broken, so that he would not have a son to reign on his throne, and my covenant with my ministers the Levites.	Jer 33:1–13 in the MT corresponds to Jer 40:1–13 in the LXX, but there is no text in the LXX corresponding to Jer 33:14–26 in the MT.
Jer 33:25	Thus says the LORD: Only if I had not established my *covenant* with day and night and the ordinances of heaven and earth,	
Ezek 20:37	I will make you pass under the staff, and will bring you within the bond of the *covenant*.	And I will drive you under my rod and bring you in by number.[f]

a. Translations are from Pietersma and Wright, eds., *New English Translation of the Septuagint*. Genesis translated by Robert J. V. Hiebert, Exodus by Larry J. Perkins, Leviticus by Dirk L. Büchner, Numbers by Peter W. Flint, Deuteronomy by Melvin K. H. Peters, Judges by Philip E. Satterthwaite, 1–2 Samuel and 1 Kings by Bernard A. Taylor, 2 Kings by Paul D. McLean, 2 Chronicles by S. Peter Cowe, Isaiah by Moisés Silva, Jeremiah by Albert Pietersma and Marc Saunders, Ezekiel by J. Noel Hubler, Daniel by R. Timothy McLay, and Zechariah by George E. Howard.

b. B text; the A text has "made for themselves *Baal-Berith* for a covenant that he should be . . . ."

c. B text; the A text has Βάαλ διαθήκης, Baal-of-Covenant.

d. B text; the A text has οἴκου τοῦ Βάαλ διαθήκης, the house of Baal-of-Covenant.

e. The translators apparently read בבית (into a house) where the MT has בברית (into a covenant) (Dillard, *2 Chronicles*, 177).

f. "The omission of 'the covenant' in LXX is as likely to be due to haplography as to dittography in MT" (Allen, *Ezekiel 20–48*, 4).

In about half of the above "exceptions," the word διαθήκη is absent simply because that portion of the MT has no counterpart in the LXX. The other irregularities do not fall in a pattern; there is no evidence of any reluctance to identify בְּרִית with διαθήκη.

Table 2

Verses in Which Διαθήκη in the LXX Has No Corresponding Word in the MT[2]

Exod 23:22	But if you listen attentively to his [the angel's] voice and do all that I say, [no corresponding text in MT; the LXX additions are a pastiche of other texts] then I will be an enemy to your enemies and a foe to your foes.	If by paying attention you listen to my voice and do all that I tell you,[g] I will be an enemy to your enemies and will resist those who resist you.
Num 25:12	Therefore say, "I hereby grant him my covenant of peace."	Thus I said, "Behold, I am giving him a covenant of peace."[h]
Deut 29:27/26	The anger of the LORD was kindled against that land, bringing on it every curse written in this book.	And the Lord became angry with wrath against that land, to bring on it according to all the curses [the A text adds "of the covenant"] written in this book.
Isa 49:6	He says, "It is too light a thing that you should be my servant to raise up the tribes of Jacob and to restore the survivors of Israel; I will give you as a light to the nations, that my salvation may reach to the end of the earth."	And he said to me, "It is a great thing for you to be called my servant so that you may set up the tribes of Iakob and turn back the dispersion of Israel. See, I have[i] made you a light of nations, that you may be for salvation to the end of the earth.

    g. Rahlfs includes a lengthy insertion at this point, a pastiche of biblical phrases, which Brenton translates: "and keep my *covenant*, you will be to me a peculiar people above all nations, for the whole earth is mine; and you will be to me a royal priesthood, and a holy nation: these words you shall speak to the children of Israel, If you will indeed hear my voice, and do all the things I will tell you" (Brenton, *Septuagint with Apocrypha*, 100–101).

    h. The A text has covenant twice: "my covenant, a covenant of peace."

    i. Rahlfs follows the B text, which copies a phrase from Isa 42:6 and 49:8: given you for a *covenant* of a people.

    2. In 19 verses, the LXX specifies "ark *of the covenant*" when the MT merely has "ark." These uses of διαθήκη are semantically unimportant, since they are in a phrase found within the MT as well (Exod 25:15; Josh 3:13, 15 (2); 4:10, 11, 16; 6:8/9, 11, 12, 13; 24:33, 1 Sam/1 Kgdms 5:4; 6:3, 18; 7:1 (2), 2 Sam/2 Kgdms 6:10, 1 Kings/3 Kgdms 2:26, 1 Chr 15:27; 16:4).

These occurrences of διαθήκη are semantically insignificant, since they repeat phrases found elsewhere in the MT. Isa 49:6 is noteworthy in that it repeats the otherwise unique idea that a person could be a covenant.

Table 3

LXX Verses in Which Διαθήκη *Corresponds to a Word Other Than* בְּרִית

Exod 27:21a	In the tent of meeting, outside the curtain that is before the covenant [עֵדֻת],[j] Aaron and his sons shall tend it from evening to morning before the LORD.	In the tent of witness outside of the veil that is over the *covenant*, Aaron and his sons shall burn it from evening until morning before the Lord. This is a perpetual precept for your descendants from the sons of Israel.
Exod 31:7	the tent of meeting, and the ark of the covenant [עֵדֻת], and the mercy seat that is on it, and all the furnishings of the tent,	the tent of witness and the ark of the covenant and the propitiatory that is on it and the furnishings of the tent
Exod 39:35/ LXX 39:15	the ark of the covenant [עֵדֻת] with its poles and the mercy seat;	And the ark of the covenant and its staves
Lev 26:11	I will place my dwelling [מִשְׁכָּנִי] in your midst, and I shall not abhor you.	And I will place my tent[k] among you, and my soul shall not abhor you.
Deut 9:5	It is not because of your righteousness or the uprightness of your heart that you are going in to occupy their land; but because of the wickedness of these nations the LORD your God is dispossessing them before you, in order to fulfill the promise [דָּבָר] that the LORD made on oath to your ancestors, to Abraham, to Isaac, and to Jacob.	It is not because of your righteousness or the holiness of your heart that you are going in to inherit their land, but because of the impiety of these nations the Lord will destroy them utterly before you, and in order that he may uphold the *covenant* that the Lord swore to your fathers, to Abraam and Isaak and Iakob.

Deut 29:20	The LORD will be unwilling to pardon them, for the LORD's anger and passion will smoke against them. All the curses written in this book [בַּסֵּפֶר] will descend on them, and the LORD will blot out their names from under heaven.	God will not want to pardon him, but the Lord's anger and his zeal will then blaze out against that person. And all the imprecations of this *covenant*, written in the book of this law will attach themselves to him, and the Lord will blot out his name from the earth beneath the sky.
1 Sam/1 Kgdms 11:2	But Nahash the Ammonite said to them, "On this condition I will make a treaty [אֶכְרוֹת]ˡ with you, namely that I gouge out everyone's right eye, and thus put disgrace upon all Israel."	And Naas the Ammanite said to them, "By this I will make a *covenant* with you, by gouging out of you every right eye, and I will put disgrace upon Israel."
1 Sam/1 Kgdms 22:8	"Is that why all of you have conspired against me? No one discloses to me when my son makes a league [כְרָת]ᵐ with the son of Jesse, none of you is sorry for me or discloses to me that my son has stirred up my servant against me, to lie in wait, as he is doing today."	For you are all in collusion against me, and there is no one who uncovers my ear when my son makes a *covenant* with the son of Iessai, and there is no one of you who feels sorry for me or uncovers my ear because my son stirred up my slave against me as an enemy, as this day.
2 Sam/2 Kgdms 10:19	When all the kings who were servants of Hadadezer saw that they had been defeated by Israel, they made peace [שָׁלֵם] with Israel, and became subject to them. So the Arameans were afraid to help the Ammonites any more.	And all the kings who were slaves of Hadraazar saw that they stumbled before Israel, and they deserted to Israel [B2 text says και διέθεντο διαθήκην], and became subject to them. And Syria was afraid to save the sons of Ammon again.
1 Kings/3 Kgdms 8:9	There was nothing in the ark except the two tablets of stone that Moses had placed there at Horeb, where the LORD made a covenant [כָּרַת] with the Israelites, when they came out of the land of Egypt.	There was nothing in the ark except the two stone tablets, tablets *of the covenant*, that Moyses had placed there at Choreb—which things the Lord arranged with the sons of Israel, when they came out of the land of Egypt.

2 Kings/4 Kgdms 11:4	But in the seventh year Jehoiada summoned the captains of the Carites and of the guards and had them come to him in the house of the LORD. He made a covenant [בְּרִית] with them and put them under oath in the house of the LORD; then he showed them the king's son.	And in the seventh year Iodae the priest sent and took the commanders of hundreds, Chorri and Rasim, and brought them to him into the Lord's house. And he made a *covenant* of the Lord with them and made them swear in the sight of the Lord; and Iodae showed them the son of the king.
2 Chr 25:4a	But he did not put their children to death, according to what is written [כָּתַב] in the law, in the book of Moses, where the LORD commanded,	And he did not kill their sons according to the *covenant* of the Lord's law, as it is written, as the Lord commanded,
2 Chr 29:10	Now it is in my heart to make a covenant [בְּרִית] with the LORD, the God of Israel, so that his fierce anger may turn away from us.	As a result of these things, it is now in my heart to make a *covenant* [Brenton's text has διαθήκην μου, διαθήκην Κυρίου] with the Lord, God of Israel, and he will turn the anger of his wrath from us.
Jer 34:16/ LXX 41:16	but then you turned around and profaned my name when each of you took back your male and female slaves, whom you had set free according to their desire, and you brought them again into subjection to be your slaves.	And you turned and profaned my name [A text has τὴν διαθήκη] when each of you turned back his male servant and each his female servant, whom you had sent off free, for their own self, as male and female servants for you.
Ezek 16:29	You multiplied your whoring [תַּזְנוּת] with Chaldea, the land of merchants; and even with this you were not satisfied.	And you multiplied your *covenants*[n] with the land of the Chaldeans, and you were not even satisfied with them.

Dan 9:13	Just as it is written in the law [תּוֹרַת] of Moses, all this calamity has come upon us. We did not entreat the favor of the LORD our God, turning from our iniquities and reflecting on his fidelity.	According to what is written in the *covenant* of Moyses, all the evils have come upon us. And we did not seek the face of the Lord our God, to turn away from our sins and to consider your righteousness, O Lord.º
Dan 9:27a	"He shall make a strong covenant [בְּרִית] with many for one week, and for half of the week he shall make sacrifice and offering cease."	And the *covenant* will prevail for many and it will return again and be rebuilt broad and long. And at the consummation of times . . . . [text uncertain] And in half of the week the sacrifice and the libation will cease.ᵖ
Zech 11:14	Then I broke my second staff Unity, annulling the family ties [אַחֲוָה] between Judah and Israel.	And I cast away the second rod, Line, to disband the tie [A text has διαθήκην μου] between Ioudas and between Israel.ᑫ

j. עֵדוּת is usually translated "testimony"; in 31:7 and 39:35/15, "ark of the testimony" is a variant name of the ark of the covenant. The LXX, like the NRSV, has standardized the terminology. Goldingay includes עֵדוּת in his dictionary article ("Covenant," especially 771, 776–77).

k. Some texts, including Rahlfs, have τὴν διαθήκην.

l. Literally, "I will cut"; "treaty" is understood from the previous verse, "cut a covenant [בְּרִית]." The LXX word διαθήκη is technically an addition, but clearly corresponds to the Hebrew בְּרִית.

m. "Covenant" is again understood from the use of "cut"; the phrase "cut a covenant" was used in 1 Sam 18:3.

n. For the functional equivalence of "whoring" and "making a covenant," see the LXX of Judg 8:33.

o. The Old Greek version has "covenant"; Theodotion has "law," like the MT.

p. This is the Old Greek version; some Greek texts are longer, repeating part of the verse, including the word διαθήκην. Montgomery says that the duplicated words in some copies have come from a marginal note—perhaps an alternate translation of the obscure Hebrew text (*Commentary on Daniel*, 402–3).

q. The use of διαθήκη may have been influenced by v. 10: breaking the first staff annulled a covenant.

These verses do not add anything to our understanding of the concept of the covenant in the Second Temple period, but they do illustrate the importance of the concept at the time, in that the translators inserted the concept in places where it was not originally present.

Some translators (or copyists of variant Hebrew texts) implied that the covenant was equivalent to God's presence (Lev 26:11), equivalent to the promise given to the patriarchs (Deut 9:5), and equivalent to what is written in the book (Deut 29:20; 2 Chron 25:4; Dan 9:13). Such substitutions were rare, but still show the importance of the word διαθήκη. Just as in the Hebrew text, διαθήκη can be used for secular agreements as well (2 Sam 10:19; Ezek 16:29).

Table 4
Uses of Διαθήκη in LXX Books Not in the MT

Bar 2:35	"I will make an everlasting *covenant* with them to be their God and they shall be my people; and I will never again remove my people Israel from the land that I have given them."
Daniel 3:34/ Pr Azar 1:11	For your name's sake do not give us up forever, and do not annul your *covenant*.
1 Macc 1:11	In those days certain renegades came out from Israel and misled many, saying, "Let us go and make a *covenant* with the Gentiles around us, for since we separated from them many disasters have come upon us."
1 Macc 1:15	and removed the marks of circumcision, and abandoned the holy *covenant*. They joined with the Gentiles and sold themselves to do evil.
1 Macc 1:57	Anyone found possessing the book of the *covenant*, or anyone who adhered to the law, was condemned to death by decree of the king.
1 Macc 1:63	They chose to die rather than to be defiled by food or to profane the holy *covenant*; and they did die.
1 Macc 2:20	I and my sons and my brothers will continue to live by the *covenant* of our ancestors.
1 Macc 2:27	Then Mattathias cried out in the town with a loud voice, saying: "Let every one who is zealous for the law and supports the *covenant* come out with me!"
1 Macc 2:50	Now, my children, show zeal for the law, and give your lives for the *covenant* of our ancestors.
1 Macc 2:54	Phinehas our ancestor, because he was deeply zealous, received the *covenant* of everlasting priesthood.

1 Macc 4:10	And now, let us cry to Heaven, to see whether he will favor us and remember his *covenant* with our ancestors and crush this army before us today.
1 Macc 11:9	He sent envoys to King Demetrius, saying, "Come, let us make a *covenant* with each other, and I will give you in marriage my daughter who was Alexander's wife, and you shall reign over your father's kingdom."
2 Macc 1:2	May God do good to you, and may he remember his *covenant* with Abraham and Isaac and Jacob, his faithful servants.
2 Macc 7:36	For our brothers after enduring a brief suffering have drunk of ever-flowing life, under God's *covenant*; but you, by the judgment of God, will receive just punishment for your arrogance.
2 Macc 8:15	if not for their own sake, then for the sake of the *covenants* made with their ancestors, and because he had called them by his holy and glorious name.
Sir 11:20	Stand by your *agreement* [חוק]ʳ and attend to it, and grow old in your work.
Sir 14:12	Remember that death does not tarry, and the *decree* [חוק] of Hades has not been shown to you.
Sir 14:17	All living beings become old like a garment, for the *decree* [חוק] from of old is, "You must die!"
Sir 16:22	Who is to announce his acts of justice? Or who can await them? For his *decree* [חוק] is far off.
Sir 17:12	He established with them an eternal *covenant,* and revealed to them his decrees.
Sir 24:23	All this is the book of the *covenant* of the Most High God, the law that Moses commanded us as an inheritance for the congregations of Jacob.
Sir 28:7	Remember the commandments, and do not be angry with your neighbor; remember the *covenant* of the Most High, and overlook faults.
Sir 38:33	They do not sit in the judge's seat, nor do they understand the *decisions* [διαθήκην] of the courts [κρίματος]; they cannot expound discipline or judgment, and they are not found among the rulers.

Sir 39:8	He will show the wisdom of what he has learned, and will glory in the law of the Lord's *covenant*.
Sir 41:19	[Be ashamed] of theft, in the place where you live. Be ashamed of breaking an oath or *agreement* [בְּרִית], and of leaning on your elbow at meals; of surliness in receiving or giving,
Sir 42:2	Do not be ashamed of the law of the Most High and his *covenant* [חֹק], and of rendering judgment to acquit the ungodly;
Sir 44:11	their wealth will remain with their descendants, and their inheritance with their children's children [εον ταῖς διαθήκαις].[s]
Sir 44:18	Everlasting *covenants* were made with him [Noah] that all flesh should never again be blotted out by a flood.
Sir 44:20 (2)	He [Abraham] kept the law of the Most High, and entered into a *covenant* [בְּרִית] with him; he certified the *covenant* [חֹק] in his flesh [i.e., was circumcised], and when he was tested he proved faithful.
Sir 44:22	To Isaac also he gave the same assurance for the sake of his father Abraham. The blessing of all people and the *covenant* [בְּרִית] he made to rest on the head of Jacob.
Sir 45:5	He allowed him [Moses] to hear his voice, and led him into the dark cloud, and gave him the commandments face to face, the law of life and knowledge, so that he might teach Jacob the *covenant* [חֹק], and Israel his decrees.
Sir 45:7	He made an everlasting covenant [חֹק] with him [Aaron], and gave him the priesthood of the people. He blessed him with stateliness, and put a glorious robe on him.
Sir 45:15	Moses ordained him, and anointed him with holy oil; it was an everlasting covenant [בְּרִית] for him and for his descendants as long as the heavens endure, to minister to the Lord and serve as priest and bless his people in his name.
Sir 45:17	In his commandments he gave him authority and statutes [חוּק] and judgments [εον διαθήκαις κριμάτων; cf. 38:33], to teach Jacob the testimonies, and to enlighten Israel with his law.
Sir 45:24	Therefore a covenant [חֹק] of friendship was established with him [Phineas], that he should be leader of the sanctuary and of his people, that he and his descendants should have the dignity of the priesthood forever.

Sir 45:25	Just as a covenant [בְּרִית] was established with David son of Jesse of the tribe of Judah, that the king's heritage passes only from son to son, so the heritage of Aaron is for his descendants alone.
Sir 47:11	The Lord took away his sins, and exalted his power forever; he gave him [David] a covenant [חוֹק] of kingship and a glorious throne in Israel.
Wis 18:22	He conquered the wrath not by strength of body, not by force of arms, but by his word he subdued the avenger, appealing to the oaths and covenants given to our ancestors.ᵗ

    r. A scroll from the Cairo Genizah contains most of Sirach; I show the Hebrew word when it is given in the supplement to the Hatch-Redpath concordance. No equivalent was given for verses in chs. 17–39; no equivalents were given for 44:11, 18 due to textual problems. I verified this data in Beentjes, *Book of Ben Sira*. The usage in Sirach is unusual not so much in the use of διαθήκη, but in the Hebrew: חוֹק is used not only in its common meaning of "decree," but also for various ancestral covenants.

    s. The NRSV footnote says that the translation "children's children" is based on the Hebrew; "meaning of Gk uncertain"; Brenton renders it "and their children are within the covenant." The NRSV and NETS include that concept in the next verse: "Their descendants stand by the covenants; their children also, for their sake."

    t. Wis 18:22 uses διαθήκη for the ancestral covenants, but Wis 12:21 is unique in using συνθήκη for God's covenants with the ancestors. All other LXX uses of συνθήκη are for secular agreements: Isa 28:15, an agreement with death; Isa 30:1, an alliance with Egypt; Dan 11:6, an alliance between rulers; Dan 11:17, between people; 1 Macc 10:26, between nations; Wis 1:16, with death. "In II Macc, *synthēkē* is exclusively employed for treaties between men [12:1; 13:25; 14:20, 26, 27], whereas *diathēkē* is reserved for God's covenant" (Winston, *Wisdom of Solomon*, 321).

These verses show that διαθήκη is used most often to refer to a covenant with God, but may also be used for other agreements, just as בְּרִית is used in the MT. Although חֹק is never rendered as διαθήκη in earlier books, the translator of Sirach has quite reasonably used διαθήκη when חוֹק was used for an ancestral covenant. However, the translator went further and used διαθήκη for other occurrences of חוֹק as well; this simply underscores the fact that διαθήκη was not restricted to divine covenants.³

    3. Quell says: "The free rendering by διαθήκη of related or similar legal terms does not involve any material error, since the conception bound up with בְּרִית-διαθήκη includes legal relationship of all kinds" (*TDNT* 2:106). Schwemer writes that in Sirach, "'Gesetz und Bund' konnten wie ein Hendiadyoin verstanden werden ... und sie geradezu austauschbar werden" ("Zum Verhältnis," 78, 86). Similarly, she says that in 2 En. 31:1, "Gebot und Bund nicht nur synonym für die durch Mose gegebene Sinai-Tora, sondern auch für deren kultischen Aspekt verwendet werden" (ibid., 80).

Appendix E

"Covenant" in the Epistle of Barnabas

COVENANT HAS A LARGER ROLE IN THE *EPISTLE OF BARNABAS* THAN IN any other document in the Apostolic Fathers.[1] This epistle makes the radical statement that the Israelites completely disqualified themselves from the covenant even before Moses came down from the mountain:

> They lost it completely in the following manner, after Moses already had received it—for the scripture says: And Moses was on the mountain fasting for forty days and forty nights, and he received the covenant from the Lord, stone tablets inscribed by the finger of the Lord's hand. But when they turned to idols, they lost it. For the Lord speaks thus: Moses, Moses, descend immediately, for your people whom you led out from the land of Egypt have sinned. And Moses understood, and he hurled the two tablets from his hands. And the covenant (of the tablets) was smashed to bits so that the covenant of Jesus, the Beloved One, might be sealed in our heart, in hope of his faith. (*Barn.* 4:6c–8).[2]

This passage appears to say that the Israelites did not have a valid covenant with God—the original covenant went into a hiatus and went into effect only after Jesus gave the correct interpretation to his followers. This approach to the covenant might be called *negation*—more radical than the supersession taught in Hebrews or the termination taught by Paul.[3] Pseudo-Barnabas argues that the Jews were misled by

---

1. "The term διαθήκη occurs 13 or 14 times in the epistle, and only twice in the rest of the 'sub-apostolic' literature" (Paget, *Epistle of Barnabas*, 59). *Barnabas* was most likely written by a Gentile (see *Barn.* 16:7) early in the second century (Treat, "Barnabas," 612–13).

2. Translation by Kraft, *Barnabas and the Didache*, 90. As might be expected, *Barnabas* ignores Exod 34 and other covenant renewals.

3. Wilson classifies both *Barnabas* and Hebrews under the term *supersession* in *Related Strangers*, 110. However, he notes that Pseudo-Barnabas "does not think in terms of a new covenant, but of *one* covenant, never possessed by the Jews but reserved for Christians" (137–38; see also Paget, *Barnabas*, 220). Thus one covenant does not

"a wicked angel" into an incorrectly literalistic understanding of the law (9:4b). Even though *Barn.* 2:6 speaks of a "new law," it is new only in the sense that it is now correctly understood.[4] *Barnabas* 13:1 says, "Let us see . . . if the covenant is for us [Christians] or for them [the Jews]." *Barnabas* 14:1 argues that the Jewish people "were not worthy to receive it because of their sins."[5] He asks, "How did we receive it?" and answers, "We might receive it through Jesus, who inherits the Lord's covenant" (14:4–5). In other words, it is not for "them."

Ehrman says that *Barnabas* "portrays Judaism as a false religion from the very beginning. According to this author, Jews . . . have never been the people of God and have never understood their own Scriptures."[6] Kraft argues for a less antagonistic view: "It is quite strange to call Pseudo-Barnabas 'anti-Jewish' on the basis of his context. He is certainly anticultic, but there were many Jews among his contemporaries who shared his attitude."[7]

Rhodes argues persuasively that Pseudo-Barnabas did not believe that the Jews were *never* God's people. "The author's assertion about the golden-calf incident is best understood as intentionally hyperbolic."[8] The evidence for this is that Pseudo-Barnabas uses evidence from Israel's post-Sinai history:

---

supersede the other—it is simply given again. He defines what he means by supersession: "to assert that Christians are the people of God" (142).

4. "Christ . . . does not bring with him a new law somehow different from the old, but merely creates the conditions in which we can understand that one law correctly" (Paget, *Barnabas*, 182). Thus the law is "new" in the same way that the new covenant in the DSS is new: a new understanding of the original intent. Wilson says, "References to a 'new law' or a 'new people' . . . could in some contexts imply that the 'old' had some sort of meaningful existence or even value. In the light of what he explicitly argues about the past, however, this cannot have been intended here, and the choice of terms is probably inadvertent" (*Related Strangers*, 129).

5. Wengst points out that the Christians also had sinfulness, but were made worthy of the covenant because "the Lord endured fleshly suffering to purify us" (5:1) (*Tradition und Theologie*, 85.

6. Ehrman, *The New Testament*, 384.

7. Kraft, *Barnabas*, 84. He argues that Pseudo-Barnabas was offering "answers to problems which had long been discussed in Judaism" (120). Kraft seems to downplay the evidence, for even anticultic Jews would not argue that the covenant was negated even before it was ratified. Wilson faults him for "a consistent misreading of the epistle" (*Related Strangers*, 347, n. 67).

8. Rhodes, *Epistle of Barnabas*, iv; and Rhodes, "Barnabas," 400.

> He continues to appeal to authority figures from the later history of Israel. He refers to events, rituals, and laws whose status ought to be moot because they took place or were instituted after the debacle at Sinai. He finds christological types that were given for Israel's recognition. He can even declare that Jesus' words and deeds were evidence of his great love for Israel. Only with the rejection of Jesus are Israel's sins made complete.... To judge from many of Barnabas's statements, even after Sinai, Israel's relationship with God—despite continual, culpable failure—remained in some sense intact.[9]

The failure of Israel at Sinai was paradigmatic, archetypical, but not a complete termination of relationship. "The golden-calf incident is the *defining* moment of a history of infidelity, of which the rejection of Jesus is the culminating event."[10] Even so, the polemics in *Barnabas* against Judaism are severe.

Why would Pseudo-Barnabas write such polemics? He says that his teaching is given "lest we be shattered to pieces as 'proselytes' to their law" (3:6). Lowy argues that the danger was real: "One can hardly escape the thought that he has a practical danger to counteract, namely, a movement which claimed proselytes [from Christianity to Judaism] by literal circumcision.... His manifold efforts hint that he is aiming at counterbalancing Jewish propaganda."[11] Wilson writes, "Christian Judaizers may have been the immediate target, but behind them lay a Judaism whose attraction (and from the author's viewpoint, threat) was immediate and pressing. Faced with this, the author emphatically denies that the covenant could be shared: it belongs not to Jews but to Christians."[12] Rhodes suggests that the author uses the golden-calf

9. Ibid., 16.

10. Ibid., 18.

11. Lowy, "Confutation of Judaism," 18, 20. Others downplay the possibility. Prostmeier writes, "Dieses Verdikt über die Juden und ihre Glaubenstradition ist einzig recht im Kontext des von der Parole in [*Barn.* 4] V 6 aufgeworfenen innerchristlichen theologischen Dissenses über die Heilsbedeutung des Christusereignisses zu lesen." But I believe that Wilson (see next note) has the better argument.

12. Wilson, *Related Strangers*, 137. "The issue was not simply antiquarian, theoretical, or even scriptural, but an urgent and pressing matter which had already made disturbing inroads into the church" (138). In a comment that coheres well with my conclusions about Hebrews, he writes, "The appearance of the covenant theme in three separate chapters suggests that it was a significant problem in its own right" (350, n. 94).

incident as a model for a contemporary problem: the possibility that the readers might turn away and forfeit the covenant.[13] "Barnabas is concerned to summon his readers to what he sees as covenantal obedience at least as much as he is concerned with denigrating Israel."[14]

Paget points out some similarities between the covenant teaching of Hebrews and *Barnabas:* 1) the covenant is made effective by the death of Jesus and given to his followers and 2) both documents note that Moses was only a servant (θέραπων) and Jesus had a higher status (Son in Heb 3:5–6, Lord in *Barn.* 14:4).[15] He also notes differences: 1) "B. does not believe there to have been two covenants, but only one" and 2) "There is less of a sense in *Barn* that Christ's death was necessary for the establishment of that covenant."[16] Backhaus points out another difference: "Die Diatheke dem Heils volk der Christen zugeeignet ist, ist jetzt nicht mehr Zielpunkt der Darlegungen, sondern deren . . . Ausgangspunkt."[17]

Barnabas, like Hebrews, is concerned only with the Sinai covenant and the Christ covenant. Neither document mentions that Abraham also had a covenant—although both Heb 6:13–18 and *Barn.* 5:6–7 assume that salvation is based on promises given to Abraham. The term διαθήκη is limited to the controversy at hand—pressures for believers to adopt Jewish laws—and the use of the term indicates that those pressures were given in the context of being faithful to the Sinai covenant. Both authors stress that people may forfeit the covenant through disobedience, just as a contract might be voided through noncompliance.

Hebrews emphasizes sacrificial laws, perhaps reflecting a date before 70, whereas *Barnabas,* written when the sacrifices were moot, does not. But the biggest difference is that *Barnabas* does not speak of a new

---

13. Rhodes, *Barnabas,* 23.

14. Ibid., 94. He argues that the author is combating people who assumed (as some Jews did) that the covenant would be valid no matter how much they disobeyed. He suggests an emendation for *Barn.* 4:6a: "Do not be like certain people . . . saying, 'Our covenant remains valid'" (132).

15. Paget, *Barnabas,* 219.

16. Ibid., 220.

17. Backhaus, "Bundesmotiv," 223.

covenant. It argues that the Christ covenant is, in all respects, what God really wanted Israel to accept. It argues for continuity not by continuing the laws of Judaism, but by eliminating them as never valid in the first place.[18]

---

18. Even if Pseudo-Barnabas believed that the old covenant remained valid, as Rhodes argues, Pseudo-Barnabas still argues that the Jews were wrong in taking the ritual commands literally.

Bibliography

Abegg, Martin G. "The Covenant of the Qumran Sectarians." Pages 81–97 in *The Concept of the Covenant in the Second Temple Period*. Edited by Stanley E. Porter and Jacqueline C. R. de Roo. SJSJ 71. Leiden: Brill, 2003.

———, Peter Flint, and Eugene Ulrich. *The Dead Sea Scrolls Bible*. San Francisco: Harper, 1999.

Alford, Henry. *The Greek Testament IV.1. The Epistle to the Hebrews, and the Catholic Epistles of St. James and St. Peter*. 1874. Repr., London: Rivingtons, 1959.

Allen, Leslie C. *Ezekiel 20–48*. WBC 29. Dallas: Word, 1990.

Aristotle. *The Art of Rhetoric*. Translated by H. C. Lawson-Tancred. New York: Penguin, 1991.

———. *Rhetoric*. Translated by J. H. Freese. No pages. Accessed 2 Jan 2008. Online: http://www.perseus.tufts.edu/cgi-bin/ptext?doc=Perseus%3Atext%3A1999. 01.0060.

Anderson, Bernhard W., with Steven Bishop. *Contours of Old Testament Theology*. Minneapolis: Fortress, 1999.

———. "The New Covenant and the Old." Pages 225–42 in *The Old Testament and Christian Faith: A Theological Discussion*. Edited by Bernhard W. Anderson. New York: Harper & Row, 1963.

Anderson, Charles P. "Who Are the Heirs of the New Age in the Epistle to the Hebrews?" Pages 255–77 in *Apocalyptic and the New Testament*. Edited by Joel Marcus and Marion L. Soards. Sheffield: JSOT Press, 1989.

Attridge, Harold W. *The Epistle to the Hebrews: A Commentary on the Epistle to the Hebrews*. Hermeneia: A Critical and Historical Commentary on the Bible. Philadelphia: Fortress, 1989.

———. "Paraenesis in a Homily (λόγος παρακλήσεως): The Possible Location of, and Socialization in, the 'Epistle to the Hebrews.'" *Semeia* 50 (1990): 211–26.

Aune, David E. *The New Testament in Its Literary Environment*. LEC 8. Philadelphia: Westminster, 1987.

———. *Westminster Dictionary of New Testament and Early Christian Literature and Rhetoric*. Louisville: Westminster John Knox, 2003.

Avemarie, Friedrich, and Hermann Lichtenberger, eds. *Bund und Tora: Zur theologischen Begriffsgeschichte in alttestamentlicher, frühjüdischer und urchristlicher Tradition*. WUNT 92. Tübingen: Mohr Siebeck, 1996.

Backhaus, Knut. "Das Bundesmotiv in der frühkirchlichen Schwellenzeit: Hebräerbrief, Barnabasbrief, Dialogus cum Tryphone." Pages 211–31 in *Der ungekündigte Bund?: Antworten des Neuen Testaments*. Edited by Hubert Frankemölle. QD 172. Freiburg: Herder, 1998.

Balz, Horst, and Gerhard Schneider. *Exegetical Dictionary of the New Testament*. Translated by Virgil P. Howard, James W. Thompson, John W. Medendorp, and Douglas W. Stott. 3 vols. Grand Rapids: Eerdmans, 1990-92.

Barclay, John M. G. *Jews in the Mediterranean Diaspora: From Alexander to Trajan (323 BCE-117 CE)*. Edinburgh: T. & T. Clark, 1996.

Barr, James. "Some Semantic Notes on the Covenant." Pages 23-38 in *Beiträge zur Alttestamentlichen Theologie: Festshrift für Walther Zimmerli zum 70. Geburtstag*. Edited by Herbert Donner, Robert Hanhart, and Rudolf Smend. Göttingen: Vandenhoeck and Ruprecht, 1977.

Barrett, C. K. "The Christology of Hebrews." Pages 110-27 in *Who Do You Say That I Am? Essays on Christology*. Edited by Mark Allan Powell and David R. Bauer. Louisville: Westminster John Knox, 1999.

Barth, Karl. *The Doctrine of Reconciliation*. Church Dogmatics, IV:1. Edited by G. W. Bromiley and T. F. Torrance. Translated by G. W. Bromiley. Edinburgh: T. & T. Clark, 1956.

Batto, Bernard F. "The Covenant of Peace: A Neglected Ancient Near Eastern Motif." *CBQ* 49 (1987): 187-211.

Bauckham, Richard. "Apocalypses." Pages 135-87 in *The Complexities of Second Temple Judaism*. Edited by D. A. Carson, P. T. O'Brien, and M. A. Seifrid. Vol. 1 of *Justification and Variegated Nomism: A Fresh Appraisal of Paul and Second Temple Judaism*. Grand Rapids: Baker, 2001.

Beentjes, Pancratius C. *The Book of Ben Sira in Hebrew: A Text Edition of All Extant Hebrew Manuscripts and a Synopsis of All Parallel Hebrew Ben Sira Texts*. VTSup 68. Leiden: Brill, 1997.

Bénétreau, Samuel. *L'Épître aux Hébreux. Commentaire Évangelique de la Bible*. 2 vols. Vaux-sur-Seine, France: Edifac, 1989-90.

Binder, Donald D. *Into the Temple Courts: The Place of the Synagogues in the Second Temple Period*. SBLDS 169. Atlanta: Society of Biblical Literature, 1999.

Black, C. Clifton, II. "The Rhetorical Form of the Hellenistic Jewish and Early Christian Sermon: A Response to Lawrence Wills." *HTR* 81 (1988): 1-18.

Bockmuehl, Markus. "The Church in Hebrews." Pages 133-51 in *A Vision for the Church: Studies in Early Christian Ecclesiology in Honour of J. P. M. Sweet*. Edited by Markus Bockmuehl and Michael B. Thompson. Edinburgh: T. & T. Clark, 1997.

———. "1QS and Salvation at Qumran." Pages 381-414 in *The Complexities of Second Temple Judaism*. Edited by D. A. Carson, P. T. O'Brien, and M. A. Seifrid. Vol. 1 of *Justification and Variegated Nomism: A Fresh Appraisal of Paul and Second Temple Judaism*. Grand Rapids: Baker, 2001.

Botterweck, G. Johannes, Helmer Ringgren, and Heinz-Josef Fabry, editors. *Theological Dictionary of the Old Testament*. Translated by John T. Willis, David E. Green, and Douglas W. Stott. 15 vols. Grand Rapids: Eerdmans, 1974-2006.

Braun, Herbert. *An die Hebräer*. HNT 14. Tübingen: Mohr (Siebeck), 1984.

Brenton, Lancelot C. L. *The Septuagint with Apocrypha: Greek and English*. 1851. Repr. Peabody: Hendrickson, 1987.

Brown, Colin, editor. *New International Dictionary of New Testament Theology*. 4 vols. Grand Rapids: Zondervan, 1975-1985.

Brown, Raymond E. and John P. Meier. *Antioch and Rome: New Testament Cradles of Catholic Christianity*. New York: Paulist, 1983.

Bruce, Frederick Fyvie. *The Epistle to the Hebrews.* Rev. ed. NICNT. Grand Rapids: Eerdmans, 1990.
——— . "'To the Hebrews': A Document of Roman Christianity?" *ANRW* 25.4: 3496–521. Part 2, *Principat*, 25.4. Edited by H. Temporini and W. Haase. New York: de Gruyter, 1987.
——— . "'To the Hebrews' or 'to the Essenes'?" *NTS* 9 (1963): 217–32.
Buchanan, George Wesley. *To the Hebrews: A New Translation with Introduction and Commentary.* AB 36. Garden City, NY: Doubleday, 1972.
Buck, Daniel E. "The Rhetorical Arrangement and Function of OT Citations in the Book of Hebrews: Uncovering Their Role in the Paraenetic Discourse of Access." PhD diss., Dallas Theological Seminary, 2002.
Bulley, Alan D. "Death and Rhetoric in the Hebrews 'Hymn to Faith.'" *SR* 25 (1996): 409–23.
Carroll, Robert P. *From Chaos to Covenant: Prophecy in the Book of Jeremiah.* New York: Crossroad, 1981.
Carson, D. A., Peter T. O'Brien, and Mark A. Seifrid, editors. *The Complexities of Second Temple Judaism.* Vol. 1 of *Justification and Variegated Nomism: A Fresh Appraisal of Paul and Second Temple Judaism.* Grand Rapids: Baker, 2001.
Casey, Juliana. *Hebrews.* NTM 18. Dublin: Veritas, 1980.
Charlesworth, James, editor. *The Old Testament Pseudepigrapha.* 2 vols. New York: Doubleday, 1983, 1985.
Chester, A. N. "Hebrews: The Final Sacrifice." Pages 57–72 in *Sacrifice and Redemption: Durham Essays in Theology.* Edited by S. W. Sykes. Cambridge: Cambridge University Press, 1991.
Choi, Phuichun Richard. "Abraham Our Father: Paul's Voice in the Covenantal Debate of the Second Temple Period." PhD diss., Fuller Theological Seminary, 1996.
Christensen, Duane L. *Deuteronomy* 21:10—34:12. WBC 6B. Nashville: Nelson, 2002.
Christiansen, Ellen Juhl. *The Covenant in Judaism and Paul: A Study of Ritual Boundaries as Identity Markers.* AGJU 27. Leiden: Brill, 1995.
——— . "The Consciousness of Belonging to God's Covenant and What It Entails According to the Damascus Document and the Community Rule." Pages 69–97 in *Qumran Between the Old and New Testaments.* Edited by Frederick H. Cryer and Thomas L. Thompson. JSOTSup 290; Copenhagen International Seminar 6. Sheffield: Sheffield Academic, 1998.
Classen, Carl Joachim. *Rhetorical Criticism of the New Testament.* Boston: Brill, 2002.
Cockerill, Gareth L. *Hebrews: A Bible Commentary in the Wesleyan Tradition.* Indianapolis: Wesleyan, 1999.
——— . "Structure and Interpretation in Hebrews 8:1—10:18: A Symphony in Three Movements." *BBR* 11 (2001): 179–201.
Colijn, Brenda B. "'Let Us Approach': Soteriology in the Epistle to the Hebrews." *JETS* 39 (1996): 571–86.
Collins, Raymond F. "The Berith-Notion of the Cairo Damascus Document and Its Comparison with the New Testament." *ETL* 39 (1963): 555–94.
Cross, Frank Moore. *From Epic to Canon: History and Literature in Ancient Israel.* Baltimore: Johns Hopkins University Press, 1998.

Croy, N. Clayton. *Endurance in Suffering: Hebrews 12.1–3 in Its Rhetorical, Religious, and Philosophical Context.* SNTSMS 98. Cambridge: Cambridge University Press, 1998.

Dahms, John V. "The First Readers of Hebrews." *JETS* 20 (1977): 365–75.

Danker, Frederick W., editor. *A Greek-English Lexicon of the New Testament and Other Early Christian Literature.* 3rd ed. Chicago: University of Chicago Press, 2000.

Das, A. Andrew. *Paul, the Law, and the Covenant.* Peabody: Hendrickson, 2001.

Davies, John Howard. *A Letter to Hebrews.* CBC. London: Cambridge University Press, 1967.

Delville, Jean-Pierre. "L'Épître aux Hébreux à la lumière du prosélytisme juif." *RCT* 10/2 (1985): 323–68.

deSilva, David A. "The Epistle to the Hebrews in Social-Scientific Perspective." *ResQ* 36 (1994): 1–21.

———. "Exchanging Favor for Wrath: Apostasy in Hebrews and Patron-Client Relationships." *JBL* 115 (1996): 91–116.

———. *Perseverance in Gratitude: A Socio-Rhetorical Commentary on the Epistle 'to the Hebrews.'* Grand Rapids: Eerdmans, 2000.

Dillard, Raymond. *2 Chronicles.* WBC 15. Waco: Word, 1987.

Donelson, Lewis R. *From Hebrews to Revelation: A Theological Introduction.* Louisville: Westminster John Knox, 2001.

Dumbrell, William J. *Covenant and Creation: A Theology of the Old Testament Covenants.* Grand Rapids: Baker, 1984.

Dunn, James D. G. "Did Paul Have a Covenant Theology? Reflections on Romans 9.4 and 11.27." Pages 287–307 in *The Concept of the Covenant in the Second Temple Period.* Edited by Stanley E. Porter and Jacqueline C. R. de Roo. SJSJ 71. Leiden: Brill, 2003.

Ehrman, Bart D. *The New Testament: A Historical Introduction to the Early Christian Writings.* 2nd ed. Oxford: Oxford University Press, 2000.

Eisenbaum, Pamela. "Heroes and History in Hebrews 11." Pages 380–96 in *Early Christian Interpretation of the Scriptures of Israel.* Edited by Craig A. Evans and James A. Sanders. Sheffield: Sheffield Academic, 1997.

Ellingworth, Paul. *The Epistle to the Hebrews: A Commentary on the Greek Text.* NIGTC. Grand Rapids: Eerdmans, 1993.

———. "The Old Testament in Hebrews: Exegesis, Method and Hermeneutics." PhD diss., University of Aberdeen, 1977.

Elliott, Mark Adam. *The Survivors of Israel: A Reconsideration of the Theology of Pre-Christian Judaism.* Grand Rapids: Eerdmans, 2000.

Enns, Peter. "Expansions of Scripture." Pages 73–98 in *The Complexities of Second Temple Judaism.* Vol. 1 of *Justification and Variegated Nomism: A Fresh Appraisal of Paul and Second Temple Judaism.* Edited by D. A. Carson, P. T. O'Brien, and M. A. Seifrid. Grand Rapids: Baker, 2001.

Evans, Craig A. "Covenant in the Qumran Literature." Pages 55–80 in *The Concept of the Covenant in the Second Temple Period.* Edited by Stanley E. Porter and Jacqueline C. R. de Roo. SJSJ 71. Leiden: Brill, 2003.

Fairweather, Janet. "The Epistle to the Galatians and Classical Rhetoric." *TynBul* 45 (1994): 1–38, 213–45.

Falk, Daniel. "Psalms and Prayers." Pages 7–56 in *The Complexities of Second Temple Judaism*, vol. 1 of *Justification and Variegated Nomism: A Fresh Appraisal of Paul and Second Temple Judaism*. Edited by D. A. Carson, P. T. O'Brien, and M. A. Seifrid. Grand Rapids: Baker, 2001.

France, Richard Thomas. "The Writer of Hebrews as a Biblical Expositor." *TB* 47 (1996): 245–76.

Freedman, David Noel. "Divine Commitment and Human Obligation: The Covenant Theme." *Interpretation* 18 (1964): 419–31.

———, editor. *Anchor Bible Dictionary*. 6 vols. New York: Doubleday, 1992.

——— and David Miano. "People of the New Covenant." Pages 7–26 in *The Concept of the Covenant in the Second Temple Period*. Edited by Stanley E. Porter and Jacqueline C. R. de Roo. SJSJ 71. Leiden: Brill, 2003.

Frey, Jörg. "Die alte und die neue διαθήκη nach dem Hebräerbrief." Pages 263–310 in *Bund und Tora: Zur theologischen Begriffsgeschichte in alttestamentlicher, frühjüdischer und urchristlicher Tradition*. Edited by Friedrich Avemarie and Hermann Lichtenberger. WUNT 92. Tübingen: Mohr Siebeck, 1996.

García Martínez, Florentino. *The Dead Sea Scrolls Translated: The Qumran Texts in English*. 2nd ed. Translated by Wilfred G. E. Watson. Leiden: Brill, 1996.

Garuti, Paolo. *Alle origini dell'omiletica Cristiana. La lettera agli Ebrei: Note di analisi retorica*. AnSBF 38. Jerusalem: Franciscan, 1995.

Gench, Frances Taylor. *Hebrews and James*. Westminster Bible Companion. Louisville: Westminster John Knox, 1996.

Goldin, Judah. "The Magic of Magic and Superstition." Pages 115–47 in *Aspects of Religious Propaganda in Judaism and Early Christianity*. Edited by Elisabeth Schüssler Fiorenza. Notre Dame: University of Notre Dame Press, 1976.

Goldingay, John. "Covenant, OT and NT." Pages 767–78 in vol. 1 of *New Interpreter's Dictionary of the Bible*. Edited by Katharine Doob Sakenfeld, Samuel D. Balentine, and Brian K. Blount. Nashville: Abingdon, 2006.

Goppelt, Leonhard. *Theology of the New Testament*. Translated by John E. Alsup. 2 vols. Grand Rapids: Eerdmans, 1982.

Gordon, Robert P. *Hebrews*. Readings: A New Biblical Commentary. Sheffield: Sheffield Academic, 2000.

Grabbe, Lester L. "Covenant in Philo and Josephus." Pages 251–66 in *The Concept of the Covenant in the Second Temple Period*. Edited by Stanley E. Porter and Jacqueline C. R. de Roo. SJSJ 71. Leiden: Brill, 2003.

Grässer, Erich. *An die Hebräer*. EKKNT 17. 3 vols. Zurich: Benziger, 1990–97.

———. *Der Alte Bund im Neuen: Exegetische Studien zur Israelfrage im Neuen Testament*. WUNT 35. Tübingen: Mohr Siebeck, 1985.

Grelot, Pierre. *Une lecture de l'épître aux Hébreux*. Lire la Bible. Paris: Cerf, 2003.

Gross, Walter. "Erneuter oder neuer Bund? Wortlaut und Aussageintention in Jer 31,31–34." Pages 41–66 in *Bund und Tora: Zur theologischen Begriffsgeschichte in alttestamentlicher, frühjüdischer und urchristlicher Tradition*. Edited by Friedrich Avemarie and Hermann Lichtenberger. WUNT 92. Tübingen: Mohr Siebeck, 1996.

Guhrt, Joachim. "Διαθήκη, diathēkē, covenant." *NIDNTT* 1:369.

Guthrie, George H. *Hebrews*. NIV Application Commentary. Grand Rapids: Zondervan, 1998.

———. *The Structure of Hebrews: A Text-Linguistic Analysis*. Leiden: Brill, 1994. Repr. Grand Rapids: Baker: 1998.

Hagner, Donald A. *Encountering the Book of Hebrews: An Exposition*. Encountering Biblical Studies. Grand Rapids: Baker, 2002.

———. "Interpreting the Epistle to the Hebrews." Pages 217–42 in *The Literature and Meaning of Scripture*. Edited by Morris A. Inch and C. Hassell Bullock. Grand Rapids: Baker, 1981.

———. *Hebrews*. NIBCNT 14. Peabody, Mass.: Hendrickson, 1990.

Hahn, Scott Walker. "A Broken Covenant and the Curse of Death: A Study of Hebrews 9:15–22." *CBQ* 66 (2004): 416–36.

———. "Covenant, Cult, and the Curse-of-Death: Διαθήκη in Heb 9:15–22." Pages 65–88 in *Hebrews: Contemporary Methods—New Insights*. Edited by Gabriella Gelardini. Leiden: Brill, 2005.

———. "Kinship by Covenant: A Biblical Theological Study of Covenant Types and Texts in the Old and New Testaments." PhD diss., Marquette University, 1995.

Halpern-Amaru, Betsy. *Rewriting the Bible: Land and Covenant in Postbiblical Jewish Literature*. Valley Forge: Trinity, 1994.

Harrington, Daniel J. "Pseudo-Philo." *OTP* 2:304–77.

Hatch, Edwin, and Henry A. Redpath. *A Concordance to the Septuagint and the Other Greek Versions of the Old Testament*. 2 vols. 1897; suppl., 1906. Repr., Graz, Austria: Akademische, 1954.

Hay, David M. "Philo of Alexandria." Pages 357–79 in *The Complexities of Second Temple Judaism*. Vol. 1 of *Justification and Variegated Nomism: A Fresh Appraisal of Paul and Second Temple Judaism*. Edited by D. A. Carson, P. T. O'Brien, and M. A. Seifrid. Grand Rapids: Baker, 2001.

Hegermann, H. "Διαθήκη, ης, ή, Diathēkē, Covenant; Testament." *EDNT* 1:299.

Hewitt, Thomas. *The Epistle to the Hebrews*. TNTC 15. Grand Rapids: Eerdmans, 1960.

Hillers, Delbert R. *Covenant: The History of a Biblical Idea*. Baltimore: John Hopkins University Press, 1969.

Hughes, John J. "Hebrews IX 15 ff. and Galatians III 15ff.: A Study in Covenant Practice and Procedure." *NovT* 21 (1979): 27–96.

Hughes, Philip Edgcumbe. *A Commentary on the Epistle to the Hebrews*. Grand Rapids: Eerdmans, 1977.

Hurst, Lincoln D. *The Epistle to the Hebrews: Its Background of Thought*. SNTSMS 65. Cambridge University Press, 1990.

Isaacs, E. "1 (Ethiopic Apocalypse of) Enoch." *OTP* 1:5–89.

Isaacs, Marie E. *Reading Hebrews and James: A Literary and Theological Commentary*. Reading the New Testament. Macon: Smyth & Helwys, 2002.

Jenni, Ernst, and Claus Westermann, editors. *Theological Lexicon of the Old Testament*. Translated by Mark E. Biddle. 3 vols. Peabody: Hendrickson, 1997.

Jewett, Robert. *Letter to Pilgrims: A Commentary on the Epistle to the Hebrews*. New York: Pilgrim, 1981.

Johnson, Luke Timothy. *Hebrews: A Commentary*. NTL. Louisville: Westminster John Knox, 2006.

Johnson, Richard W. *Going Outside the Camp: The Sociological Function of the Levitical Critique in the Epistle to the Hebrews*. JSNTSup 209. London: Sheffield Academic, 2001.

Kennedy, George A. *New Testament Interpretation Through Rhetorical Criticism.* Chapel Hill: University of North Carolina Press, 1984.
———. *Progymnasmata: Greek Textbooks of Prose Composition and Rhetoric.* Atlanta: Society of Biblical Literature, 2003.
Keown, Gerald L., Pamela J. Scalise, and Thomas G. Smothers. *Jeremiah 26–52.* WBC 27. Dallas: Word, 1995.
Kim, Eui Won. "An Eschatological Examination of the New Covenant Based on the Dead Sea Scrolls." PhD diss., New York University, 1981.
Kim, Lloyd. *Polemic in the Book of Hebrews: Anti-Judaism, Anti-Semitism, Supersessionism?* PTMS 64. Eugene, OR: Pickwick, 2006.
Kistemaker, Simon J. *Exposition of the Epistle to the Hebrews.* NTC 19. Grand Rapids: Baker, 1984.
Kittel, Gerhard, and Gerhard Friedrich, editors. *Theological Dictionary of the New Testament.* Translated by Geoffrey W. Bromiley. 10 vols. Grand Rapids: Eerdmans, 1964–1976.
Knoppers, Gary N. "Ancient Near Eastern Royal Grants and the Davidic Covenant: A Parallel?" *JAOS* 116 (1996): 670–97.
Koester, Craig R. *The Epistle to the Hebrews: A New Translation with Introduction and Commentary.* AB 36. New York: Doubleday, 2001.
———. "Hebrews, Rhetoric, and the Future of Humanity." *CBQ* 64 (2002): 103–23.
Kohlenberger, John R. III, and James A. Swanson. *The Hebrew-English Concordance to the Old Testament.* Grand Rapids: Zondervan, 1998.
Kraft, Robert A. *Barnabas and the Didache.* Vol. 3 of *The Apostolic Fathers: A New Translation and Commentary.* Edited by Robert M. Grant. New York: Thomas Nelson, 1965.
Kutsch, Ernst. "Bund." *TRE* 7:397–410.
Lalleman-de Winkel, Hetty. *Jeremiah in Prophetic Tradition: An Examination of the Book of Jeremiah in the Light of Israel's Prophetic Traditions.* CBET 26. Leuven: Peeters, 2000.
Lane, William L. *Hebrews: A Call to Commitment.* Peabody, Mass.: Hendrickson, 1985.
———. *Hebrews 1–8.* WBC 47A. Dallas: Word, 1991.
———. *Hebrews 9–13.* WBC 47B. Dallas: Word, 1991.
Larsson, Edvin. "How Mighty Was the Mighty Minority?" Pages 93–105 in *Mighty Minorities? Minorities in Early Christianity, Positions and Strategies.* Edited by David Hellholm, Halvor Moxnes, and Turid Karlsen Seim. Oslo: Scandinavian University Press, 1995.
Lehne, Susanne. *The New Covenant in Hebrews.* JSNTSup 44. Sheffield: Sheffield Academic, 1990.
Levenson, Jon Douglas. *Theology of the Restoration of Ezekiel 40–48.* Missoula: Scholars Press, 1976.
Levison, John R. "Torah and Covenant in Pseudo Philo's Liber Antiquitatum Biblicarum." Pages 111–28 in *Bund und Tora: Zur theologischen Begriffsgeschichte in alttestamentlicher, frühjüdischer und urchristlicher Tradition.* Edited by Friedrich Avemarie and Hermann Lichtenberger. WUNT 92. Tübingen: Mohr Siebeck, 1996.
Lichtenberger, Hermann. "Alter Bund und Neuer Bund." *NTS* 41 (1995): 400–414.
Lincoln, Andrew T. *Hebrews: A Guide.* London: Clark, 2006.

Lindars, Barnabas. "The Rhetorical Structure of Hebrews." *NTS* 35 (1989): 382–406.
———. *The Theology of the Letter to the Hebrews*. New Testament Theology. Cambridge: Cambridge University Press, 1991.
Lohfink, Norbert. *The Covenant Never Revoked: Biblical Reflections on Christian-Jewish Dialogue*. New York: Paulist, 1991.
Longenecker, Richard N. *Galatians*. WBC 41. Dallas: Word, 1990.
Lowy, S. "The Confutation of Judaism in the Epistle of Barnabas." *JJS* 11 (1960): 1–33.
Lundbom, Jack R. *Jeremiah 21–36: A New Translation and Commentary*. AB 21B. New York: Doubleday, 1999.
———. "New Covenant." *ABD* 4:1088–94.
Mack, Burton. *Wisdom and Hebrew Epic: Ben Sira's Hymn in Praise of the Fathers*. Chicago: University of Chicago Press, 1985.
Mackie, Scott D. "Confession of the Son of God in Hebrews." *NTS* 53 (2007): 114–29.
Malina, Bruce J. "Rhetorical Criticism and Social-Scientific Criticism: Why Won't Romanticism Leave Us Alone?" Pages 72–99 in *Rhetoric, Scripture and Theology: Essays from the 1994 Pretoria Conference*. Edited by S. E. Porter and T. H. Olbricht. JSNTSup 131. Sheffield: Sheffield Academic, 1996.
Mann, Thomas W. *The Book of the Torah: The Narrative Integrity of the Pentateuch*. Atlanta: John Knox, 1988.
Manson, William. *The Epistle to the Hebrews: An Historical and Theological Reconsideration*. London: Hodder & Stoughton, 1951.
Marohl, Matthew J. *Faithfulness and the Purpose of Hebrews: A Social Identity Approach*. PTMS 82. Eugene, OR: Pickwick, 2008.
Martin-Achard, Robert. "Quelques remarques sur la nouvelle alliance chez Jérémie." Pages 141–64 in *Questions disputées d'Ancien Testament: Méthode et théologie*. Edited by C. Brekelmans. BETL 33. Louvain: Leuven University Press, 1974.
März, Claus-Peter. *Hebräerbrief*. Die Neue Echter Bibel. Würzburg: Echter, 1989.
Maxey, Lee Zachary. "The Rhetoric of Response: A Classical Rhetorical Reading of Hebrews 10:32—12:13." PhD diss., Claremont Graduate University, 2002.
McConville, Gordon J. "בְּרִית (b*rît), Treaty, Agreement, Alliance, Covenant (#1382)." *NIDOTTE* 1:747–55.
McCullough, J. C. "Hebrews in Recent Scholarship." *IBS* 16 (1994): 66–86, 108–20.
McKenzie, Steven L. *Covenant*. Understanding Biblical Themes. St. Louis: Chalice, 2000.
McNamara, Martin. "Some Targum Themes." Pages 303–56 in *The Complexities of Second Temple Judaism*. Vol. 1 of *Justification and Variegated Nomism: A Fresh Appraisal of Paul and Second Temple Judaism*. Edited by D. A. Carson, P. T. O'Brien, and M. A. Seifrid. Grand Rapids: Baker, 2001.
Mendenhall, George E., and Gary A. Herion. "Covenant." *ABD* 1:1179–202.
Michel, Otto. *Der Brief an die Hebräer: Übersetzt und erklärt*. 13th ed. KEK. Göttingen: Vandenhoeck & Ruprecht, 1936, 1975.
Mitchell, Alan C. *Hebrews*. SP 13. Collegeville, Minn.: Liturgical, 2007.
Mitchell, Margaret M. *Paul and the Rhetoric of Reconciliation: An Exegetical Investigation of the Language and Composition of 1 Corinthians*. HUT 28. Tübingen: Mohr Siebeck, 1991.
Moffatt, James. *A Critical and Exegetical Commentary on the Epistle to the Hebrews*. International Critical Commentary. New York: Scribner's Sons, 1924.

Montefiore, Hugh W. *The Epistle to the Hebrews*. Black's New Testament Commentaries. London: A & C Black, 1964.
Montgomery, James A. *A Critical and Exegetical Commentary on the Book of Daniel*. Edinburgh: Clark, 1927.
Morris, Leon. "Hebrews." Pages 1–158 in vol. 12 of *Expositor's Bible Commentary*. Edited by Frank Gaebelein and J. D. Douglas. Grand Rapids: Zondervan, 1981.
Morrison, Michael D. *Sabbath, Circumcision, and Tithing: Which Old Testament Laws Apply to Christians?* San Jose, CA.: Writers Club, 2002.
Moule, C. F. D. "Sanctuary and Sacrifice in the Church of the New Testament." *JTS*, n.s., 1 (1950): 29–41.
Murphy, Frederick J. "The Eternal Covenant in Pseudo-Philo." *JSP* 3 (1988): 43–57.
Murphy-O'Connor, Jerome. "The New Covenant in the Letters of Paul and the Essene Documents." Pages 194–204 in *To Touch the Text: Biblical and Related Studies in Honor of Joseph A. Fitzmyer, S.J.* Edited by Maurya P. Horgan and Paul J. Kobelski. New York: Crossroad, 1989.
Murray, Robert. "Jews, Hebrews and Christians: Some Needed Distinctions." *NovT* 24 (1982): 194–208.
Nicholson, Ernest W. *God and His People: Covenant and Theology in the Old Testament*. Oxford: Clarendon, 1986.
Nickelsburg, George W. E. *Jewish Literature Between the Bible and the Mishnah: A Historical and Literary Introduction*. 2nd ed. Minneapolis: Fortress, 2005.
Nolland, John. *Luke 1–9:20*. WBC 35A. Dallas: Word, 1989.
Olbricht, Thomas H. "An Aristotelian Rhetorical Analysis of 1 Thessalonians." Pages 216–36 in *Greeks, Romans, and Christians: Essays in Honor of Abraham J. Malherbe*. Edited by D. L. Balch, E. Ferguson, and W. A. Meeks. Minneapolis: Fortress, 1990.
———. "Hebrews as Amplification." Pages 375–87 in *Rhetoric and the New Testament*. Edited by S. E. Porter and T. H. Olbricht. JSOTSup 90. Sheffield: JSOT Press, 1993.
Paget, James Carleton. *The Epistle of Barnabas: Outlook and Background*. WUNT, 2nd series, 64. Tübingen: Mohr (Siebeck), 1994.
———. "Jewish Christianity." Pages 731–75 in *The Early Roman Period*. Vol. 3 of *The Cambridge History of Judaism*. Edited by William Horbury. Cambridge: Cambridge University Press, 1999.
Peterson, David. *Hebrews and Perfection: An Examination of the Concept of Perfection in the 'Epistle to the Hebrews.'* SNTSMS 47. Cambridge: Cambridge University Press, 1982.
Pfitzner, Victor C. *Hebrews*. Abingdon New Testament Commentaries. Nashville: Abingdon, 1997.
Pietersma, Albert, and Benjamin G. Wright. *New English Translation of the Septuagint and the Other Greek Translations Traditionally Included Under That Title*. New York: Oxford University Press, 2007.
Pinçon, Bertrand. *Du nouveau dans l'ancien: Essai sur la notion l'alliance nouvelle dans le Livre de Jérémie et dans quelques relectures au cours de l'Exil*. Profac 61. Lyon: Université Catholique de Lyon, 2000.
Porter, Stanley E. "The Concept of Covenant in Paul." Pages 269–85 in *The Concept of the Covenant in the Second Temple Period*. Edited by Stanley E. Porter and Jacqueline C. R. de Roo. SJSJ 71. Leiden: Brill, 2003.

———. "The Date of the Composition of Hebrews and Use of the Present Tense-Form." Pages 295–313 in *Crossing the Boundaries: Essays in Biblical Interpretation*. Edited by Stanley E. Porter, Paul Joyce, and David E. Orton. Biblical Interpretation Series 8. Leiden: Brill, 1994.

———. "Paul of Tarsus and His Letters." Pages 533–85 in *Handbook of Classical Rhetoric in the Hellenistic Period, 330 B.C.–A.D. 400*. Edited by Stanley E. Porter. Leiden: Brill, 1997.

——— and Jacqueline C. R. de Roo, editors. *The Concept of the Covenant in the Second Temple Period*. SJSJ 71. Leiden: Brill, 2003.

Potter, H. D. "The New Covenant in Jeremiah XXXI 31–34." *VT* 33 (1983): 347–57.

Priest, J. "Testament of Moses." *OTP* 1:919–34.

Rayburn, Robert S. "The Contrast Between the Old and New Covenants in the New Testament." PhD diss., University of Aberdeen, 1978.

Reed, Jeffrey T. "The Epistle." Pages 171–93 in *Handbook of Classical Rhetoric in the Hellenistic Period (330 b.c.–a.d. 400)*. Edited by Stanley E. Porter. Leiden: Brill, 1997.

Rhodes, James N. "Barnabas, Epistle of." Pages 399–400 in vol. 1 of *New Interpreter's Dictionary of the Bible*. Edited by Katharine Doob Sakenfeld, Samuel D. Balentine, and Brian K. Blount. Nashville: Abingdon, 2006.

———. *The Epistle of Barnabas and the Deuteronomic Tradition: Polemics, Paraenesis, and the Legacy of the Golden-Calf Incident*. WUNT, 2nd series, 188. Tübingen: Mohr Siebeck, 2004.

Robertson, O. Palmer. *The Christ of the Covenants*. Phillipsburg: Presbyterian & Reformed, 1980.

de Roo, Jacqueline C. R. "God's Covenant with the Forefathers." Pages 191–202 in *The Concept of the Covenant in the Second Temple Period*. Edited by Stanley E. Porter and Jacqueline C. R. de Roo. SJSJ 71. Leiden: Brill, 2003.

Salevao, Iutisone. *Legitimation in the Letter to the Hebrews: The Construction and Maintenance of a Symbolic Universe*. JSNTSup 219. London: Sheffield Academic, 2002.

Sanders, E. P. *Paul and Palestinian Judaism: A Comparison of Patterns of Religion*. Minneapolis: Fortress, 1977.

Schenck, Kenneth. *Understanding the Book of Hebrews: The Story Behind the Sermon*. Louisville: Westminster John Knox, 2003.

Schenker, Adrian. "Der nie aufgehobene Bund: Exegetische Beobachtungen zu Jer 31,31–34." Pages 85–112 in *Der neue Bund im Alten: Studien zur Bundestheologie der beiden Testamente*. Edited by Erich Zenger. Freiburg: Herder, 1993.

Schierse, Franz Joseph. *The Epistle to the Hebrews* (Bound with The Epistle of St. James, by Otto Knoch). Translated by Benen Fahy. New Testament for Spiritual Reading 21. London: Burns & Oates, 1969.

Schiffman, Lawrence H. "The Concept of Covenant in the Qumran Scrolls and Rabbinic Literature." Pages 257–78 in *The Idea of Biblical Interpretation*. Edited by Hindy Najman and Judith H. Newman. Leiden: Brill, 2003.

Schmidt, Thomas E. "Moral Lethargy and the Epistle to the Hebrews." *WTJ* 54 (1992): 167–73.

Schmithals, Walter. "Über Empfänger und Anlass des Hebräerbriefes." Pages 321–42 in *Eschatologie und Schöpfung: Festschrift für Erich Grässer*. Edited by M. Evang, H. Merklein, and M. Wolter. BZNW 89. Berlin: de Gruyter, 1997.

Schunack, Gerd. *Der Hebräerbrief.* ZBKNT 14. Zurich: Theologischer Verlag, 2002.
Schwemer, Anna Maria. "Zum Verhältnis von Diatheke und Nomos in den Schriften der jüdischen Diaspora Ägyptens in hellenistisch-römischer Zeit." Pages 67–110 in *Bund und Tora: Zur theologischen Begriffsgeschichte in alttestamentlicher, frühjüdischer und urchristlicher Tradition.* Edited by Friedrich Avemarie and Hermann Lichtenberger. WUNT 92. Tübingen: Mohr Siebeck, 1996.
Scott, Ernest F. *The Epistle to the Hebrews: Its Doctrine and Significance.* Edinburgh: Clark, 1922.
Seid, Timothy W. "Synkrisis in Hebrews 7: The Rhetorical Structure and Strategy." Pages 322–47 in *The Rhetorical Interpretation of Scripture: Essays from the 1996 Malibu Conference.* Edited by S. E. Porter and D. L. Stamps. JSNTSup 180. Sheffield: Sheffield Academic, 1999.
Smith, Robert H. *Hebrews.* ACNT. Minneapolis: Augsburg, 1984.
Sohn, Seock-Tae. "'I Will Be Your God and You Will Be My People': The Origin and Background of the Covenant Formula." Pages 355–72 in *Ki Baruch Hu: Ancient Near Eastern, Biblical, and Judaic Studies in Honor of Baruch A. Levine.* Edited by Robert Chazan, William W. Hallo, and Lawrence H. Schiffman. Winona Lake, IN: Eisenbrauns, 1999.
Son, Kiwoong. *Zion Symbolism in Hebrews: Hebrews 12:18-24 as a Hermeneutical Key to the Epistle.* Paternoster Biblical Monographs. Milton Keynes, UK: Paternoster, 2005.
Spicq, Ceslas. *L'Épître aux Hébreux.* Sources Bibliques. Paris: Gabalda, 1977.
Spilsbury, Paul. "Josephus." Pages 241–60 in *The Complexities of Second Temple Judaism.* Vol. 1 of *Justification and Variegated Nomism: A Fresh Appraisal of Paul and Second Temple Judaism.* Edited by D. A. Carson, P. T. O'Brien, and M. A. Seifrid. Grand Rapids: Baker, 2001.
Stanley, Steven K. "A New Covenant Hermeneutic: The Use of Scripture in Hebrews 8–10." PhD diss., University of Sheffield, 1994.
———. "The Structure of Hebrews from Three Perspectives." *TynBul* 45 (1994): 245–71.
Stowers, Stanley K. *Letter Writing in Greco-Roman Antiquity.* LEC 5. Philadelphia: Westminster, 1986.
Strobel, August. *Der Brief an die Hebräer.* Das Neue Testament Deutsch 9/2. 13th ed. Göttingen: Vandenhoeck & Ruprecht, 1991.
Stylianopoulos, Theodore G. "Shadow and Reality: Reflections on Hebrews 10:1–18." *GOTR* 17 (1972): 215–30.
Sumney, Jerry L. "The Argument of Colossians." Pages 339–52 in *Rhetorical Argumentation in Biblical Texts.* Edited by A. Eriksson, T. H. Olbricht, and W. Übelacker. Emory Studies in Early Christianity 8. Harrisburg: Trinity Press International, 2002.
Tate, Marvin E. *Psalms 51-100.* WBC 20. Dallas: Word, 1990.
Thielman, Frank. *Paul and the Law: A Contextual Approach.* Downers Grove, IL: InterVarsity, 1994.
Thompson, James. *The Letter to the Hebrews.* Living Word Commentary 15. Austin: Sweet, 1971.
Thurén, Jukka. *Das Lobopfer der Hebräer: Studien zum Aufbau und Anliegen von Hebräerbrief 13.* Åbo: Åbo Akademi, 1973.

Thurén, Lauri. "The General New Testament Writings." Pages 587–607 in *Handbook of Classical Rhetoric in the Hellenistic Period, 330 B.C.–A.D. 400*. Edited by S. E. Porter. Leiden: Brill, 1997.

———. *The Rhetorical Strategy of 1 Peter with Special Regard to Ambiguous Expressions*. Åbo: Åbo Akademi, 1990.

Treat, Jay Curry. "Barnabas, Epistle of." *ABD* 1:611–14.

Trotter, Andrew H., Jr. *Interpreting the Epistle to the Hebrews*. Guides to New Testament Exegesis. Grand Rapids: Baker, 1997.

Übelacker, Walter G. *Der Hebräerbrief als Appell*. ConBNT 21. Stockholm: Almqvist & Wiksell, 1989.

———. "Paraenesis or Paraclesis—Hebrews as a Test Case." Pages 319-52 in *Early Christian Paraenesis in Context*. Edited by Troels Engberg-Petersen and James Starr. Berlin: de Gruyter, 2004.

VanderKam, James C. "Covenant." Pages 151–55 in vol. 1 of *Encyclopedia of the Dead Sea Scrolls*. Edited by Lawrence H. Schiffman and James C. VanderKam. 2 vols. Oxford: Oxford University Press, 2000.

VanGemeren, Willem, editor. *New International Dictionary of Old Testament Theology and Exegesis*. 5 vols. Grand Rapids: Zondervan, 1997.

Vanhoye, Albert. "Le Dieu de la nouvelle alliance dans l'épître aux Hébreux." Pages 315–30 in *La notion biblique de Dieu: Le Dieu de la Bible et le Dieu des philosophes*. Edited by J. Coppens. BETL 41. Gembloux, Belgium: Duculot, 1974.

———. "La 'teliôsis' du Christ: Point capital de la christologie sacerdotale d'Hébreux." *NTS* 42 (1996): 321–38.

Vermes, Geza. *The Complete Dead Sea Scrolls in English*. Rev. ed. London: Penguin, 2004.

Vogel, Manuel. *Das Heil des Bundes: Bundestheologie im Frühjudentum und im frühen Christentum*. Texte und Arbeiten zum neutestamentlichen Zeitalter 18. Tübingen: Francke, 1996.

Walker, Peter. "Jerusalem in Hebrews 13:9–14 and the Dating of the Epistle." *TynBul* 45 (1994): 39–71.

———. "A Place for Hebrews? Context for a First-Century Sermon." Pages 231–49 in *The New Testament in Its First Century Setting: Essays on Context and Background*. Edited by P. J. Williams, Andrew D. Clarke, Peter M. Head, and David Instone-Brewer. Grand Rapids: Eerdmans, 2004.

Walters, John R. "The Rhetorical Arrangement of Hebrews." *AsTJ* 51 (1996): 59–70.

Watson, Duane Frederick. *Invention, Arrangement, and Style: Rhetorical Criticism of Jude and 2 Peter*. SBLDS 104. Atlanta: Scholars Press, 1988.

———. "Rhetorical Criticism of Hebrews and the Catholic Epistles Since 1978." *CurBS* 5 (1997): 175–207.

Watts, John D. W. *Isaiah 34–66*. WBC 25. Waco: Word, 1987.

Weiss, Hans-Friedrich. *Der Brief an die Hebräer: Übersetzt und Erklärt*. 15th ed. KEK 13. Göttingen: Vandenhoeck & Ruprecht: 1991.

Welbourn, L. "On the Date of 1 Clement." *BR* 29 (1984): 35–54.

Wengst, Klaus. *Tradition und Theologie des Barnabasbriefes*. Berlin: de Gruyter, 1971.

Westcott, Brooke Foss. *The Epistle to the Hebrews: The Greek Text with Notes and Essays*. 2nd ed. London: Macmillan, 1892. Repr. Grand Rapids: Eerdmans, 1980.

Williamson, Paul R. "Covenant." Pages 139–55 in *Dictionary of the Old Testament: Pentateuch*. Edited by David W. Baker and T. Desmond Alexander. Downers Grove, IL: InterVarsity, 2003.

Wills, Lawrence. "The Form of the Sermon in Hellenistic Judaism and Early Christianity." *HTR* 77 (1984): 177–99.

Wilson, Robert McLachlan. *Hebrews*. New Century Bible Commentary. Grand Rapids: Eerdmans, 1987.

Wilson, Stephen G. *Related Strangers: Jews and Christians 70–170 c.e.* Minneapolis: Fortress, 1995.

Winston, David. *The Wisdom of Solomon*. AB 43. Garden City: Doubleday, 1979.

Wintermute, O. S. "Jubilees." *OTP* 2:35–142.

Witherington, Ben, III. *Letters and Homilies for Jewish Christians: A Socio-Rhetorical Commentary on Hebrews, James and Jude*. Downers Grove: InterVarsity, 2007.

Wolff, Christian. *Jeremia im Frühjudentum und Urchristentum*. TUGAL 118. Berlin: Akademie, 1976.

Wright, G. Ernest. "The Theological Study of the Bible." Pages 983–89 in *The Interpreter's One-Volume Commentary on the Bible*. Edited by Charles M. Laymon. Nashville: Abingdon, 1971.

Wright, R. B. "Psalms of Solomon." *OTP* 2:639–70.

Young, Norman H. "'Bearing His Reproach' (Heb 13.9–14)." *NTS* 48 (2002): 243–61.

Yu, Young Ki. "The New Covenant: The Promise and Its Fulfillment." PhD diss., University of Durham, 1989.

www.ingramcontent.com/pod-product-compliance
Lightning Source LLC
Chambersburg PA
CBHW070255230426
43664CB00014B/2538